I0131682

# QuickBooks
## FOR
# ACCOUNTING
# PROFESSIONALS

## PRESENTED BY:
## CRAIG M. KERSHAW, CPA, MBA

QuickBooks for Accounting Professionals

For permission requests, write to:
The CFO Source, LLC
5515 Hudson Drive
Eldersburg, MD 21784
http://www.cfosource.net/

Ordering Information:
Quantity sales. Special discounts are available on quantity purchases by corporations, associations, and others. Orders by U.S. trade bookstores and wholesalers. For details, contact the publisher at the address above.

Editing by Debra L Hartmann with The Pro Book Editor. (https://theprobookeditor.com)
Cover and Interior Design by IAPS (http://www.iaps.rocks)

Print ISBN: 978-0-9977388-3-4
eBook ISBN: 978-0-9977388-2-7

1. Main category—Business & Money > Bookkeeping
2. Other category—Computers & Technology > QuickBooks

First Edition

# Table of Contents

# About the Author

Craig Kershaw, CPA, MBA is the managing partner of The CFO Source, a Baltimore based consulting firm that provides senior level financial expertise to small and medium size businesses. Craig has over 20 years of experience at the CFO and Controller level in the transportation, construction, and service industries. He has worked with medium size businesses to Fortune 500 companies and demonstrated excellence across the full range of financial management responsibilities—financing, treasury, accounting, risk management, and information technology. Craig has been involved in start-up ventures, arranging financing, real estate lease negotiations, and complex multi-million-dollar insurance transactions.

Craig has been a QuickBooks Pro Advisor since 2009, and has helped numerous clients set up, trouble shoot, and fine tune their accounting. The CFO Source's clients look to the firm to get the most from their investment in QuickBooks with ongoing training of their accounting staff. Craig's efforts in QuickBooks training started as "how to" instructions for clients looking for advice on how to record specific "oddball" transactions. The growing list of instructions has been put into a series of books, allowing users to understand the breadth of capabilities QuickBooks provides.

Craig teaches continuing professional education courses to members of the Maryland Association of CPAs using his QuickBooks series of books and has been training business owners and their staff on the use of QuickBooks since 2005. Craig is a regular contributor of QuickBooks articles to the Maryland Construction Networks "Networked and Connected" newsletter.

# Preface

## Who This Book is For

QuickBooks for Accountants was written as a resource for accounting professionals—CPAs, controllers, accounting managers, and bookkeepers will find insights and guidance that will help them get their jobs done faster and more accurately. This reference manual will enable accountants at all levels to increase their QuickBooks expertise and become invaluable to the companies they work for.

The author drew on years of experience as a CFO, Controller, and QuickBooks Pro Advisor to select topics that would be the most helpful for accountants. Some of the areas covered include:

- setting up new companies,
- customizing and memorizing reports,
- specialized reports for sales and income taxes,
- troubleshooting and fixing issues created by untrained users,
- budgeting,
- issuing 1099s, and
- understanding cash basis accounting.

To get the most out of this book, readers should have a basic understanding of QuickBooks. The book goes beyond the basics of how to process transactions to focus on the functionality that is of most use to accountants. For help with the basics, it is suggested to make use of the built-in help within the QuickBooks program and the tutorials available at the QuickBooks website.

## Versions Referenced

This book focuses on the tools in the Pro, Premier, and Enterprise versions. The book does not address functionality in the QuickBooks Online, Mac Desktop, or Point of Sale products.

A few of the QuickBooks functionalities presented in this book are only available in the Accountant's Desktop and/or Enterprise versions of QuickBooks. Readers should explore these functionalities, and we think they will agree that these tools are worth the small amount of additional expense to have available. Those presented in this book include:

- reclassifying Transactions,
- fixing Unapplied Customer Payments and Credits,
- fixing Incorrectly Recorded Sales Tax payments, and
- combined Reports.

# Chapter One

# Chart of Accounts

## Overview

The chart of accounts is the backbone of QuickBooks. Correctly setting it up and understanding how it works is critical to accurate accounting and reporting. Your chart of accounts can be customized to produce tailored financial statements within the framework of the account types available. Setting up your chart of accounts should take in mind all of the desired financial reports, as well as the ability of QuickBooks to track sales and expenses with a greater level of detail outside of the usual financial statements.

## Account Types in QuickBooks

When setting up accounts in QuickBooks, each account must be assigned an account type. Account Types determine the financial report each account will appear on and their order in reports. Account Types are fixed, so the user cannot change the title of an account type, add additional account types, or change the order of appearance of account types on standard financial statements. In addition, account types have specific attributes to facilitate record keeping, functionality, and transaction processing. Below is a listing of account types shown in the order in which the account types appear on the respective financial statement. The typical usage of each account type is shown as well as a description of functionality specific to the account type.

# Profit and Loss

| Account Types | Description/Functionality |
|---|---|
| Income | Sales earned from normal business operations - sales of services or products |
| Cost of Goods Sold | Direct costs related to providing services or product sales - inventory costs, direct labor, construction job costs |
| Expense | Indirect or "Overhead" expenses, ie - rent, telephone, office, supplies, administrative salaries |
| Other Income | Income not from normal business operations - interest, dividends, special refunds, gains on sales of assets |
| Other Expense | Expenses not related to normal operations - income taxes, legal settlements, losses on sales of assets |

# Balance Sheet

| Account Types | Description/Functionality |
|---|---|
| Bank | For cash accounts - checking, savings, petty cash |
| | Write checks, make deposits, perform bank reconciliations |
| Accounts Receivable | Used to track amounts due from customers |
| | Reports - listings and agings of amounts due from customers |
| | Customer Name must be used to record transactions to this account |
| Other Current Asset | Assets such as prepaid expenses, inventory, advances to employees |
| Fixed Asset | Long lived assets - vehicles, equipment, land, buildings and computers |
| Other Assets | Assets such as lease deposits, goodwill and other intangibles |
| Accounts Payable | Used to track amounts due to vendors for purchases made on account |
| | Reports - listings and agings of amounts due to vendors |
| | Issue checks to vendors |
| | Vendor Name must be used to record transactions to this account |
| Other Current Liability | Short term liabilities - lines of credit, payroll and sales tax liabilities, accrued expenses |
| Credit Card | Amounts due under credit cards - track liability for expenses and purchases due or paid with credit cards |
| Long Term Liability | Loans, mortgages, and notes payable |
| | Use the QuickBooks Loan Manager to issue checks, record interest and principal payments, track loan balances |
| Equity | Investment in the company and withdraws by the owners/shareholders |

# Chart of Accounts Considerations

**Should You Use Account Numbers or Not?**

The use of account numbers in QuickBooks is an option found in the Accounting Preference section. There are some advantages to using a numbering system:

- Speeds up data entry – for example, if Office Supplies is account number 6210, typing that number when doing data entry will bring up that account in fewer keystrokes.
- Determines the ordering of accounts shown on financial statements – QuickBooks displays accounts on financial statements in alphabetic order if account numbers are not used. If numbers are used, accounts are grouped in numeric order.

**Should You Use Sub-Accounts?**

- Sub-Accounts allow for grouping and subtotaling of similar accounts. For example, salaries, payroll taxes, workers compensation, and employee healthcare costs can be set up as sub-accounts to a "Payroll Costs" account.

**Are Multiple Accounts Receivable and Payable Accounts Needed?**

For many companies, having only one accounts receivable and one accounts payable account works fine. However, if you need to know the total of AR or AP within various categories, multiple accounts can be set up so QuickBooks will present the user with a drop-down box to select which of the AR or AP accounts to be used when entering bills or creating customer invoices:

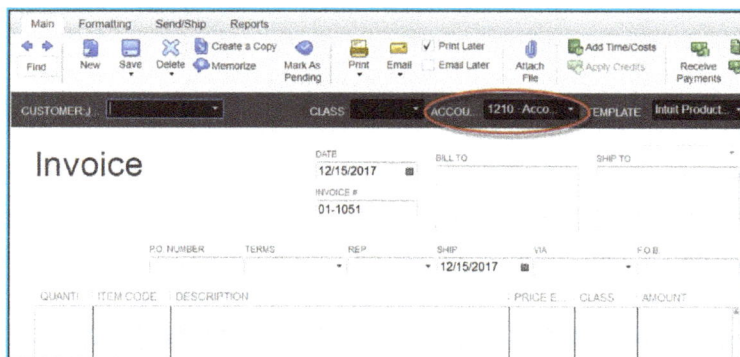

**Changing Account Types**

It's not uncommon that accounts are set up with incorrect account types resulting in the account either showing up in the wrong section of a financial statement or on the wrong statement altogethezr. In most cases, this can be corrected by editing the account and selecting the correct account type. In some cases, however, the user cannot change the account type that has been initially selected due to the following restrictions:

- You cannot change an account to or from Accounts Receivable or Accounts Payable.
- You cannot change the account type of automatically created accounts such as Undeposited Funds or Sales Tax Payable.
- You cannot change an account that has sub-accounts unless you first change all the sub-accounts to accounts, make the change, and edit the accounts back to sub-accounts under the revised account.

# Common Chart of Accounts Problems
# (And How to Fix Them)

### Duplicate Accounts/Accounts with Similar Names

Several methods are available to deal with this:

**Deleting an account.** This will work, but only if the account has not been used in a transaction.

> To delete: go to Lists, select Chart of Accounts, and left click once on the account you would like to delete. If you then right click on the account, a dialogue box will open. Choose the Delete option.

**Inactivating an account.** This can be a good option if the account has already been used. After inactivating an account, it will still appear in reports to accommodate showing data collected while it was active. If making reports more streamlined is your goal, this approach may not get the result you were looking for, especially if you are trying to remove several accounts from reports.

> To inactivate an account: select the account as stated in the above deleting example except select the Make Account Inactive option.

**Merging accounts.** This process merges one account into another, eliminating all traces of the merged account. For example, if you want to merge the account Bank Fees into Bank Service Charges, all transactions will show as Bank Service Charges. (BEWARE: This cannot be reversed!)

> To merge accounts: go to Lists, select Chart of Accounts, right click on the account you would like to merge, and select Edit Account. In the Account Name field, type the name of the account you would like this account to merge into using the exact name of the desired account, then click Save and Close. You will get this message: "This name is already being used. Would you like to merge them?" Click Yes. (see image on next page)

| Account Name | Bank Service Charges | |
|---|---|---|
| | ☐ Subaccount of | ▼ |

OPTIONAL

| Description | |
|---|---|
| Note | |
| Tax-Line Mapping | <Unassigned> ▼ How do I choose the r |

**Merge**

⚠ This name is already being used. Would you like to merge them?

Yes     **No**

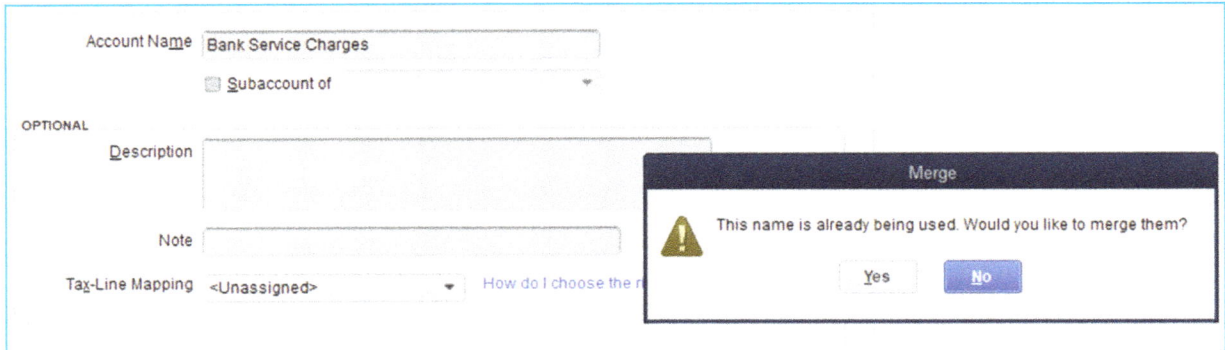

## Chart of Accounts "Too Large"

Using the chart of accounts to segregate too much data can make for multi-page financial statements that are so data rich they lack usefulness. Functionality exists in several other areas of QuickBooks to provide detailed reporting to supplement your financial statements, so you don't need the Chart of Accounts to drill down to every bit of detail. A variety of report types are available, including the following:

**Jobs** – Tracking the revenue and related expenses for contracts is the most common use for job codes. Separate P&Ls can be run for each job code. Job codes could also be used for tracking:

- Equipment repairs by piece of equipment
- Revenues and expenses related to non-profit grants and donations
- Spending on fixed asset purchases such as the construction of new facilities

Jobs are set up as subsets of customers in the Customer Center. In the case of the three examples above, a "dummy" customer would need to be set up and then jobs set up underneath the customer.

**Classes** – Class codes are used by many organizations to group revenues and expenses by division or department. Separate P & Ls can be run for each class code. To use class codes, access your Accounting Preferences and select the "use class tracking" option. To have meaningful Profit and Loss statements by class, all transactions should be class coded. QuickBooks will prompt users when class codes are not used, but will accept transactions without them. When running a P&L by class, a separate column labeled "Unclassified" will be shown that will include transactions not given class codes.

**Job Types** – If your company organizes by projects or "jobs," then these codes allow you to group like projects for reporting. For example, a contractor could have job types such as residential, commercial, and government.

**Item Codes** – One of the functions item codes serve is to provide sales and cost detail that is not appropriate for summary level financial statements. For example, if you sell 20 different varieties of a product, you can show the sales of all 20 as one line on your financial statement but also get detailed reporting at the item code level.

## Accounts Show Negative Balances on Reports

There can be several reasons why an account would show a negative balance on a Profit & Loss or Balance Sheet report. In most cases, negative balances should be investigated. Sometimes the negative figure is correct, and in other cases, the negative is due to setup problems within QuickBooks. Here's a rundown of possible explanations:

**The accounting is correct as shown** – For example, an accumulated depreciation account on the asset side of a balance sheet should show a negative balance, as would a prepaid insurance account if the expenses charged to the account exceed the payments.

**Incorrect Account Type** – Each account type is set up to appear in a specific report with a "normal" balance. For example, the account type Income is set to appear at the top of the income statement and shows as a positive if the account has a credit balance. If an account being used to record expenses is incorrectly assigned an account type of Income, it will appear on reports with a negative balance. The fix in this example is to change the account type to Expense.

**Item Code pointing to wrong type of account** – When item codes are used for invoicing customers, the transaction is recorded as a credit. If the item code used to generate the invoice points to an account with an account type of Expense, a negative balance will appear.

**Transactions charged to wrong account** – Selecting the wrong account can cause negatives to appear on financial statements. For example, coding a disbursement to a revenue account would cause the revenue account to show a negative balance.

Notes:

# Chapter Two
# QuickBooks Transaction Types

Every QuickBooks transaction is assigned a transaction "Type" code that designates the nature of the transaction and the module the transaction originated from. The codes are fixed by the program, so new ones cannot be added nor can existing codes be changed. The codes are not assigned by the user, but rather generated automatically by the modules within QuickBooks. These codes don't really have an impact on reporting other than appearing on detailed transaction reports to indicate what module in QB the transaction was made in.

Understanding these codes is useful in analyzing transactions. Transaction type codes make sense in the normal flow of transactions and can be a flag if a code appears that doesn't make sense for that type of account. For example, when recording a Vendor Bill, the transaction type code assigned is "Bill." It makes sense that an expense account would show a transaction type code of Bill, while if that code appears for a revenue account, it would be cause for investigation since Vendor bills are not typically coded as revenues.

When reviewing transaction detail reports, Type codes appear as shown below.

| Type | Date | Num | Adj | Name | Memo | Class | Clr | Split | Debit | Credit | Balance |
|------|------|-----|-----|------|------|-------|-----|-------|-------|--------|---------|
| **4110 · Construction Income** | | | | | | | | | | | |
| Invoice | 12/01/2020 | 01-1... | | Cruz, Albert:Cot... | -MULTIPLE- | Revenu... | | 1210 Acco... | 0.00 | | 0.00 |
| Invoice | 12/01/2020 | 01-1... | | Cruz, Albert:Cot... | 10% due up... | Revenu... | | 1210 Acco... | | 33,500.00 | 33,500.00 |
| Total 4110 · Construction Income | | | | | | | | | 0.00 | 33,500.00 | 33,500.00 |
| **5110 · Job Related Costs** | | | | | | | | | | | |
| Bill | 12/12/2020 | | | Cruz, Albert:Cot... | Painting | Materi... | | 2010 Acco... | 1,163.04 | | -1,163.04 |
| Bill | 12/15/2020 | 908 | | Cruz, Albert:Cot... | Excavation | Materi... | | 2010 Acco... | 2,300.00 | | -3,463.04 |
| Bill | 12/15/2020 | | | Cruz, Albert:Cot... | Cabinets &... | Subcon... | | 2010 Acco... | 12,532.00 | | -15,995.04 |
| Total 5110 · Job Related Costs | | | | | | | | | 15,995.04 | 0.00 | -15,995.04 |
| **5200 · Job Labor Costs** | | | | | | | | | | | |
| **5210 · Job Labor (Gross Wages)** | | | | | | | | | | | |
| Paycheck | 12/08/2020 | 489 | | Cruz, Albert:Cot... | | Labor C... | | 1130 Payr... | 1,721.00 | | -1,721.00 |
| Paycheck | 12/08/2020 | 488 | | Cruz, Albert:Cot... | | Labor C... | | 1130 Payr... | 1,760.00 | | -3,481.00 |
| Paycheck | 12/08/2020 | 490 | | Cruz, Albert:Cot... | | Labor C... | | 1130 Payr... | 1,700.00 | | -5,181.00 |
| Total 5210 · Job Labor (Gross Wages) | | | | | | | | | 5,181.00 | 0.00 | -5,181.00 |

*Quality-Built Construction — Transaction Detail By Account — December 1 - 15, 2020 — Accrual Basis*

A listing of QuickBooks transaction type codes is provided as Appendix A.

## Notes on Transaction Types

Estimate, Sales Order, and Purchase Order codes are non posting, meaning that these codes will not be found on financial statement reports. These codes will appear on reports such as "Transaction list by Customer" (for estimates) or "Transaction List by Vendor" (for purchase orders).

The reduction of inventory related to the sale of product will appear on QuickBooks reports with a transaction type code of Invoice. Customer Invoices generated with Inventory Part item codes will record both the sale of the product with the accompanying creation of a receivable and record the cost of goods sold and reduction in inventory. Below is a sample transaction that shows the Invoice type transaction code for a sale from inventory:

**Wholesale/Distributor Sample File**
**Transaction Journal**
All Transactions

| Trans # | Type | Date | Num | Name | Memo | Item | Item Description | Account | Class | Sales Price | Debit | Credit |
|---------|------|------|-----|------|------|------|-----------------|---------|-------|-------------|-------|--------|
| 1285 | Invoice | 12/20/2019 | 71142 | Baker's Profession... | | | | Accounts Receiva... | | | 344.50 | |
| | | | | Baker's Profession... | Chestnut wi... | Chande... | Chestnut with Mar... | Revenue | | 325.00 | | 325.00 |
| | | | | Baker's Profession... | Chestnut wi... | Chande... | Chestnut with Mar... | Inventory Asset | | | | 96.49 |
| | | | | Baker's Profession... | Chestnut wi... | Chande... | Chestnut with Mar... | Cost of Goods | | | 96.49 | |
| | | | | Comptroller of Ma... | Sales Tax | Marylan... | Sales Tax | Sales Tax Payable | | 6.0% | | 19.50 |
| | | | | | | | | | | | 440.99 | 440.99 |
| **TOTAL** | | | | | | | | | | | 440.99 | 440.99 |

Notes:

## Chapter Three

# Getting the Most Out of Reports

QuickBooks not only provides users with a wide selection of reports, it also provides numerous ways to modify reports to make them more useful. After running a report from the main menu "Reports" option, the user has a wide variety of tools available to customize the report in numerous ways. These include establishing date ranges, presentation formats, filtering for selected criteria, and summarizing data. Users can also "Memorize" reports that have been customized for later use.

## Modifying Reports

### The Expand/Collapse Function

This functionality allows the user to toggle back and forth between more or less detail on the same report. On financial statements, sub-accounts can be either shown in detail (Expand mode) or collapsed to a summary (Collapse mode). Shown next is a Profit & Loss in the Expand format. Expand and Collapse are toggle buttons, so when the button shows Expand, you would click that to get the expanded view and it would then change to Collapse so you know to click that to change back to collapsed view. It will always show the opposite of the view you are currently in. In the example images shown next, sub-accounts are shown for Job Labor Costs and Car/Truck Expense.

Here's the same report in Collapse mode:

Note on the Collapsed Report, sub-accounts do not appear, so the report is shorter because only the totals in the main accounts show.

The user also has the option of choosing to collapse some sub-accounts into their parent account while leaving other accounts detailed. This is done in Expand mode, by clicking on the small gray triangles to the left of the accounts for toggling them individually between collapse and expand.

## Changing the Order of Accounts on Reports

The default presentation on reports when account numbers are not used is to show accounts in alphabetical order within account type groupings. A common request of accountants is that they want Accumulated Depreciation and Accumulated Amortization accounts shown last in the grouping of related accounts on the balance sheet. Since these accounts start with an "A" the accounts show first by default. Below is the asset section sample company balance sheet showing the accounts in the default order.

Assigning account numbers can resolve this because accounts are shown in numerical order, not alphabetically. However, some users prefer not to use account numbers. For those users, the ordering of the accounts on reports can be changed using a drag and drop approach in the Chart of Accounts.

To change the order of an account without using account numbers, first bring up the Chart of Accounts in the list area. Before you reorder accounts, the Chart of Accounts needs to be in its "Original Order," which sorts the list first by Account Type and then alphabetically by Account, if account numbers are not used. There are two ways to get the list in the Original Order. Refer to the Chart of Accounts shown next.

Clicking on the black diamond in the upper left is the quickest way to resort the list. If the black diamond does not show, clicking on the word "Name" at the top of the Chart of Accounts will make it appear.

If you prefer to see the re-sort applied step by step, click the "Account" button in the lower left, then select "Re-sort List." Answering "OK" to the message below will put the Chart of Accounts in the original order.

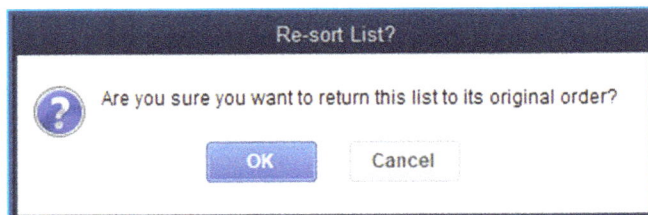

After the Chart of Accounts is sorted, reorder the accounts by placing your cursor on the black diamond to the left of the account you wish to reorder. The black diamond for Accumulated Depreciation is shown boxed in red in the next example image.

| NAME | TYPE |
| --- | --- |
| First National Bank | Bank |
| Accounts Receivable | Accounts Receivable |
| Inventory | Other Current Asset |
| Inventory Asset | Other Current Asset |
| Prepaid Expenses | Other Current Asset |
| Undeposited Funds | Other Current Asset |
| Accumulated Depreciation | Fixed Asset |
| Buildings | Fixed Asset |
| Furniture and Equipment | Fixed Asset |
| Land | Fixed Asset |
| Tractors and Trailers | Fixed Asset |
| Warehouse Equipment | Fixed Asset |
| Deferred Financing Costs | Other Asset |
| Accum Amort - Def Financing | Other Asset |
| Deferred Financing - Orig Cost | Other Asset |

When the cursor is placed on a black diamond, a four-way black arrow like the shape below will appear:

Once the four-way black arrow is showing, left click and hold down, then drag the account to the position in the list desired. Below shows the Chart of Accounts reordered for the Accumulated Depreciation and Accumulated Amortization accounts.

| NAME | TYPE |
| --- | --- |
| First National Bank | Bank |
| Accounts Receivable | Accounts Receivable |
| Inventory | Other Current Asset |
| Inventory Asset | Other Current Asset |
| Prepaid Expenses | Other Current Asset |
| Undeposited Funds | Other Current Asset |
| Buildings | Fixed Asset |
| Land | Fixed Asset |
| Furniture and Equipment | Fixed Asset |
| Tractors and Trailers | Fixed Asset |
| Warehouse Equipment | Fixed Asset |
| Accumulated Depreciation | Fixed Asset |
| Deferred Financing Costs | Other Asset |
| Deferred Financing - Orig Cost | Other Asset |
| Accum Amort - Def Financing | Other Asset |
| Security Deposits Receivable | Other Asset |

Accounts can only be reordered within the Account Type the account has been set up for. For example, the Land Account, which is set up with a Fixed Asset account type, cannot be moved to the Other Asset area.

Attempting to move an account to an area it is not set up for will generate the following message:

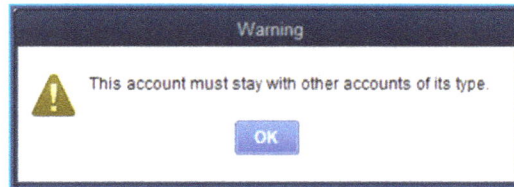

Here's the balance sheet after reordering the accounts:

| | Dec 31, 17 |
|---|---|
| **ASSETS** | |
| Current Assets | |
| Checking/Savings | 421,382.50 |
| Other Current Assets | 80,000.00 |
| **Total Current Assets** | 501,382.50 |
| Fixed Assets | |
| Buildings | 220,000.00 |
| Land | 80,000.00 |
| Accumulated Depreciation | -5,640.00 |
| **Total Fixed Assets** | 294,360.00 |
| Other Assets | |
| Deferred Financing Costs | |
| Deferred Financing - Orig Cost | 30,000.00 |
| Accum Amort - Def Financing | -3,000.00 |
| **Total Deferred Financing Costs** | 27,000.00 |
| **Total Other Assets** | 27,000.00 |
| **TOTAL ASSETS** | 822,742.50 |

# Customizing Standard Reports

QuickBooks comes with a long list of "standard," already created reports that can be customized in numerous ways when a few changes will be more efficient than creating a custom report. If a data field is not available on standard reports, it may be available when creating custom reports covered later in this chapter.

After a report is displayed, click on the "Customize Report" tab in the report menu as shown below:

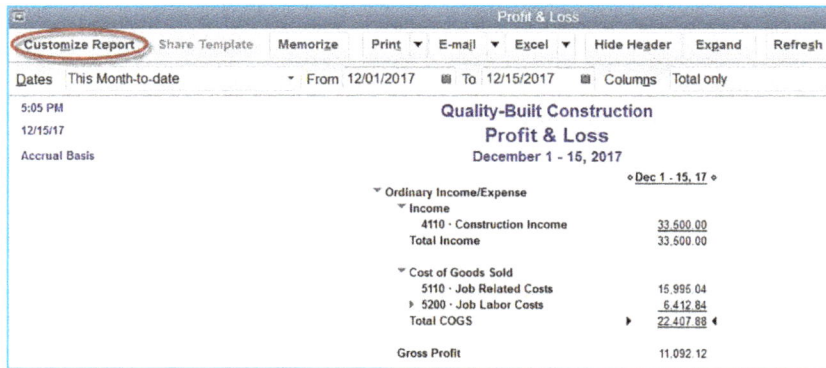

Clicking on Customize Report brings up the Modify Report screen with four tabs, each having different functionality.

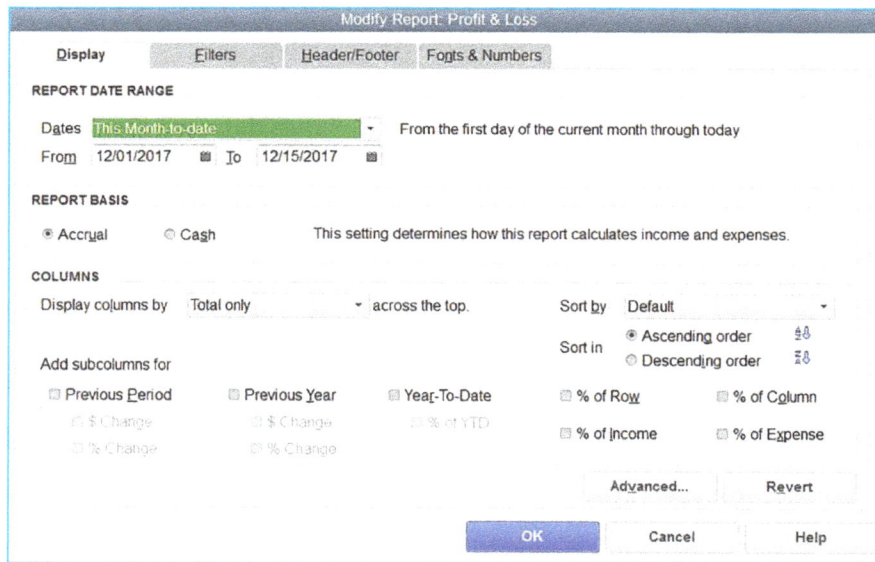

In the Display options, the user can:

- select a date range,
- choose Accrual or Cash Reporting (the default for this can be set in the Reports and Graphs Preference section),
- set display by time period (week, month, quarter) or data field such as class,
- access the Advanced menu to select whether zeroes should be shown.

Selecting the Filters Tab brings up the following screen:

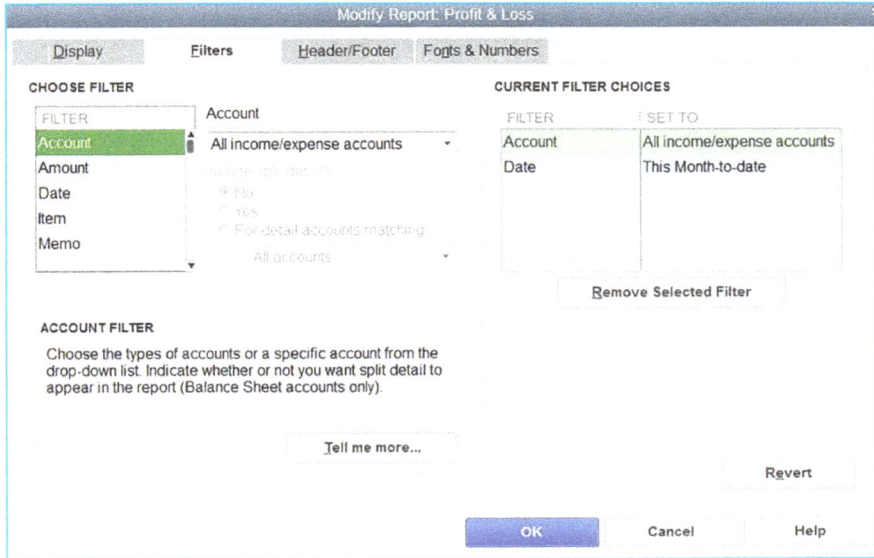

In the Filters tab, the user can choose one or multiple data fields to apply as filters for the report. In addition, each data field selected can be filtered for one or more attributes. For example, a report could be filtered for only income (sales) accounts, and then also filtered for specific Names (Customers).

The Header/Footer tab displays the following screen:

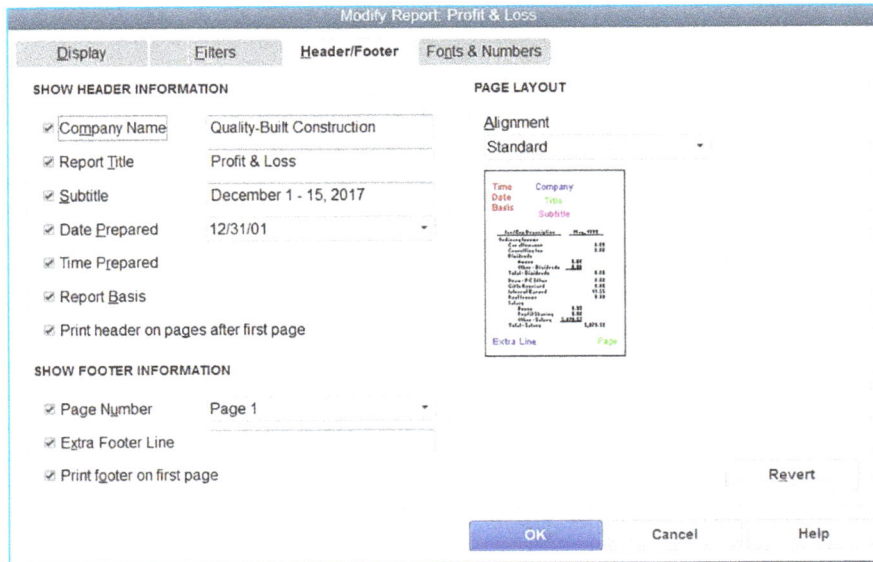

© The CFO Source, LLC 2017

In this tab, the user can change the standard header and footer titles for the report, add page numbers, and change alignment.

The Fonts & Numbers tab shows the following screen:

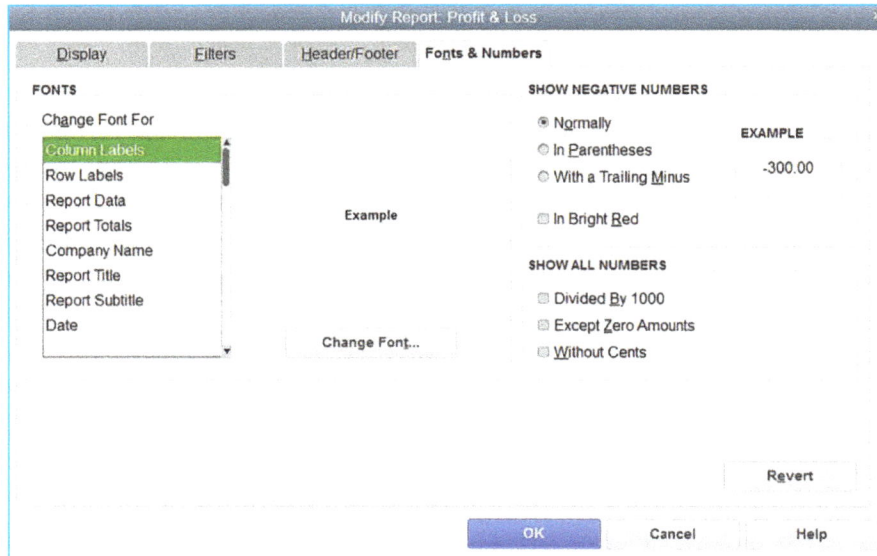

In this tab, the user can select:

- how negative numbers will be displayed,
- to show cents or round to thousands,
- change the font of selected label.

# Transaction Detail by Account Report

This report is very useful in analyzing or "drilling down" into the account balances shown on reports, and is similar to the General Ledger Report in that both show the details of transactions that make up an account balance. However, the General Ledger report does not allow for the subtotaling of transactions.

By double clicking on an amount shown in the report, all of the transactions adding up to that balance are shown.

Once the report is generated, it can be customized in several ways. To illustrate, the Profit & Loss report below will be used.

---

**Carl's Computer Shop**
**Profit & Loss**
June 1 through December 15, 2019

| | Jun 1 - Dec 15, 19 |
|---|---|
| ▼ Ordinary Income/Expense | |
| ▼ Income | |
| ▼ Sales | |
| Assembled Systems ▶ | 173,540.00 ◀ |
| Merchandise | 81,957.67 |
| Service | 164,378.00 |
| Total Sales | 419,875.67 |
| Total Income | 419,875.67 |

By double clicking on the Assembled Systems Sales amount, the default Transaction Detail by Account Report is generated. Note the total of the report matches the P&L amount:

Transaction Detail By Account

Customize Report | Comment on Report | Share Template | Memorize | Print ▼ | E-mail ▼ | Excel ▼ | Hide Header | Expand | Refresh

Dates Custom ▼ From 06/01/2019 To 12/15/2019 Total By Account list ▼ Sort By Default ▼

:24 PM
2/15/19
Accrual Basis

**Carl's Computer Shop**
**Transaction Detail By Account**
June 1 through December 15, 2019

| Type | Date | Num | Name | Memo | Class | Debit | Credit | Balance |
|---|---|---|---|---|---|---|---|---|
| **Sales** | | | | | | | | |
| **Assembled Systems** | | | | | | | | |
| Sales Receipt | 06/02/2019 | 2007-1020 | Morris, Katherine | Entry level com... | Bayshore Store | | 8,950.00 | 8,950.00 |
| Sales Receipt | 07/07/2019 | 2007-1025 | Milner, Eloyse | -MULTIPLE- | San Tomas Store | | 35,375.00 | 44,325.00 |
| Sales Receipt | 08/04/2019 | 2007-1027 | Reese, Pamela | Midrange comp... | Bayshore Store | | 3,585.00 | 47,910.00 |
| Sales Receipt | 08/18/2019 | 2007-1028 | Morgenthaler, Jenny | Power User co... | Bayshore Store | | 8,685.00 | 56,595.00 |
| Invoice | 08/18/2019 | 2007-106 | Jones Law Office | Power User co... | Bayshore Store | | 14,475.00 | 71,070.00 |
| Invoice | 09/08/2019 | 2007-107 | Lew Plumbing - C | Midrange comp... | Bayshore Store | | 5,975.00 | 77,045.00 |
| Sales Receipt | 09/08/2019 | 2007-1029 | Lucchini, Bill | Power User co... | Bayshore Store | | 14,475.00 | 91,520.00 |
| Sales Receipt | 10/06/2019 | 2007-1030 | Jimenez, Cristina | -MULTIPLE- | Bayshore Store | | 8,060.00 | 99,580.00 |
| Sales Receipt | 10/13/2019 | 2007-1031 | Oliveri, Tom | Power User co... | Bayshore Store | | 14,475.00 | 114,055.00 |
| Sales Receipt | 10/13/2019 | 2007-1034 | Tumacder, Jacint | Power User co... | Bayshore Store | | 5,790.00 | 119,845.00 |
| Invoice | 10/20/2019 | 2007-1042 | Easley, Paula | Midrange comp... | San Tomas Store | | 4,780.00 | 124,625.00 |
| Sales Receipt | 11/03/2019 | 2007-1037 | Lee, Laurel | Entry level com... | Bayshore Store | | 4,475.00 | 129,100.00 |
| Invoice | 11/10/2019 | 2007-108 | Jones Law Office | Midrange comp... | Bayshore Store | | 5,975.00 | 135,075.00 |
| Sales Receipt | 11/24/2019 | 2007-1042 | Tumacder, Jacint | Midrange comp... | San Tomas Store | | 3,585.00 | 138,660.00 |
| Invoice | 11/24/2019 | 2007-1043 | Oliveri, Tom | -MULTIPLE- | Bayshore Store | | 17,555.00 | 156,215.00 |
| Sales Receipt | 12/03/2019 | 2007-1043 | Morris, Katherine | Entry level com... | Bayshore Store | | 895.00 | 157,110.00 |
| Sales Receipt | 12/03/2019 | 2007-1045 | Wilks, Daniel | Midrange comp... | Bayshore Store | | 5,975.00 | 163,085.00 |
| Sales Receipt | 12/03/2019 | 2007-1048 | Wood, Emily | Midrange comp... | Bayshore Store | | 5,975.00 | 169,060.00 |
| Credit Memo | 12/08/2019 | 2007-1040C | Oliveri, Tom | Midrange comp... | Bayshore Store | 2,390.00 | | 166,670.00 |
| Sales Receipt | 12/15/2019 | 2007-1051 | Oliveri, Tom | Entry level com... | Bayshore Store | | 895.00 | 167,565.00 |
| Invoice | 12/15/2019 | 2007-113 | Jones Law Office | Midrange comp... | Bayshore Store | | 5,975.00 | 173,540.00 |
| Total Assembled Systems | | | | | | 2,390.00 | 175,930.00 | 173,540.00 |
| Total Sales | | | | | | 2,390.00 | 175,930.00 | 173,540.00 |
| TOTAL | | | | | | 2,390.00 | 175,930.00 | 173,540.00 |

## Adding Columns

One useful way to customize this report is to add columns that display information needed for the analysis being undertaken. For example, if income transactions are being analyzed, the item code used for billing could be useful as well as the payment information. For payroll related reports, employee names and payroll item codes could assist in analysis. Columns not useful to the analysis can also be removed as part of the customization.

To add or remove columns that will appear on the report, select Customize Report from the upper left of the report, then the Display option to bring up the following screen:

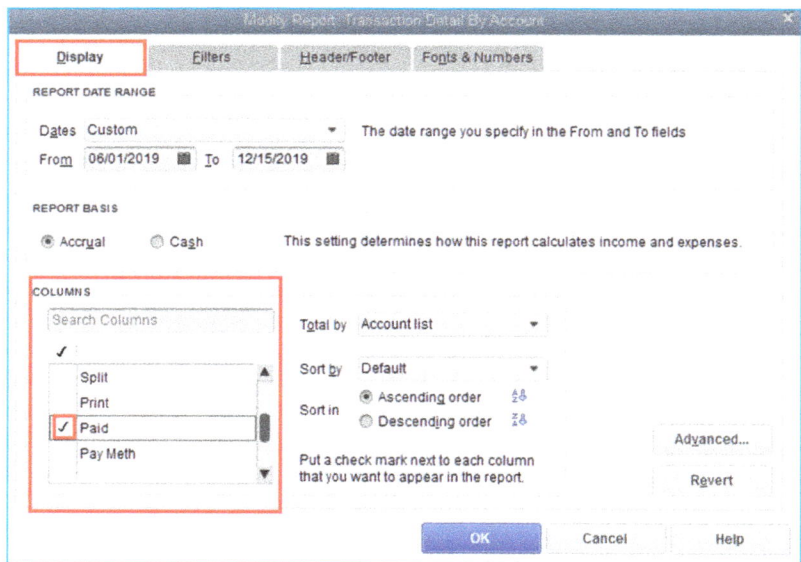

In the Columns section, the user can select which columns to add or remove from the report by checking or un-checking the available options. In the above example, "Paid" was checked off so that it can be determined if the invoices listed on the report are paid or unpaid.

This shows the Transaction Detail by Account report with the Paid column added:

**Carl's Computer Shop**
**Transaction Detail By Account**
June 1 through December 15, 2019

| Type | Date | Num | Name | Memo | Class | Paid | Debit | Credit | Balance |
|---|---|---|---|---|---|---|---|---|---|
| **Sales** | | | | | | | | | |
| **Assembled Systems** | | | | | | | | | |
| Sales Rece... | 06/02/2019 | 2007-1020 | Morris, Katherine | Entry level computer... | Bayshore Store | Unpaid | | 8,950.00 | 8,950.00 |
| Sales Rece... | 07/07/2019 | 2007-1025 | Milner, Eloyse | -MULTIPLE- | San Tomas Store | Unpaid | | 35,375.00 | 44,325.00 |
| Sales Rece... | 08/04/2019 | 2007-1027 | Reese, Pamela | Midrange computer ... | Bayshore Store | Unpaid | | 3,585.00 | 47,910.00 |
| Sales Rece... | 08/18/2019 | 2007-1028 | Morgenthaler, J... | Power User compute... | Bayshore Store | Unpaid | | 8,685.00 | 56,595.00 |
| Invoice | 08/18/2019 | 2007-106 | Jones Law Office | Power User compute... | Bayshore Store | Paid | | 14,475.00 | 71,070.00 |
| Invoice | 09/08/2019 | 2007-107 | Lew Plumbing - C | Midrange computer ... | Bayshore Store | Unpaid | | 5,975.00 | 77,045.00 |
| Sales Rece... | 09/08/2019 | 2007-1029 | Lucchini, Bill | Power User compute... | Bayshore Store | Unpaid | | 14,475.00 | 91,520.00 |
| Sales Rece... | 10/06/2019 | 2007-1030 | Jimenez, Cristina | -MULTIPLE- | Bayshore Store | Unpaid | | 8,060.00 | 99,580.00 |
| Sales Rece... | 10/13/2019 | 2007-1031 | Oliveri, Tom | Power User compute... | Bayshore Store | Unpaid | | 14,475.00 | 114,055.00 |
| Sales Rece... | 10/13/2019 | 2007-1034 | Tumacder, Jacint | Power User compute... | Bayshore Store | Unpaid | | 5,790.00 | 119,845.00 |
| Invoice | 10/20/2019 | 2007-1042 | Easley, Paula | Midrange computer ... | San Tomas Store | Unpaid | | 4,780.00 | 124,625.00 |
| Sales Rece... | 11/03/2019 | 2007-1037 | Lee, Laurel | Entry level computer... | Bayshore Store | Unpaid | | 4,475.00 | 129,100.00 |
| Invoice | 11/10/2019 | 2007-108 | Jones Law Office | Midrange computer ... | Bayshore Store | Unpaid | | 5,975.00 | 135,075.00 |
| Sales Rece... | 11/24/2019 | 2007-1042 | Tumacder, Jacint | Midrange computer ... | San Tomas Store | Unpaid | | 3,585.00 | 138,660.00 |
| Invoice | 11/24/2019 | 2007-1043 | Oliveri, Tom | -MULTIPLE- | Bayshore Store | Unpaid | | 17,555.00 | 156,215.00 |
| Sales Rece... | 12/03/2019 | 2007-1043 | Morris, Katherine | Entry level computer... | Bayshore Store | Unpaid | | 895.00 | 157,110.00 |
| Sales Rece... | 12/03/2019 | 2007-1045 | Wilks, Daniel | Midrange computer ... | Bayshore Store | Unpaid | | 5,975.00 | 163,085.00 |
| Sales Rece... | 12/03/2019 | 2007-1048 | Wood, Emily | Midrange computer ... | Bayshore Store | Unpaid | | 5,975.00 | 169,060.00 |
| Credit Memo | 12/08/2019 | 2007-104... | Oliveri, Tom | Midrange computer ... | Bayshore Store | Paid | 2,390.00 | | 166,670.00 |
| Sales Rece... | 12/15/2019 | 2007-1051 | Oliveri, Tom | Entry level computer... | Bayshore Store | Unpaid | | 895.00 | 167,565.00 |
| Invoice | 12/15/2019 | 2007-113 | Jones Law Office | Midrange computer ... | Bayshore Store | Unpaid | | 5,975.00 | 173,540.00 |
| **Total Assembled Systems** | | | | | | | 2,390.00 | 175,930.00 | 173,540.00 |
| **Total Sales** | | | | | | | 2,390.00 | 175,930.00 | 173,540.00 |
| **TOTAL** | | | | | | | 2,390.00 | 175,930.00 | 173,540.00 |

**"Names" versus "Source Names"**

The default on the Transaction Detail by Account report is to show the "Name" related to the transaction. For job costed transactions, however, there are two names related to transactions as follows:

- Customer:Job names – appears as "Name"
- Vendor and Employee names – appear as "Source Name"

To add the additional Source Name column, select Customize Report from the upper left of the report, then the Display option to show the following screen, and select Source Name in addition to Name:

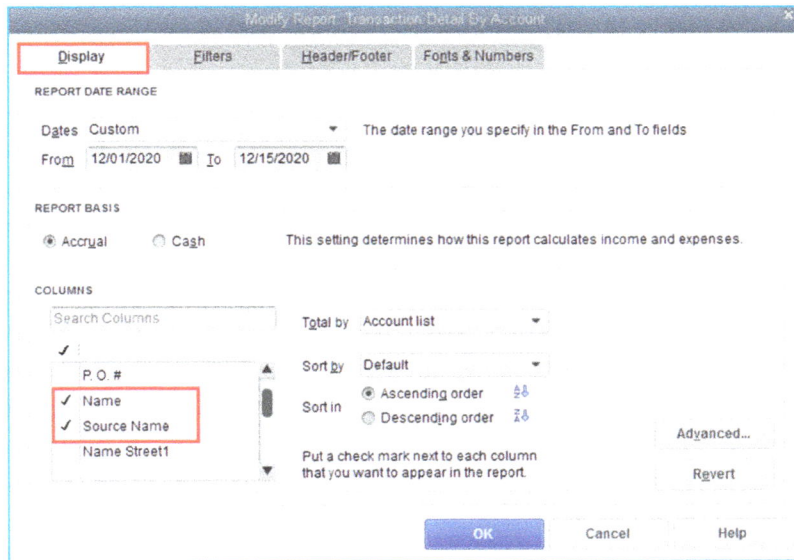

Below is a Transaction Detail by Account report that has been modified to show both the "Name" and "Source Name" columns. Note that Name and Source Name are the same for the income transactions, but expense transactions show a Customer:Job name and a Vendor or Employee name.

**Quality-Built Construction**
**Transaction Detail By Account**
December 1 - 15, 2020

| Type | Date | Num | Name | Source Name | Debit | Credit | Balance |
|---|---|---|---|---|---|---|---|
| **4110 · Construction Income** | | | | | | | |
| Invoice | 12/01/2020 | 01-10... | Cruz, Albert:Cottage - New Construction | Cruz, Albert:Cottage - New Construction | 0.00 | | 0.00 |
| Invoice | 12/01/2020 | 01-10... | Cruz, Albert:Cottage - New Construction | Cruz, Albert:Cottage - New Construction | | 33,500.00 | 33,500.00 |
| Invoice | 12/15/2020 | 01-10... | Cruz, Albert:Cottage - New Construction | Cruz, Albert:Cottage - New Construction | | 50,000.00 | 83,500.00 |
| Total 4110 · Construction Income | | | | | 0.00 | 83,500.00 | 83,500.00 |
| **5110 · Job Related Costs** | | | | | | | |
| Bill | 12/12/2020 | | Cruz, Albert:Cottage - New Construction | Color-Brite Paint Company | 1,163.04 | | -1,163.04 |
| Bill | 12/15/2020 | 908 | Cruz, Albert:Cottage - New Construction | Bay City Backhoe Service | 2,300.00 | | -3,463.04 |
| Bill | 12/15/2020 | | Cruz, Albert:Cottage - New Construction | Laurel's Cabinets | 12,532.00 | | -15,995.04 |
| Total 5110 · Job Related Costs | | | | | 15,995.04 | 0.00 | -15,995.04 |
| **5200 · Job Labor Costs** | | | | | | | |
| **5210 · Job Labor (Gross Wages)** | | | | | | | |
| Paycheck | 12/08/2020 | 489 | Cruz, Albert:Cottage - New Construction | Teichman, Tim | 1,721.00 | | -1,721.00 |
| Paycheck | 12/08/2020 | 488 | Cruz, Albert:Cottage - New Construction | Pepper, Chris | 1,760.00 | | -3,481.00 |
| Paycheck | 12/08/2020 | 490 | Cruz, Albert:Cottage - New Construction | Mitchell, Clark | 1,700.00 | | -5,181.00 |
| Total 5210 · Job Labor (Gross Wages) | | | | | 5,181.00 | 0.00 | -5,181.00 |

Additionally, expense transactions that are not job costed will show the same information in the "Name" and "Source Name" columns. As shown below on a non-job costed vendor transaction, the vendor name appears in both columns.

**Quality-Built Construction**
**Transaction Detail By Account**
November 1 through December 15, 2020

| Type | Date | Name | Source Name | Debit | Credit | Balance |
|------|------|------|-------------|-------|--------|---------|
| **6490 · Office Supplies** | | | | | | |
| Bill | 11/03/2020 | Office Mart | Office Mart | 227.00 | | 227.00 |
| Credit Card Ch... | 11/03/2020 | Reliable Office Supplies | Reliable Office Supplies | 52.12 | | 279.12 |
| Bill | 11/17/2020 | Office Mart | Office Mart | 227.00 | | 506.12 |
| Bill | 12/01/2020 | Office Mart | Office Mart | 227.00 | | 733.12 |
| Bill | 12/15/2020 | Office Mart | Office Mart | 227.00 | | 960.12 |
| Total 6490 · Office Supplies | | | | 960.12 | 0.00 | 960.12 |
| **TOTAL** | | | | 960.12 | 0.00 | 960.12 |

**Sorting and Sub-Totaling**

Two additional customizations that allow the user to better organize this report are available.

The "Sort By" option sorts the report by any one of the columns shown on the report. Shown below is the report sorted by the Paid column:

Share Template   Memorize   Print ▾   E-mail ▾   Excel ▾   Hide Header   Expand   Refresh

06/01/2019 ▦ To 12/15/2019 ▦  Total By Account list ▾   Sort By Paid ▾

**Carl's Computer Shop**
**Transaction Detail By Account**
June 1 through December 15, 2019

| Type | Date | Num | Name | Memo | Class | Paid | Debit | Credit | Balance |
|------|------|-----|------|------|-------|------|-------|--------|---------|
| **Sales** | | | | | | | | | |
| **Assembled Systems** | | | | | | | | | |
| Invoice | 08/18/2019 | 2007-106 | Jones Law Office | Power User compute... | Bayshore Store | Paid | | 14,475.00 | 14,475.0 |
| Credit Memo | 12/08/2019 | 2007-104... | Oliveri, Tom | Midrange computer ... | Bayshore Store | Paid | 2,390.00 | | 12,085.0 |
| Sales Receipt | 06/02/2019 | 2007-1020 | Morris, Katherine | Entry level computer... | Bayshore Store | Unpaid | | 8,950.00 | 21,035.0 |
| Sales Receipt | 07/07/2019 | 2007-1025 | Milner, Eloyse | -MULTIPLE- | San Tomas Store | Unpaid | | 35,375.00 | 56,410.0 |
| Sales Receipt | 08/04/2019 | 2007-1027 | Reese, Pamela | Midrange computer ... | Bayshore Store | Unpaid | | 3,585.00 | 59,995.0 |
| Sales Receipt | 08/18/2019 | 2007-1028 | Morgenthaler, J... | Power User compute... | Bayshore Store | Unpaid | | 8,685.00 | 68,680.0 |
| Invoice | 09/08/2019 | 2007-107 | Lew Plumbing - C | Midrange computer ... | Bayshore Store | Unpaid | | 5,975.00 | 74,655.0 |
| Sales Receipt | 09/08/2019 | 2007-1029 | Lucchini, Bill | Power User compute... | Bayshore Store | Unpaid | | 14,475.00 | 89,130.0 |
| Sales Receipt | 10/06/2019 | 2007-1030 | Jimenez, Cristina | -MULTIPLE- | Bayshore Store | Unpaid | | 8,060.00 | 97,190.0 |
| Sales Receipt | 10/13/2019 | 2007-1031 | Oliveri, Tom | Power User compute... | Bayshore Store | Unpaid | | 14,475.00 | 111,665.0 |
| Sales Receipt | 10/13/2019 | 2007-1034 | Tumacder, Jacint | Power User compute... | Bayshore Store | Unpaid | | 5,790.00 | 117,455.0 |
| Sales Receipt | 11/03/2019 | 2007-1037 | Lee, Laurel | Entry level computer... | Bayshore Store | Unpaid | | 4,475.00 | 121,930.0 |
| Sales Receipt | 11/24/2019 | 2007-1042 | Tumacder, Jacint | Midrange computer ... | San Tomas Store | Unpaid | | 3,585.00 | 125,515.0 |
| Sales Receipt | 12/03/2019 | 2007-1043 | Morris, Katherine | Entry level computer... | Bayshore Store | Unpaid | | 895.00 | 126,410.0 |
| Sales Receipt | 12/03/2019 | 2007-1045 | Wilks, Daniel | Midrange computer ... | Bayshore Store | Unpaid | | 5,975.00 | 132,385.0 |
| Sales Receipt | 12/03/2019 | 2007-1048 | Wood, Emily | Midrange computer ... | Bayshore Store | Unpaid | | 5,975.00 | 138,360.0 |
| Sales Receipt | 12/15/2019 | 2007-1051 | Oliveri, Tom | Entry level computer... | Bayshore Store | Unpaid | | 895.00 | 139,255.0 |
| Invoice | 12/15/2019 | 2007-113 | Jones Law Office | Midrange computer ... | Bayshore Store | Unpaid | | 5,975.00 | 145,230.0 |
| Invoice | 11/10/2019 | 2007-108 | Jones Law Office | Midrange computer ... | Bayshore Store | Unpaid | | 5,975.00 | 151,205.0 |
| Invoice | 10/20/2019 | 2007-1042 | Easley, Paula | Midrange computer ... | San Tomas Store | Unpaid | | 4,780.00 | 155,985.0 |
| Invoice | 11/24/2019 | 2007-1043 | Oliveri, Tom | -MULTIPLE- | Bayshore Store | Unpaid | | 17,555.00 | 173,540.0 |
| **Total Assembled Systems** | | | | | | | 2,390.00 | 175,930.00 | 173,540.0 |
| **Total Sales** | | | | | | | 2,390.00 | 175,930.00 | 173,540.0 |
| **TOTAL** | | | | | | | 2,390.00 | 175,930.00 | 173,540.0 |

The "Total By" option creates totals by some but not all of the columns. For example, the Name and Class columns can be totaled, but not the Type or Memo columns. This is also the case for fields added to the report in customization.

Before using the "Total By" option, it is suggested to click on the expand button as the feature requires this in some cases. The message below is generated when "expanding" the report is required.

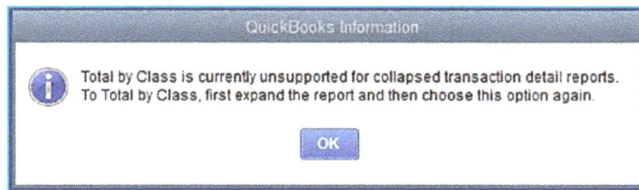

QuickBooks Information

Total by Class is currently unsupported for collapsed transaction detail reports. To Total by Class, first expand the report and then choose this option again.

OK

Below is the same report with totals by Class after the report was expanded. Note that the report has totals by Class, and the transactions within each Class are sorted by Paid status.

Carl's Computer Shop
Transaction Detail By Account
June 1 through December 15, 2019

| Type | Date | Num | Name | Memo | Class | Paid | Debit | Credit | Balance |
|------|------|-----|------|------|-------|------|-------|--------|---------|
| **Bayshore Store** | | | | | | | | | |
| Invoice | 08/18/2019 | 2007-106 | Jones Law Office | Power User compute... | Bayshore Store | Paid | | 14,475.00 | 14,475.00 |
| Credit Memo | 12/08/2019 | 2007-104... | Oliveri, Tom | Midrange computer ... | Bayshore Store | Paid | 2,390.00 | | 12,085.00 |
| Sales Receipt | 06/02/2019 | 2007-1020 | Morris, Katherine | Entry level computer... | Bayshore Store | Unpaid | | 8,950.00 | 21,035.00 |
| Sales Receipt | 08/04/2019 | 2007-1027 | Reese, Pamela | Midrange computer ... | Bayshore Store | Unpaid | | 3,585.00 | 24,620.00 |
| Sales Receipt | 08/18/2019 | 2007-1028 | Morgenthaler, J... | Power User compute... | Bayshore Store | Unpaid | | 8,685.00 | 33,305.00 |
| Invoice | 09/08/2019 | 2007-107 | Lew Plumbing - C | Midrange computer ... | Bayshore Store | Unpaid | | 5,975.00 | 39,280.00 |
| Sales Receipt | 09/08/2019 | 2007-1029 | Lucchini, Bill | Power User compute... | Bayshore Store | Unpaid | | 14,475.00 | 53,755.00 |
| Sales Receipt | 10/06/2019 | 2007-1030 | Jimenez, Cristina | Midrange computer ... | Bayshore Store | Unpaid | | 3,585.00 | 57,340.00 |
| Sales Receipt | 10/06/2019 | 2007-1030 | Jimenez, Cristina | Entry level computer... | Bayshore Store | Unpaid | | 4,475.00 | 61,815.00 |
| Sales Receipt | 10/13/2019 | 2007-1031 | Oliveri, Tom | Power User compute... | Bayshore Store | Unpaid | | 14,475.00 | 76,290.00 |
| Sales Receipt | 10/13/2019 | 2007-1034 | Tumacder, Jacint | Power User compute... | Bayshore Store | Unpaid | | 5,790.00 | 82,080.00 |
| Sales Receipt | 11/03/2019 | 2007-1037 | Lee, Laurel | Entry level computer... | Bayshore Store | Unpaid | | 4,475.00 | 86,555.00 |
| Sales Receipt | 12/03/2019 | 2007-1043 | Morris, Katherine | Entry level computer... | Bayshore Store | Unpaid | | 895.00 | 87,450.00 |
| Sales Receipt | 12/03/2019 | 2007-1045 | Wilks, Daniel | Midrange computer ... | Bayshore Store | Unpaid | | 5,975.00 | 93,425.00 |
| Sales Receipt | 12/03/2019 | 2007-1048 | Wood, Emily | Midrange computer ... | Bayshore Store | Unpaid | | 5,975.00 | 99,400.00 |
| Sales Receipt | 12/15/2019 | 2007-1051 | Oliveri, Tom | Entry level computer... | Bayshore Store | Unpaid | | 895.00 | 100,295.00 |
| Invoice | 12/15/2019 | 2007-113 | Jones Law Office | Midrange computer ... | Bayshore Store | Unpaid | | 5,975.00 | 106,270.00 |
| Invoice | 11/10/2019 | 2007-108 | Jones Law Office | Midrange computer ... | Bayshore Store | Unpaid | | 5,975.00 | 112,245.00 |
| Invoice | 11/24/2019 | 2007-1043 | Oliveri, Tom | Power User compute... | Bayshore Store | Unpaid | | 11,580.00 | 123,825.00 |
| Invoice | 11/24/2019 | 2007-1043 | Oliveri, Tom | Midrange computer ... | Bayshore Store | Unpaid | | 5,975.00 | 129,800.00 |
| **Total Bayshore Store** | | | | | | | 2,390.00 | 132,190.00 | 129,800.00 |
| **San Tomas Store** | | | | | | | | | |
| Sales Receipt | 07/07/2019 | 2007-1025 | Milner, Eloyse | Entry level computer... | San Tomas Store | Unpaid | | 8,950.00 | 8,950.00 |
| Sales Receipt | 07/07/2019 | 2007-1025 | Milner, Eloyse | Midrange computer ... | San Tomas Store | Unpaid | | 11,950.00 | 20,900.00 |
| Sales Receipt | 07/07/2019 | 2007-1025 | Milner, Eloyse | Power User compute... | San Tomas Store | Unpaid | | 14,475.00 | 35,375.00 |
| Sales Receipt | 11/24/2019 | 2007-1042 | Tumacder, Jacint | Midrange computer ... | San Tomas Store | Unpaid | | 3,585.00 | 38,960.00 |
| Invoice | 10/20/2019 | 2007-1042 | Easley, Paula | Midrange computer ... | San Tomas Store | Unpaid | | 4,780.00 | 43,740.00 |
| **Total San Tomas Store** | | | | | | | 0.00 | 43,740.00 | 43,740.00 |
| **TOTAL** | | | | | | | 2,390.00 | 175,930.00 | 173,540.00 |

# QuickBooks Custom Reports

In addition to standard reports, custom summary and detail reports can also be created. Custom reports have options for formatting and selection of details that are not available in standard reports. From Reports in the main menu, simply select either Summary or Transaction Detail to begin creating a custom report.

**Custom Summary Reports** – allows a wide variety of data fields to be displayed as either rows or columns. As such, a report can be structured that "flips" the standard P & L view of data. For example, instead of accounts appearing as rows like in a typical P & L, accounts can be selected to appear as columns instead. The user also has all the other functions available for customizing reports such as filtering, changing headers/footers, and fonts.

As an example, a summary level report will be developed showing sales by Customer as rows and sales by Account (Income statement) as columns, along with the percentage of sales each customer accounts for.

From Reports in the main menu, select the Summary option to bring up the Summary Report screen as shown below. Note that "Income Statement" has been selected for columns and "Customer" has been selected for rows. Note also that the "% of Column" box has been checked.

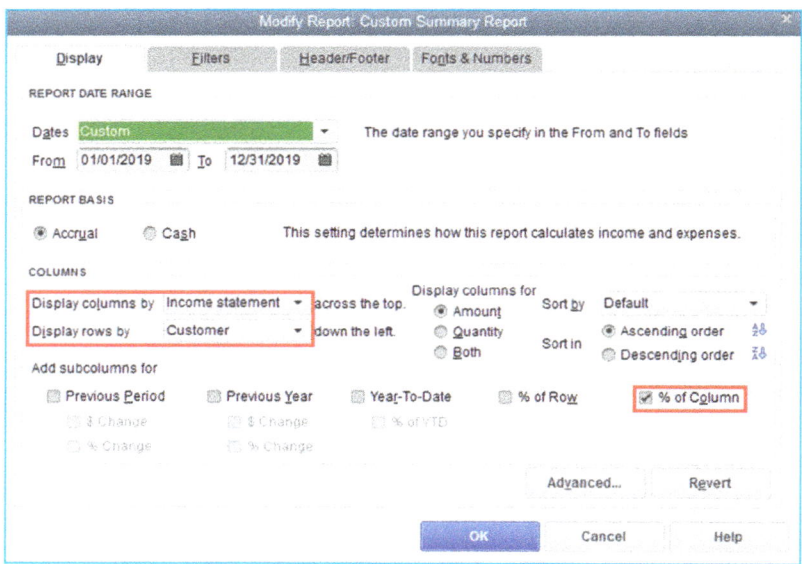

The next step is to apply filters so that only income accounts appear on the report. In the Filters tab, "All ordinary income accounts" have been selected as shown below.

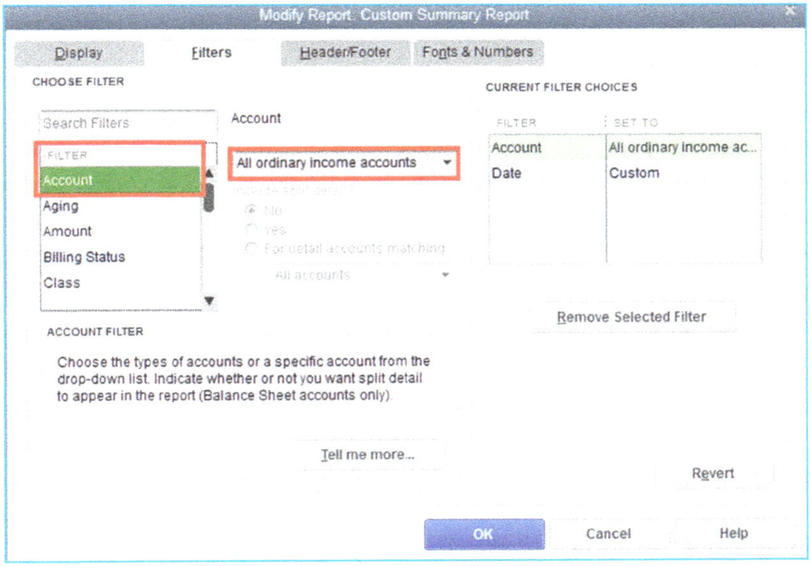

The last step is to change the title of the report. The new title is shown below in the Header/Footer tab:

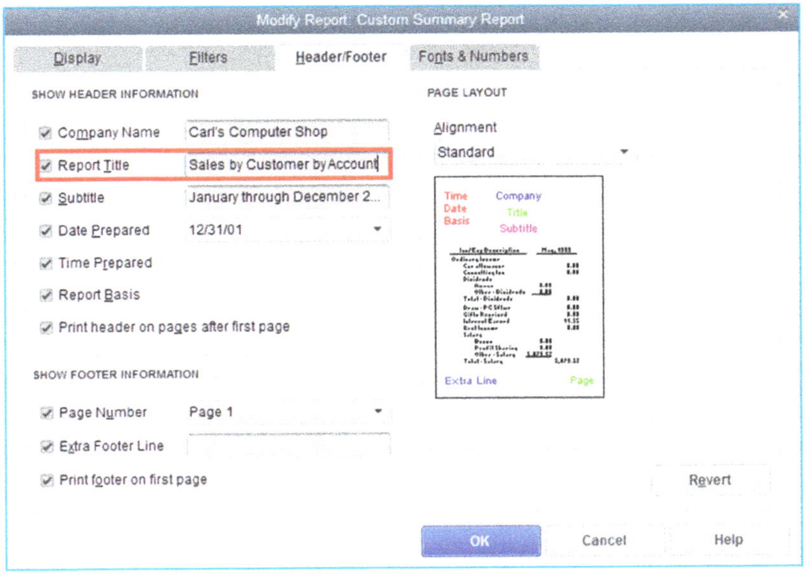

Below is the resulting customized report:

**Carl's Computer Shop**
**Sales by Customer by Account**
January through December 2019

| | Assembled Systems (Sales) | | Merchandise (Sales) | | Service (Sales) | | Total Sales | | Total Income | |
|---|---|---|---|---|---|---|---|---|---|---|
| | Jan - Dec 19 | % of Column | Jan - Dec 19 | % of Column | Jan - Dec 19 | % of Column | Jan - Dec 19 | % of Column | Jan - Dec 19 | % of Column |
| Chidester, Jim | 2,895.00 | 1.3% | 1,610.00 | 1.5% | 2,403.00 | 1.1% | 6,908.00 | 1.3% | 6,908.00 | 1.3% |
| Duncan, Dave | 0.00 | 0.0% | 0.00 | 0.0% | 11,180.00 | 5.2% | 11,180.00 | 2% | 11,180.00 | 2% |
| Dunn, Eric C.W. | 4,475.00 | 2% | 0.00 | 0.0% | 0.00 | 0.0% | 4,475.00 | 0.8% | 4,475.00 | 0.8% |
| Easley, Paula | 5,975.00 | 2.6% | 10,784.67 | 10.2% | 6,267.00 | 2.9% | 23,026.67 | 4.2% | 23,026.67 | 4.2% |
| Jimenez, Cristina | 10,745.00 | 4.7% | 3,288.00 | 3.1% | 22,469.00 | 10.6% | 36,502.00 | 6.7% | 36,502.00 | 6.7% |
| Jones Law Office | 38,375.00 | 16.8% | 3,587.00 | 3.4% | 6,410.00 | 3% | 48,372.00 | 8.9% | 48,372.00 | 8.9% |
| Lamb, Brad | 0.00 | 0.0% | 12,912.00 | 12.2% | 23,685.00 | 11.1% | 36,597.00 | 6.7% | 36,597.00 | 6.7% |
| Lee, Laurel | 8,950.00 | 3.9% | 3,948.00 | 3.7% | 4,709.00 | 2.2% | 17,607.00 | 3.2% | 17,607.00 | 3.2% |
| Lew Plumbing - C | 5,975.00 | 2.6% | 6,564.00 | 6.2% | 9,490.00 | 4.5% | 22,029.00 | 4% | 22,029.00 | 4% |
| Lucchini, Bill | 28,950.00 | 12.7% | 4,586.00 | 4.3% | 6,629.00 | 3.1% | 40,165.00 | 7.4% | 40,165.00 | 7.4% |
| Luke, Noelani | 0.00 | 0.0% | 0.00 | 0.0% | 8,105.00 | 3.8% | 8,105.00 | 1.5% | 8,105.00 | 1.5% |
| Milner, Eloyse | 35,375.00 | 15.5% | 0.00 | 0.0% | 10,305.00 | 4.8% | 45,680.00 | 8.4% | 45,680.00 | 8.4% |
| Morgenthaler, Je... | 14,950.00 | 6.6% | 7,437.00 | 7% | 46,688.00 | 21.9% | 69,075.00 | 12.6% | 69,075.00 | 12.6% |
| Morris, Katherine | 15,820.00 | 6.9% | 4,687.00 | 4.4% | 15,112.00 | 7.1% | 35,619.00 | 6.5% | 35,619.00 | 6.5% |
| Oliveri, Tom | 30,535.00 | 13.4% | 11,144.00 | 10.6% | 15,629.00 | 7.3% | 57,308.00 | 10.5% | 57,308.00 | 10.5% |
| Prentice, Adelaide | 0.00 | 0.0% | 8,370.00 | 7.9% | 2,700.00 | 1.3% | 11,070.00 | 2% | 11,070.00 | 2% |
| Reese, Pamela | 3,585.00 | 1.6% | 3,746.98 | 3.6% | 975.00 | 0.5% | 8,306.98 | 1.5% | 8,306.98 | 1.5% |
| Ruff, Bryan | 0.00 | 0.0% | 0.00 | 0.0% | 5,400.00 | 2.5% | 5,400.00 | 1% | 5,400.00 | 1% |
| Smith, Lee | 0.00 | 0.0% | 0.00 | 0.0% | 6,790.00 | 3.2% | 6,790.00 | 1.2% | 6,790.00 | 1.2% |
| Tumacder, Jacint | 9,375.00 | 4.1% | 13,232.00 | 12.5% | 1,638.00 | 0.8% | 24,245.00 | 4.4% | 24,245.00 | 4.4% |
| Wilks, Daniel | 5,975.00 | 2.6% | 7,784.00 | 7.4% | 2,300.00 | 1.1% | 16,059.00 | 2.9% | 16,059.00 | 2.9% |
| Wood, Emily | 5,975.00 | 2.6% | 1,862.00 | 1.8% | 4,080.00 | 1.9% | 11,917.00 | 2.2% | 11,917.00 | 2.2% |
| TOTAL | 227,930.00 | 100.0% | 105,542.65 | 100.0% | 212,964.00 | 100.0% | 546,436.65 | 100.0% | 546,436.65 | 100.0% |

**Custom Transaction Detail Report** – this screen is identical in appearance to the "Transaction Detail by Account" screen generated when drilling down on balances in standard reports. The difference is that there are more data fields available to display as columns. If a data field is not available on standard reports, it may be available in the Custom option.

# Memorizing (and Retrieving) Reports

After getting a report just the way you want it, you can save the report's settings—what QuickBooks calls "Memorizing"—so you don't have to recreate the customizations every time you need a particular report.

To memorize a report, click on the "Memorize" tab in the report menu while the report is open. This brings up the Memorize Report box where you can give your report a name for later use. Once saved, memorized reports can be accessed by selecting Memorized Reports under Reports on the main menu.

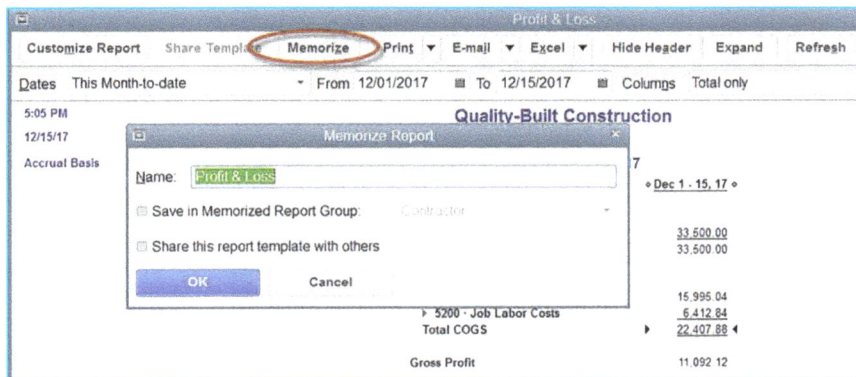

When a change is made to a memorized report, it can be saved as a new report or the original report can be replaced with the new one.

While the report is open, click on the Memorize tab, which will bring up the following screen:

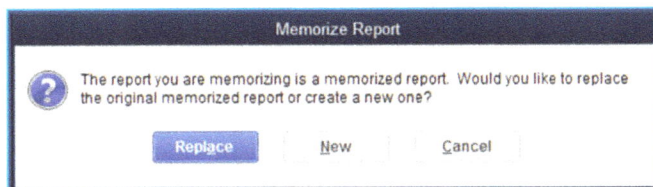

**IMPORTANT TIP** – The collapsing of sub-accounts as discussed earlier *does not* get memorized. When reports that have been customized by collapsing sub-accounts are memorized and later retrieved, the collapsed sub-accounts will reappear.

Users who create a large number of memorized reports will find the predefined Memorized Report Groups and/or create New Groups options useful so individual reports can easily be located. For example, it may be helpful to have report groups for sales reports, budget reports, accounts receivable reports, etc.

To set up a new memorized report group, start at the main menu and select Reports, then Memorized Reports, then Memorized Report List, which will bring up the Memorized Report screen below:

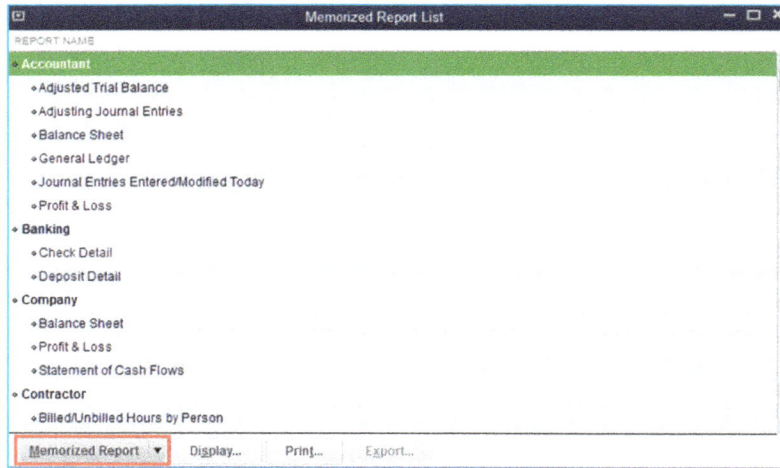

Clicking on the drop-down arrow in the lower left of the Memorized Report box shown in the above screen will give the option of creating a new group.

# Showing Comments on Reports

Accountants preparing reports for management are often called upon to provide explanations about variances or issues that exist. Comments can be added to reports so that explanations can be communicated using "Commented Reports." As an example, an Accounts Receivable Aging report will be commented on with notes on the collectability of older customer balances.

To create a Commented Report, after generating a report, click on the "Comment on Report" tab in the upper left of the report menu as shown below:

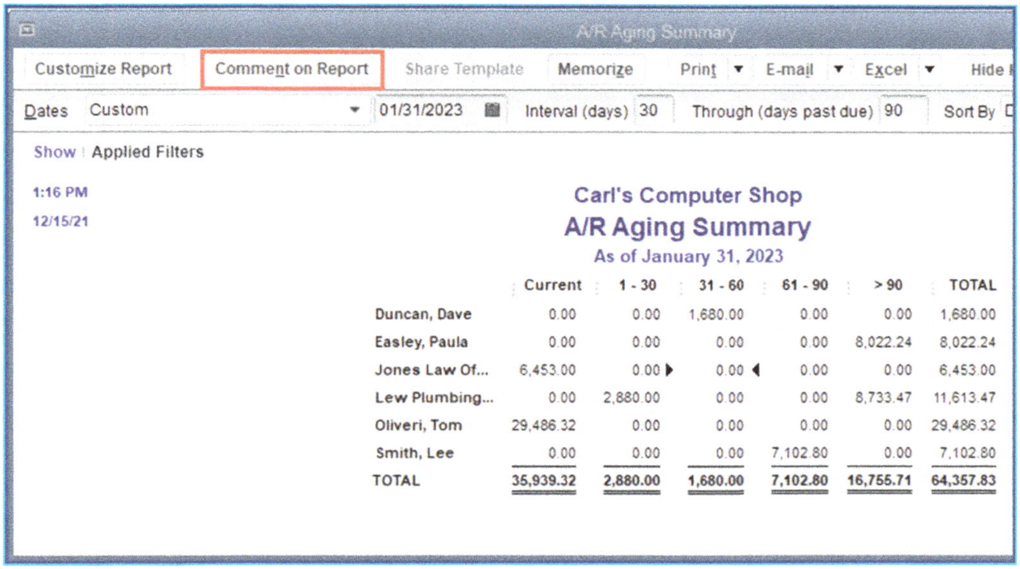


Carl's Computer Shop
A/R Aging Summary
As of January 31, 2023

| | Current | 1 - 30 | 31 - 60 | 61 - 90 | > 90 | TOTAL |
|---|---|---|---|---|---|---|
| Duncan, Dave | 0.00 | 0.00 | 1,680.00 | 0.00 | 0.00 | 1,680.00 |
| Easley, Paula | 0.00 | 0.00 | 0.00 | 0.00 | 8,022.24 | 8,022.24 |
| Jones Law Of... | 6,453.00 | 0.00 | 0.00 | 0.00 | 0.00 | 6,453.00 |
| Lew Plumbing... | 0.00 | 2,880.00 | 0.00 | 0.00 | 8,733.47 | 11,613.47 |
| Oliveri, Tom | 29,486.32 | 0.00 | 0.00 | 0.00 | 0.00 | 29,486.32 |
| Smith, Lee | 0.00 | 0.00 | 0.00 | 7,102.80 | 0.00 | 7,102.80 |
| TOTAL | 35,939.32 | 2,880.00 | 1,680.00 | 7,102.80 | 16,755.71 | 64,357.83 |

After clicking on the Comment on Report tab, the screen below will show a box to the right of each number.

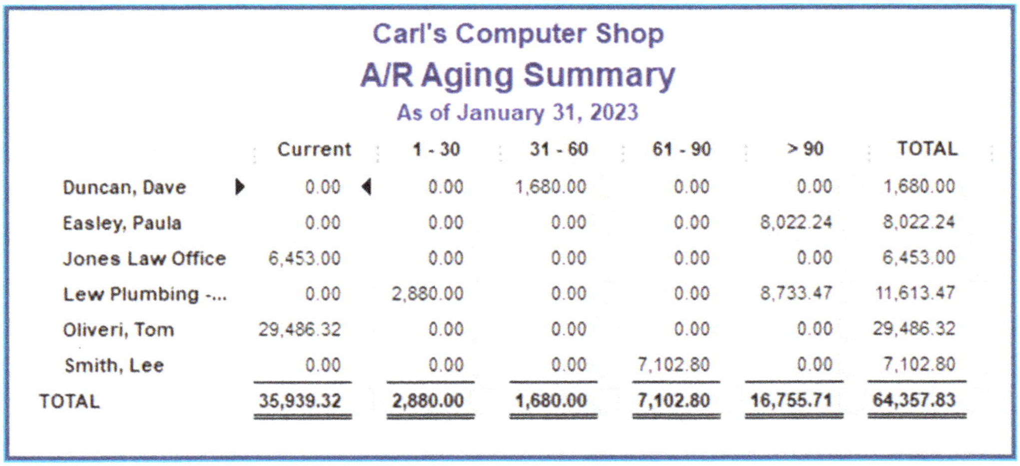

Carl's Computer Shop
A/R Aging Summary
As of January 31, 2023

| | Current | 1 - 30 | 31 - 60 | 61 - 90 | > 90 | TOTAL |
|---|---|---|---|---|---|---|
| Duncan, Dave | 0.00 | 0.00 | 1,680.00 | 0.00 | 0.00 | 1,680.00 |
| Easley, Paula | 0.00 | 0.00 | 0.00 | 0.00 | 8,022.24 | 8,022.24 |
| Jones Law Office | 6,453.00 | 0.00 | 0.00 | 0.00 | 0.00 | 6,453.00 |
| Lew Plumbing -... | 0.00 | 2,880.00 | 0.00 | 0.00 | 8,733.47 | 11,613.47 |
| Oliveri, Tom | 29,486.32 | 0.00 | 0.00 | 0.00 | 0.00 | 29,486.32 |
| Smith, Lee | 0.00 | 0.00 | 0.00 | 7,102.80 | 0.00 | 7,102.80 |
| TOTAL | 35,939.32 | 2,880.00 | 1,680.00 | 7,102.80 | 16,755.71 | 64,357.83 |

Clicking on one of the boxes will bring up the screen shown next, where comments can be inserted.

Numbers are assigned to the comments, with the first comment being number 1, the second comment number 2, etc. The comments are typed in the gray area at the bottom. In the next example, a comment has been inserted about the collectability of an older receivable. Clicking on the save button in the lower right of the screen will save the comment and allow for the insertion of another comment.

Below shows the comment screen after the insertion of three comments. Comments can be deleted by clicking on the X to the far right of the comment. If a comment is deleted, the numbering is changed accordingly. For example, if comment number 2 is deleted then comment number 3 would be renumbered as comment number 2.

After making all the comments desired, the report with the accompanying comments can be printed or emailed as a PDF file. The comments are shown on a separate page.

Below is the printed report and comments for the previous example:

**Carl's Computer Shop**
**A/R Aging Summary**
As of January 31, 2023

| | Current | 1 - 30 | 31 - 60 | 61 - 90 | > 90 | TOTAL |
|---|---|---|---|---|---|---|
| Duncan, Dave | 0.00 | 0.00 | 1,680.00 | 0.00 | 0.00 | 1,680.00 |
| Easley, Paula | 0.00 | 0.00 | 0.00 | 0.00 | 8,022.24 [1] | 8,022.24 |
| Jones Law Office | 6,453.00 | 0.00 | 0.00 | 0.00 | 0.00 | 6,453.00 |
| Lew Plumbing - C | 0.00 | 2,880.00 | 0.00 | 0.00 | 8,733.47 [2] | 11,613.47 |
| Oliveri, Tom | 29,486.32 | 0.00 | 0.00 | 0.00 | 0.00 | 29,486.32 |
| Smith, Lee | 0.00 | 0.00 | 0.00 | 7,102.80 [3] | 0.00 | 7,102.80 |
| TOTAL | 35,939.32 | 2,880.00 | 1,680.00 | 7,102.80 | 16,755.71 | 64,357.83 |

1:33 PM

12/15/21

**Carl's Computer Shop**
**A/R Aging Summary**
As of January 31, 2023

1. Customer has issues with quality of product

2. Customer has gone out of business, suggest this be written off

3. Customer has promised payment next week

Commented Reports can be saved for later use by clicking on the Save button while in the screen used to create comments. This will bring up the box below where the Commented Report can be given a name.

**Save Your Commented Report** ✕

Name: A/R Aging Summary as of 1-31-2023

| OK | Cancel |
|---|---|

To retrieve a previously saved Commented Report, from the main menu select Reports, then Commented Reports, then select the report desired from the drop-down list. One of the drawbacks of creating a Commented Report is that once created, the only edits that can be made are to change or add new comments. It is suggested that commented reports be generated only after all reports have been reviewed for a period and all necessary adjustments are made.

# Processing Multiple Reports

Many accountants are called upon to issue a package of financial reports on a monthly or quarterly basis. These could include a Summary Profit & Loss Statement, Profit & Loss by Class or Job, Balance Sheet, Accounts Receivable Aging, and Accounts Payable Aging. Calling each one up individually and selecting the appropriate date ranges can be time consuming, but the Processing Multiple Reports option streamlines this process. In order to use this functionality, reports must be either Memorized or Commented reports.

From the main menu, select Generate Multiple Reports under Reports, then Process Multiple Reports. The screen below will appear:

In the above example, reports grouped as "Accountant" reports from the list of Memorized Reports have been chosen. Further, the user can select which reports in the group to process by checking off the boxes on the left, next to the individual report name. On the right, the dates for the reports are selected.

Once the reports to be processed are selected and the desired date ranges set, the user can Display, Print, or Email the reports.

# Combining Reports From Multiple Companies

Many organizations are structured with multiple corporations having common ownership. This is done for legal, tax, financing, or other reasons. In many cases, individual QuickBooks company files are set up for each corporation. Reports from these separate companies can be combined to produce financial statements for the entire organization. The reports are generated as Excel reports, enabling accountants to then make adjustments in Excel for the elimination of intercompany balances for a true consolidated report.

Several things to keep in mind:

- This functionality is only available in the Enterprise version of QuickBooks.
- All files from which data is to be combined must be in the same year version of QuickBooks.
- Only company files with the QBW extension can be combined. Backup, Accountant's Copy, and Portable files will not work with the combine functionality.
- Each company will appear as a separate column on the report and a total "Combined" column is generated on the far right.
- Accounts appear as rows, as with individual reports. Accounts that are exact matches will show on the same row on the report; edit account names to match if it is desired for accounts to show on the same row.
- The reports can be given a custom name.
- Once reports are generated, they are not automatically updated for changes made in the QuickBooks files from where the data originated.
- Combined reports cannot be memorized.

Only the following reports are available to be combined:

- Balance Sheet Standard
- Balance Sheet Summary
- Profit & Loss Standard
- Statement of Cash Flows
- Trail Balance
- Profit & Loss by Class
- Sales by Customer Summary

## Running Combined Reports

To run a combined report, from the main menu select Reports, then Combine Reports from Multiple Companies, which will bring up the screen below:

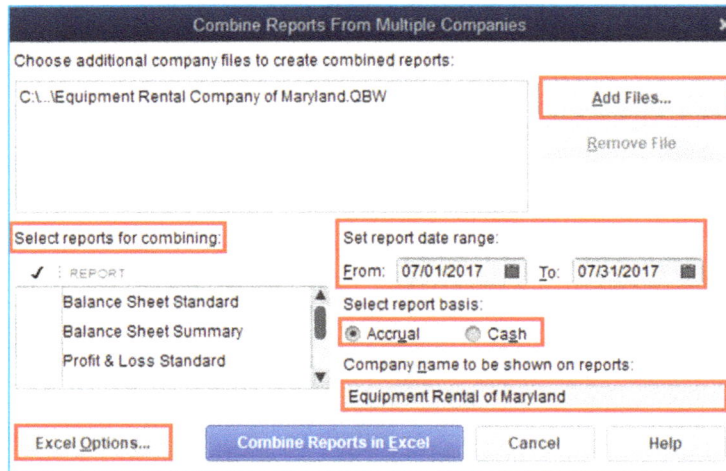

Clicking on the "Add Files" button will allow the user to select which companies are to be combined. This will bring up a drop-down menu of file names for selection in the Windows File Manager format. Double clicking on a file name will add it to the list.

The Excel options button will bring up the same screen as shown in the last image example at the end of chapter three, allowing the user to select the Excel formats desired. These selections are saved for the next report.

After selecting the desired report(s), date range, report basis, and giving the report a name, click on the blue "Combine Reports in Excel" button to generate the report(s). If multiple reports are selected, one Excel spreadsheet will be generated with a separate worksheet/tab for each report.

Combined Reports can take a few minutes to complete, and while reports are being generated, the following messages will be shown:

- Please wait while QuickBooks gathers report data. This process may take a while. Gathering reports data from company file 1 of 3.
- Exporting combined reports to Excel. Please wait.

Once the report has completed, a new Excel spreadsheet is created. Below is a sample of a combined Profit & Loss Standard report:

| | Equipment Rental of Maryland | Equipment Rental of Virginia | Equipment Rental Parent | TOTAL |
|---|---|---|---|---|
| **Equipment Rental of Maryland** | | | | 7:53 PM |
| **Combined Profit And Loss** | | | | 10/30/2017 |
| January through September 2017 | | | | Accrual Basis |
| Ordinary Income/Expense | | | | |
| Income | | | | |
| Rental Income | 145,000.00 | 225,000.00 | 0.00 | 370,000.00 |
| Total Income | 145,000.00 | 225,000.00 | 0.00 | 370,000.00 |
| Cost of Goods Sold | | | | |
| Equipment Repairs | 19,500.00 | 27,500.00 | 0.00 | 47,000.00 |
| Freight Charges | 10,000.00 | 15,000.00 | 0.00 | 25,000.00 |
| Fuel | 6,000.00 | 11,000.00 | 0.00 | 17,000.00 |
| Total COGS | 35,500.00 | 53,500.00 | 0.00 | 89,000.00 |
| Gross Profit | 109,500.00 | 171,500.00 | 0.00 | 281,000.00 |
| Expense | | | | |
| Bank Service Charges | 10.00 | 10.00 | 25.00 | 45.00 |
| Computer and Internet Expenses | 0.00 | 0.00 | 2,000.00 | 2,000.00 |
| Depreciation Expense | 5,000.00 | 8,334.00 | 700.00 | 14,034.00 |
| Insurance Expense | 0.00 | 0.00 | 3,500.00 | 3,500.00 |
| Interest Expense | 1,500.00 | 2,500.00 | 0.00 | 4,000.00 |
| Meals and Entertainment | 0.00 | 0.00 | 500.00 | 500.00 |
| Office Supplies | 200.00 | 300.00 | 300.00 | 800.00 |
| Payroll | 37,500.00 | 55,000.00 | 40,000.00 | 132,500.00 |
| Payroll Taxes | 3,375.00 | 4,950.00 | 3,250.00 | 11,575.00 |
| Postage and Delivery | 25.00 | 35.00 | 100.00 | 160.00 |
| Professional Fees | 0.00 | 0.00 | 12,500.00 | 12,500.00 |
| Rent Expense | 8,500.00 | 10,000.00 | 2,250.00 | 20,750.00 |
| Small Tools and Equipment | 125.00 | 250.00 | 0.00 | 375.00 |
| Utilities | 750.00 | 1,000.00 | 375.00 | 2,125.00 |
| Total Expense | 56,985.00 | 82,379.00 | 65,500.00 | 204,864.00 |
| Net Ordinary Income | 52,515.00 | 89,121.00 | -65,500.00 | 76,136.00 |

# Advanced Feature of Exporting Reports to Excel

When reports don't show exactly what is needed, exporting to Excel may be preferable so the user can customize beyond what is available through QuickBooks. Using the Advanced Excel Options when exporting can streamline efforts.

From the report bar, select Excel/Create New Worksheet, then click on the Advanced button to open the Advanced Excel Options dialogue box. Some pointers:

- Get all the information you need before exporting – for example, if you are exporting a transaction report for use in an Excel pivot table, you may want the account to show on each row of the report. Modify the transaction report to show Account before you do the export.
- Row height – the default option brings the report into Excel with different size rows, matching the QB report. If you want all the rows the same height, unclick the "Row Height" option.
- Space between columns – the default option brings the report into Excel with blank columns. If you do not want blank columns, unclick the "Space Between Columns" option.

© The CFO Source, LLC 2017

- Gridlines – the default option brings the gridlines into the Excel report. Unclick this option to eliminate the gridlines if so desired.
- QuickBooks Export Guide – the default option creates a worksheet with the name "QuickBooks Export Tips," which provides information about exporting to Excel, but is really not needed. Uncheck this option to prevent the extra worksheet from being part of your final Excel report.

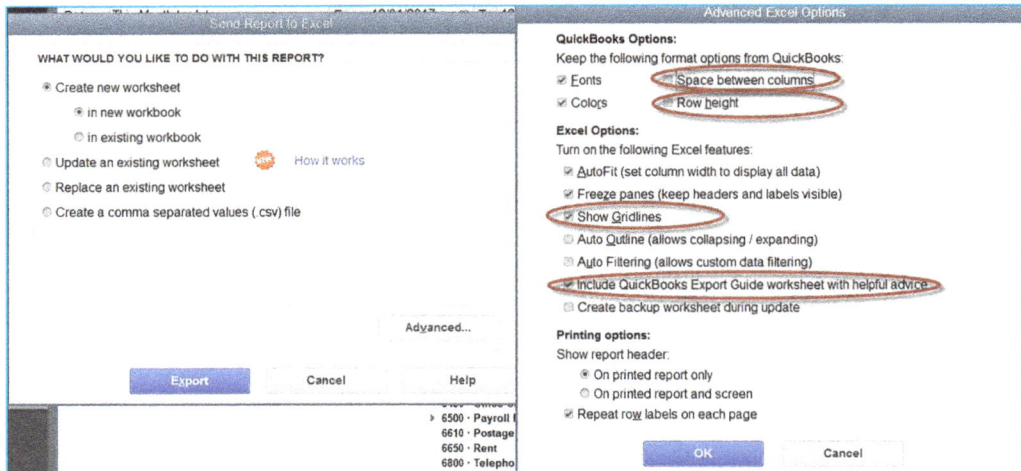

Notes:

_____

# Chapter Four
# Using the Audit Trail Report

One of the internal control weaknesses of QuickBooks is that transactions can be changed or deleted. This can be viewed as both good and bad. On the plus side, transactions can be changed or deleted to correct accounting, minimizing the need for adjusting journal entries or credit memos. The drawback is that there is no record in the drill down "transaction detail" reports showing what changes were made.

Fortunately, the Audit Trail report provides the history of both deleted and changed transactions. This can be extremely helpful when changes are made to transactions from prior time periods and accountants find that balances no longer agree with financial statements and/or tax returns. This report would be used to review changes and make corrections if necessary.

To illustrate, assume when you finalized a client's financial statements as of 12/31/2018, the accounts receivable balance was $55,000 as shown in the aging report below:

**Quality-Built Construction**
**A/R Aging Summary**
**As of December 31, 2018**

| | Current | 1 - 30 | 31 - 60 | 61 - 90 | > 90 | TOTAL |
|---|---|---|---|---|---|---|
| James Smith | 0.00 | 12,500.00 | 6,500.00 | 0.00 | 0.00 | 19,000.00 |
| Hamby, Shane | 15,000.00 | 0.00 | 0.00 | 0.00 | 0.00 | 15,000.00 |
| ▼ Molotsi, Hugh | | | | | | |
| Second Story Add... | 0.00 | 13,500.00 | 0.00 | 0.00 | 0.00 | 13,500.00 |
| Molotsi, Hugh - Oth... | 7,500.00 | 0.00 | 0.00 | 0.00 ▶ | 0.00 ◀ | 7,500.00 |
| Total Molotsi, Hugh | 7,500.00 | 13,500.00 | 0.00 | 0.00 | 0.00 | 21,000.00 |
| TOTAL | 22,500.00 | 26,000.00 | 6,500.00 | 0.00 | 0.00 | 55,000.00 |

Several months later, you returned to the client and found that the balance in accounts receivable as of 12/31/2018 had changed, with a new balance of only $40,000. As shown on the Aging Summary shown next, the receivable from Shane Hamby disappeared.

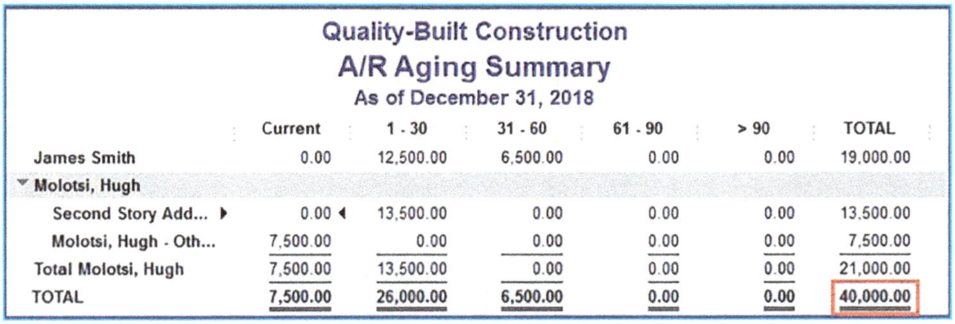

Quality-Built Construction
A/R Aging Summary
As of December 31, 2018

| | Current | 1 - 30 | 31 - 60 | 61 - 90 | > 90 | TOTAL |
|---|---|---|---|---|---|---|
| James Smith | 0.00 | 12,500.00 | 6,500.00 | 0.00 | 0.00 | 19,000.00 |
| Molotsi, Hugh | | | | | | |
| Second Story Add... | 0.00 | 13,500.00 | 0.00 | 0.00 | 0.00 | 13,500.00 |
| Molotsi, Hugh - Oth... | 7,500.00 | 0.00 | 0.00 | 0.00 | 0.00 | 7,500.00 |
| Total Molotsi, Hugh | 7,500.00 | 13,500.00 | 0.00 | 0.00 | 0.00 | 21,000.00 |
| TOTAL | 7,500.00 | 26,000.00 | 6,500.00 | 0.00 | 0.00 | 40,000.00 |

Using the Audit Trail Report, it is possible to find out what happened to the missing receivable from Shane Hamby. From the main menu, select Reports, then Accountant & Taxes, then Audit Trail, which brings up the below screen:

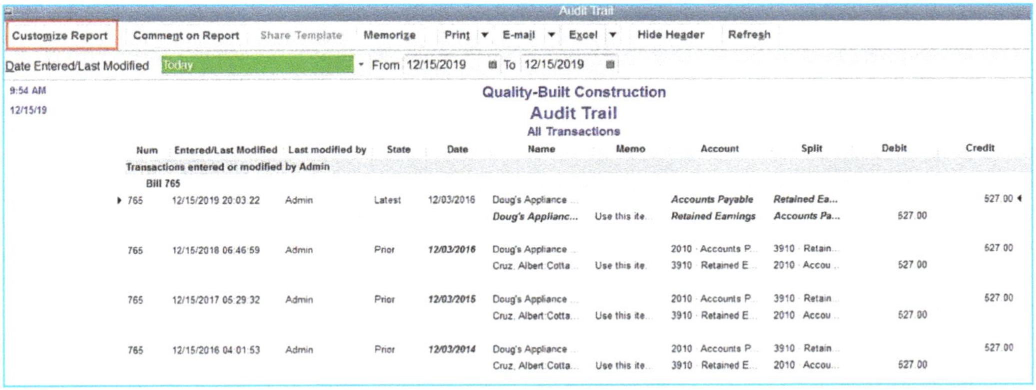


Quality-Built Construction
Audit Trail
All Transactions

| Num | Entered/Last Modified | Last modified by | State | Date | Name | Memo | Account | Split | Debit | Credit |
|---|---|---|---|---|---|---|---|---|---|---|
| Transactions entered or modified by Admin | | | | | | | | | | |
| Bill 765 | | | | | | | | | | |
| 765 | 12/15/2019 20:03:22 | Admin | Latest | 12/03/2016 | Doug's Appliance ... | | Accounts Payable | Retained Ea... | | 527.00 |
| | | | | | Doug's Applianc... | Use this ite... | Retained Earnings | Accounts Pa... | 527.00 | |
| 765 | 12/15/2018 06:46:59 | Admin | Prior | 12/03/2016 | Doug's Appliance ... | | 2010 · Accounts P... | 3910 · Retain... | | 527.00 |
| | | | | | Cruz, Albert:Cotta... | Use this ite... | 3910 · Retained E... | 2010 · Accou... | 527.00 | |
| 765 | 12/15/2017 05:29:32 | Admin | Prior | 12/03/2015 | Doug's Appliance ... | | 2010 · Accounts P... | 3910 · Retain... | | 527.00 |
| | | | | | Cruz, Albert:Cotta... | Use this ite... | 3910 · Retained E... | 2010 · Accou... | 527.00 | |
| 765 | 12/15/2016 04:01:53 | Admin | Prior | 12/03/2014 | Doug's Appliance ... | | 2010 · Accounts P... | 3910 · Retain... | | 527.00 |
| | | | | | Cruz, Albert:Cotta... | Use this ite... | 3910 · Retained E... | 2010 · Accou... | 527.00 | |

From this screen, select the Customize Report tab.

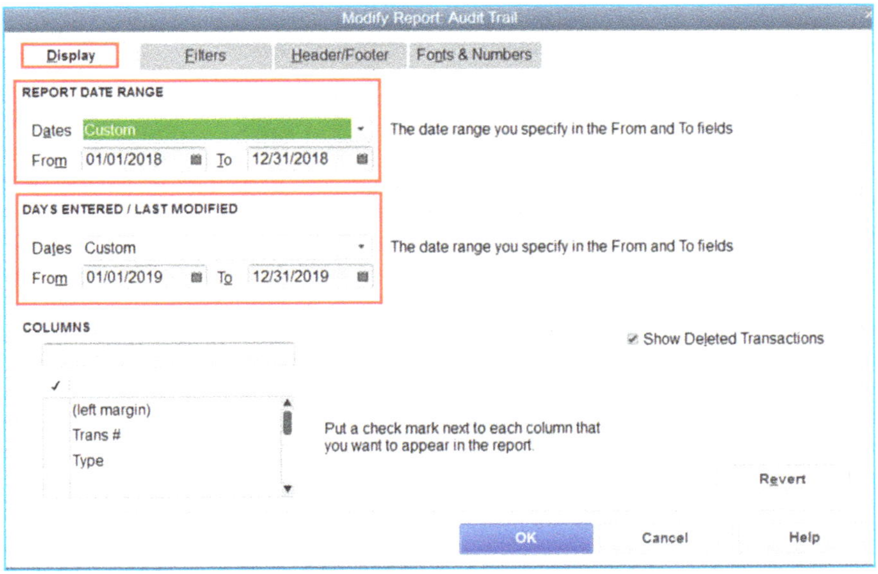

In the Display tab, there are two sections on dates:

- Report Date Range – this is the date the transaction was assigned when entered into QuickBooks.
- Date Entered/Last Modified – this is the date on which the transaction was recorded.

In the example, the report date range would be 1/1/2018 to 12/31/2018, representing all transactions for calendar year 2018. For the Date Entered/Last Modified Dates, these would be after 12/31/2018, as it is likely that the receivable transactions being researched were changed after year end.

In the Filters Tab, the user can filter for numerous criteria. In this example, the report is filtered for the Customer Name Shane Hamby. First, select Name from the filter menu as shown below:

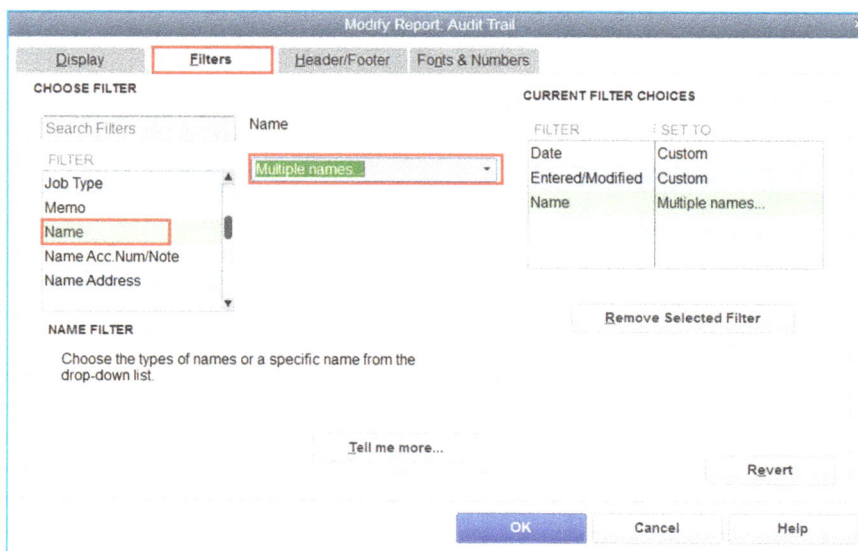

Next, click on the Multiple Names drop-down menu to bring up a list of names to choose from.

As shown below, all names connected with Shane Hamby were selected:

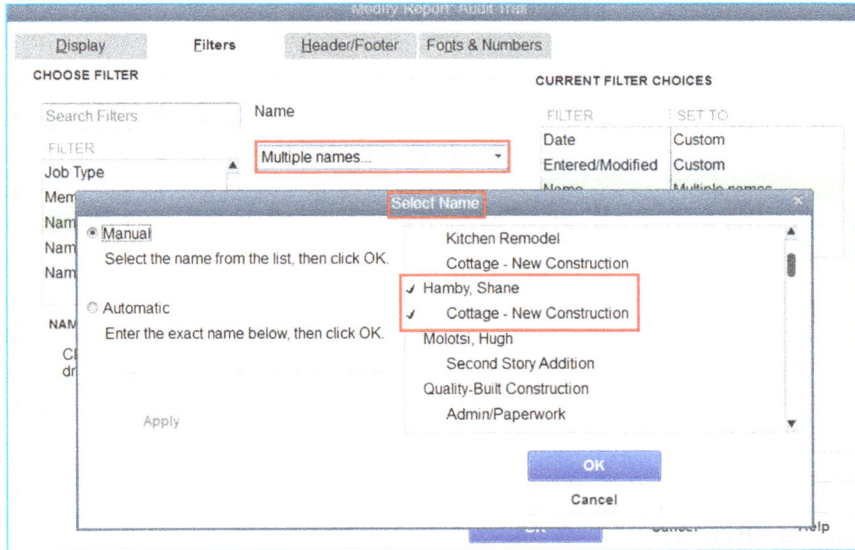

Clicking OK to confirm your selections will show the following customized report:

In this example, the Audit Trail Report shows the reason the Shane Hamby receivable disappeared from the aging report dated 12/31/2018. The update to Invoice 1120 changed the date to 1/2/2019, which would cause that invoice for $15,000 NOT to appear on an aging dated 12/31/2018.

Notes:

## Chapter Five

# Accountant's Copy Functionality

The Accountant's Copy functionality is designed so that accountants can get a copy of a client's QuickBooks file, make changes to the file, and return the changes to be incorporated into the Client's file. An important feature is the ability of both the client and the accountant to work on the file at the same time, even though two files exist—the client's file and the accountant's copy.

This functionality is meant for smaller clients who keep their company file on a local computer that is not accessible to their accountant. For larger clients who have given their accountant access to their company file either in the cloud or with a remote desktop connection, the accountant's copy functionality is likely not needed.

## The Accountant's Copy and Versions/Years of QuickBooks

Certain compatibility issues exist due to clients and accountants having a variety of QuickBooks versions. The following guidelines apply:

- The functionality only works for years 2007 and greater.
- The accountant can use either the same year version as the client or the next year. For example, if the client is using a 2014 version, the accountant can use either 2014 or 2015.
- If the client is using the most recent year, the accountant must use the most recent year as well.

A critical part of the process is setting the "Dividing Date." When an accountant's file is created, a Dividing Date must be assigned for two purposes:

- The client cannot make changes to their file using a date *on or before* the Dividing Date.
- The accountant cannot make changes to the file *after* the Dividing Date.

Typically, accountants will work on a client's file through the end of a particular time period, such as end of the year. It is suggested that the Dividing Date be set for a few days after a period end date. This allows for the creation of reversing entries and the ability to change the dates of any transactions immediately following the period ending date, if need be.

There are several file extensions related to file creation for QuickBooks Accountants. These are as follows:

- A .QBX file is created when a client creates an Accountant's Copy file to send to their accountant.
- A .QBA file is created when the accountant converts the .QBX file from their client.
- A .QBY file, also referred to as the "Changes file," is created when the accountant is finished making adjustments. This file is sent to the client and serves to import the changes into the client's regular file (.QBW).

# Creating an Accountant's Copy file

This will be done by the client from their regular QuickBooks file. From the main menu, go to File, then Create Copy, then select Accountant's Copy as shown below:

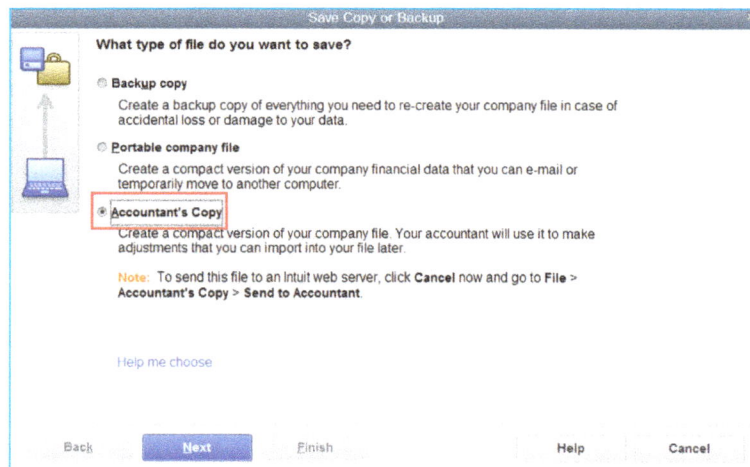

Selecting Next will bring up the screen shown next, asking the user to confirm that an accountant's file is desired.

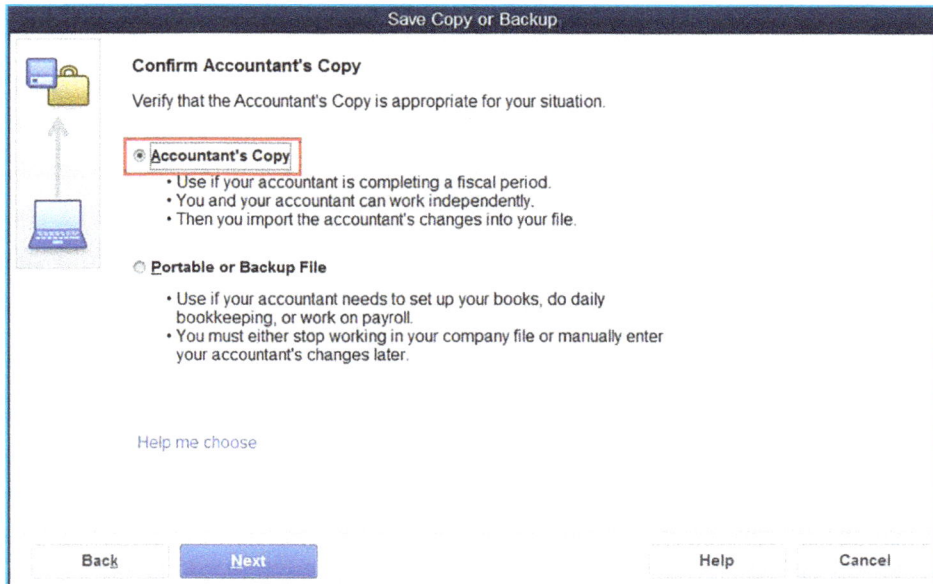

Select Next to bring up the screen where the Dividing Date is set. The "Custom" option was chosen in the first drop-down box to allow a specific date to be entered in the second field.

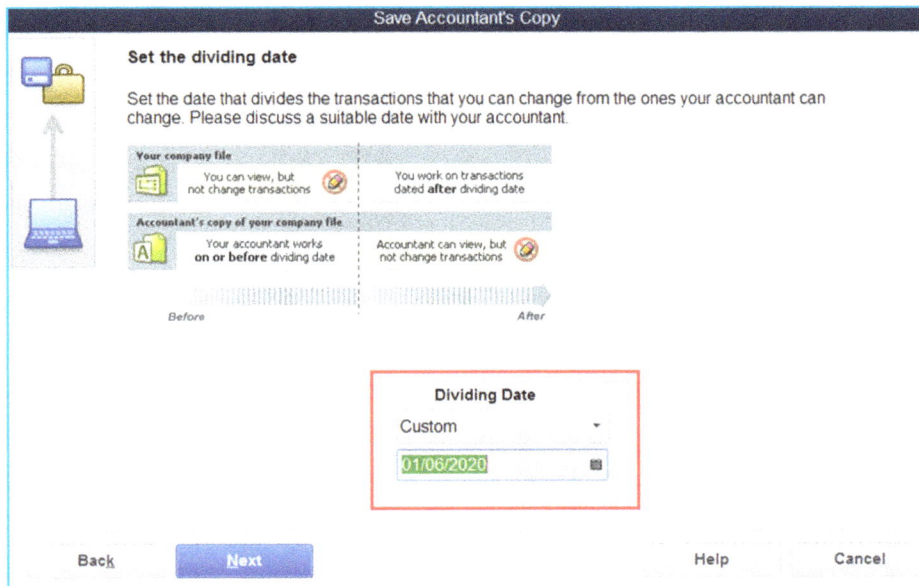

Selecting Next will bring up the following screen so that the file can be named and saved. It is suggested to give the file a name that includes the client's company name and the date the file was created.

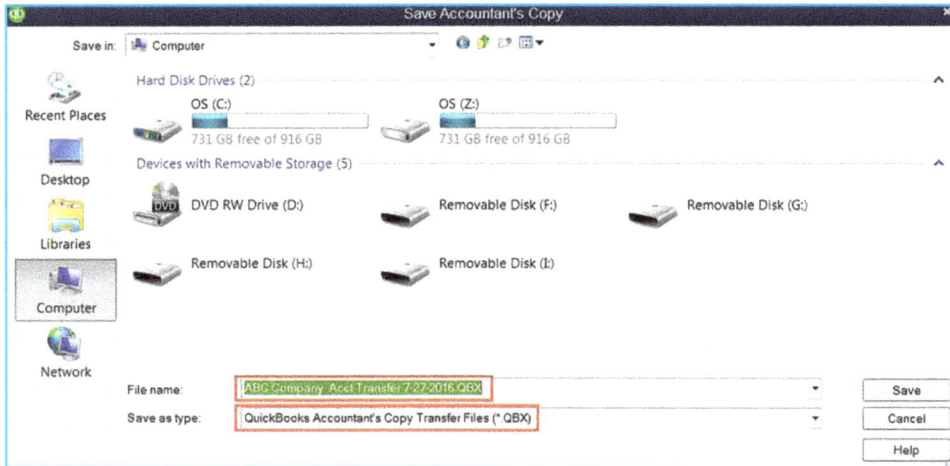

After creating the file, the client then sends the Accountant's Copy file to the accountant. This can be done by email, flash drive, shared cloud files, etc. Make sure the client provides the Admin user name and password so the file can be opened!

# Client View Until Changes are Returned

The client will see a notation at the top of their screen, next to the company name, indicating "Accountant's Changes Pending." This will remain until either the accountant's changes are imported or the client file is converted back to a regular company file.

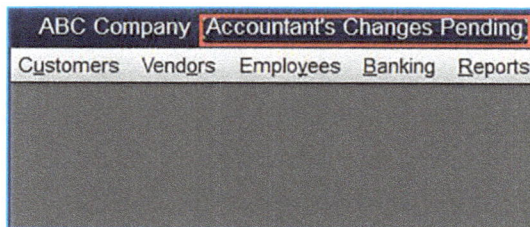

Additionally, if the client attempts to input transactions *before* the dividing date, QuickBooks will not save the transaction and the following message will appear:

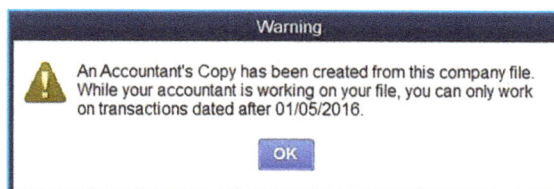

# Opening the Accountant's Copy

Once received, the accountant opens a client file as follows:

From the main menu, select File, then Open or Restore Company, then choose Convert an Accountant's Copy Transfer File.

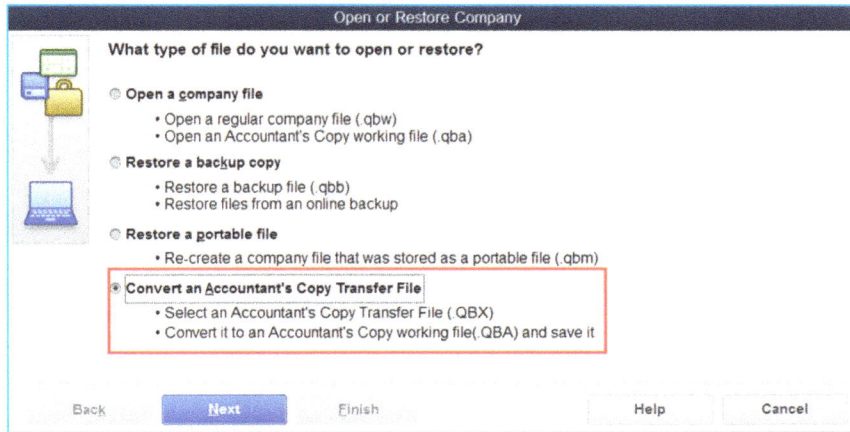

QuickBooks will display the following flowchart that provides an overview of the Accountant's file functionality.

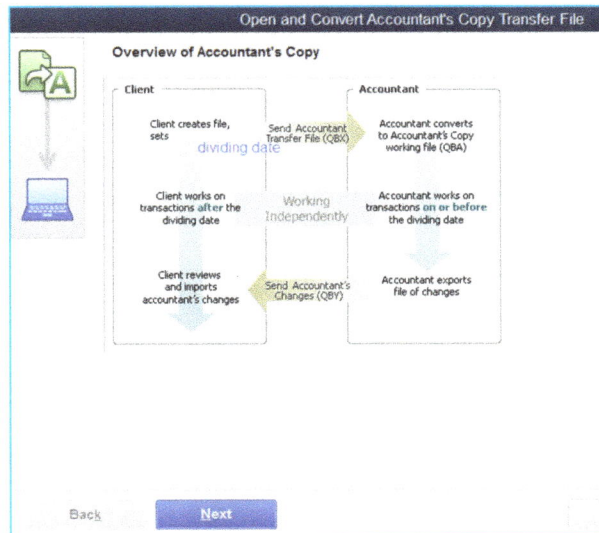

Clicking on Next will bring up the following screen of details on what Clients and Accountants can and can't do when using an Accountant's Copy.

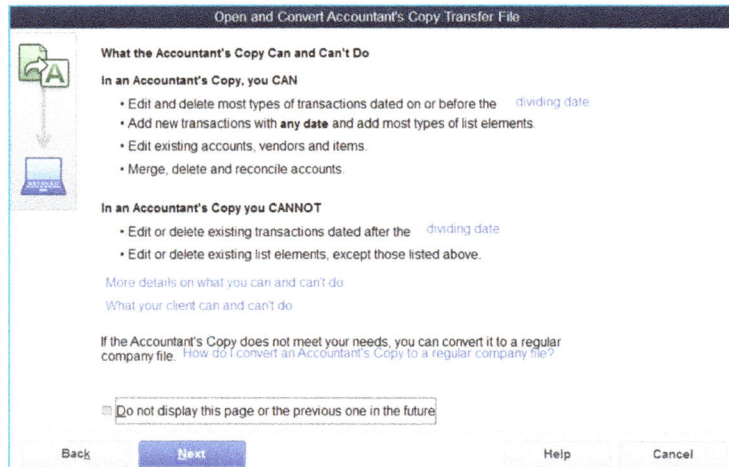

Clicking Next will enable the user to select the Accountant's Transfer file that will be converted to a .QBA file.

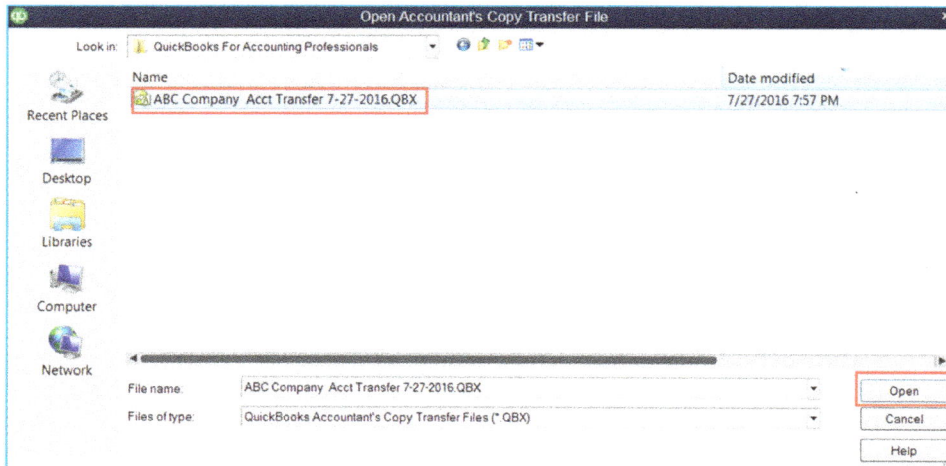

Clicking on Open will bring up the following message:

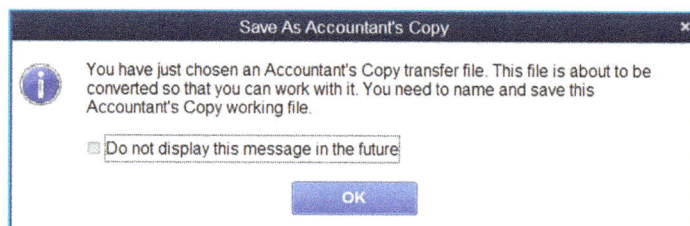

Clicking OK will bring up the screen that allows you to save and convert the file to a .QBA file.

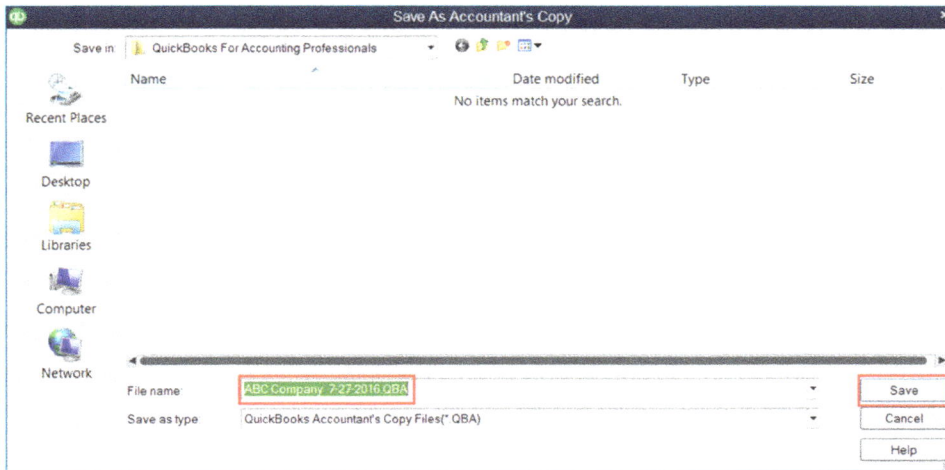

After clicking on Save, the file will be converted to a .QBA file, which can take several minutes. Once the conversion is completed, the user will be prompted for the Admin password to open the file. Upon the file opening, the following message will appear:

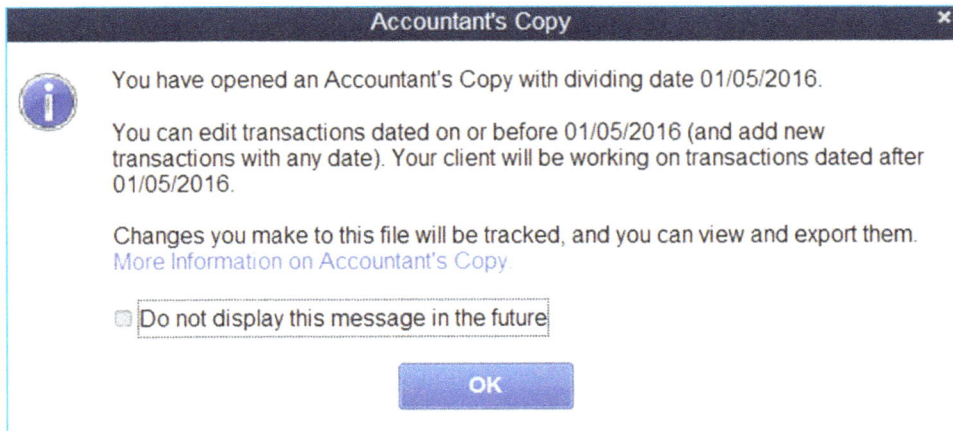

Click OK to begin using the file.

# Accountant View Until Changes are Returned

The accountant will see a notation at the top of the screen, next to the company name, indicating "Acct Copy" along with the dividing date set for the file. This will remain until either the accountant's changes are created or the client file is converted back to a regular company file.

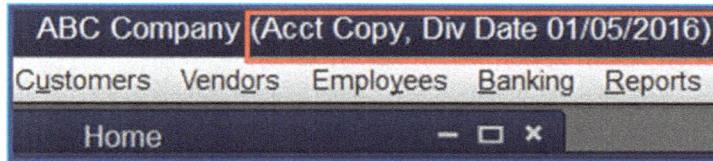

Additionally, if the Accountant attempts to edit transactions after the dividing date, QuickBooks will not save the transaction and the following message will appear:

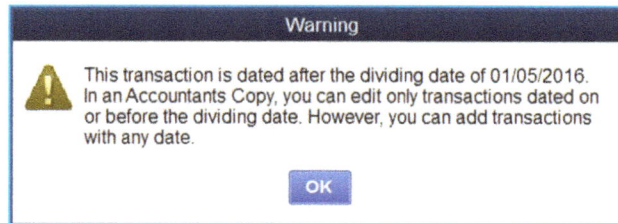

# Creating the Changes File

Once the accountant has made all the desired changes, a "changes file" is created so that the changes can be sent to the client. From the main menu, select File, then Send Company File, then Accountant's Copy, then View/Export Changes for Client. This will bring up the following screen:

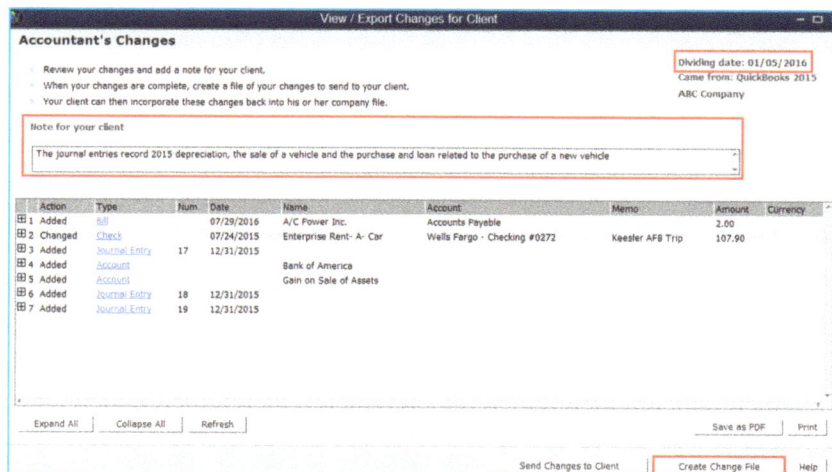

---

The accountant has the option of adding a note to accompany the file sent to the client. After reviewing the list of changes, click on "Create Change File" to bring up the screen below to select the save location and name the file as desired. Note the file type is .QBY.

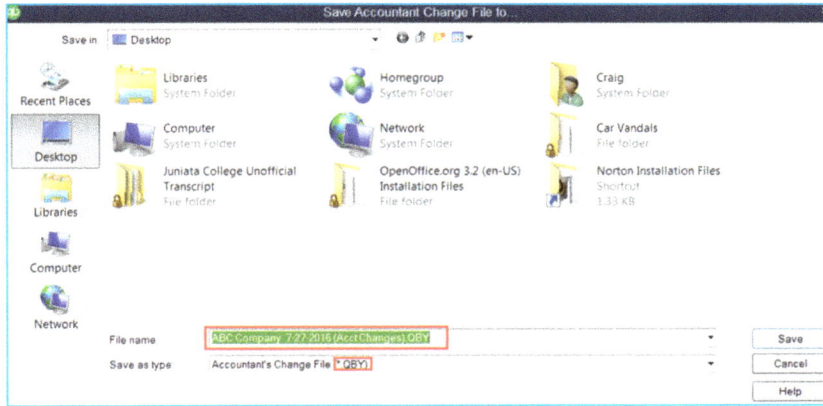

After saving the file, the following message will appear:

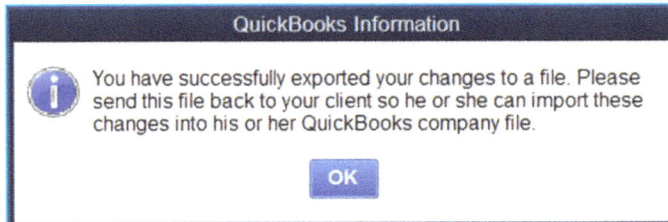

The file can be sent to the client by email, flash drive, shared cloud files, etc. from the location selected when naming the file.

# Importing the Changes File

Upon receiving the changes file, the client can import the changes into the working copy of their file so both the client's file and the accountant's file have the same data. From the main menu, select File, then Send Company File, then Accountant's Copy, then Client Activities, and finally, Import Accountant's Changes From File. This will bring up a screen to select the file previously received from the accountant. Upon selecting the file, the following screen will appear:

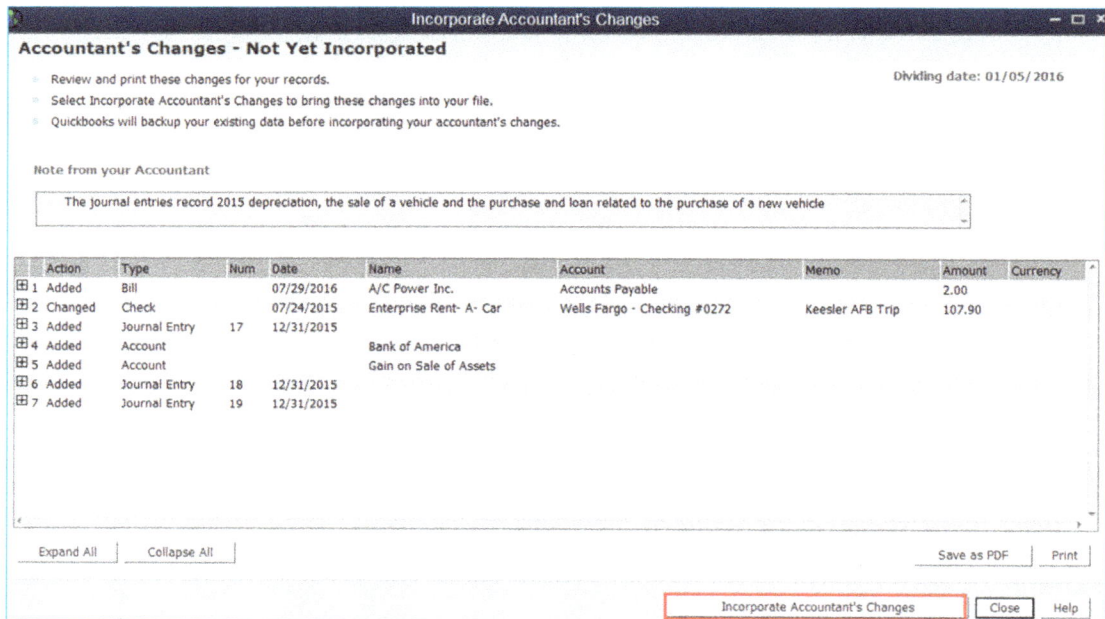

After clicking on Incorporate Accountant's Changes, the user will be asked to back up the file. After the file is backed up, the following message will appear:

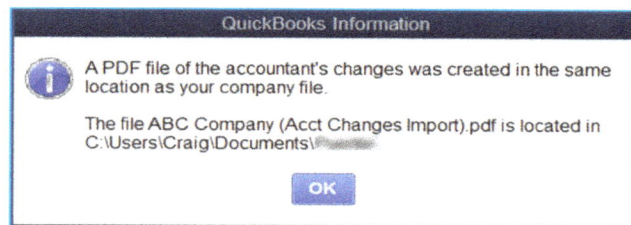

Finally, the user will get a message indicating the changes were successfully incorporated. Note that the details of the transactions can be shown (or minimized) by clicking on the + or – signs on the left of the screen.

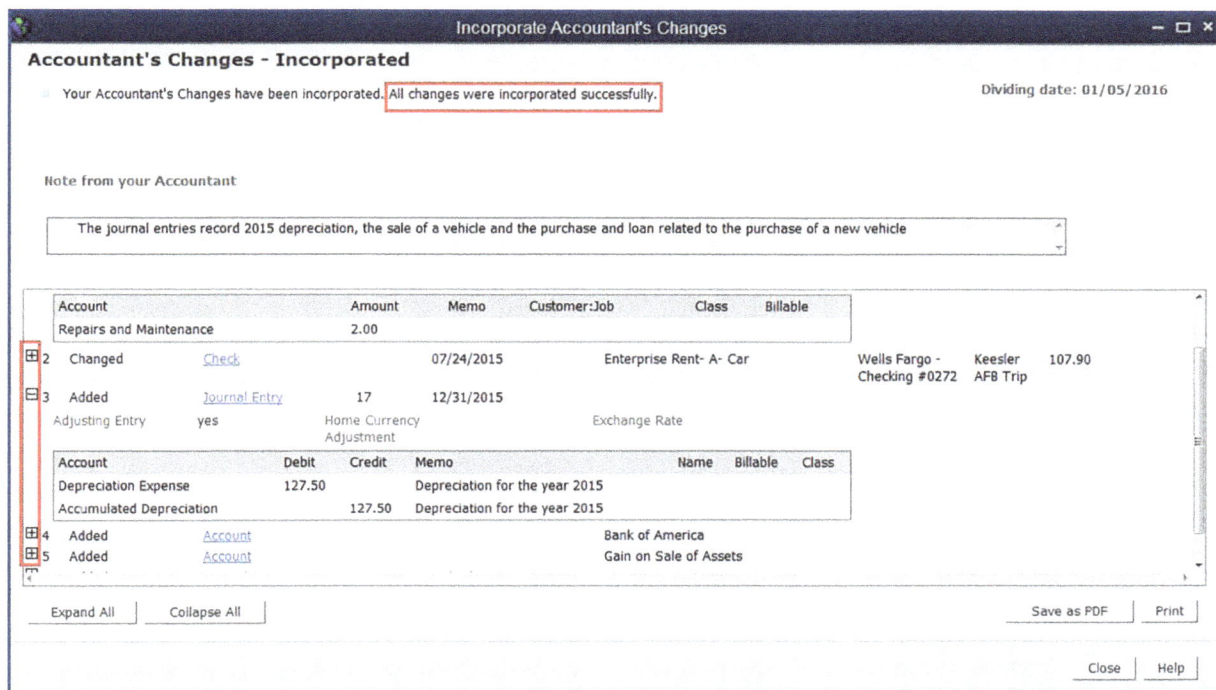

# Removing the Accountant's Copy Restrictions

If needed, the accountant's restrictions can be removed and the client's file returned to a normal state. From the main menu, select File, then Send Company File, then Accountant's Copy, then Client Activities, then finally, Remove Restrictions. Checking the box to confirm your intention and then clicking OK will remove the restrictions.

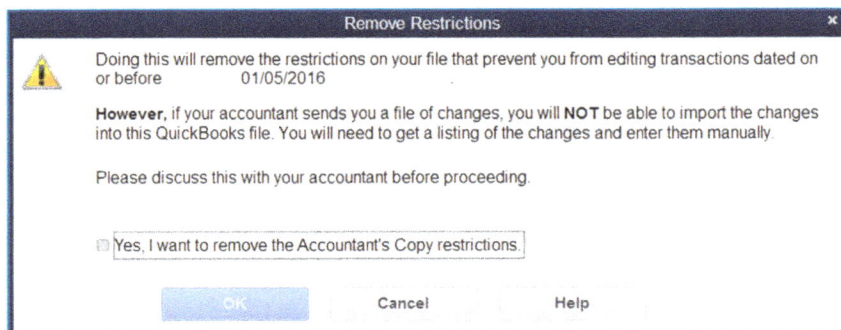

© The CFO Source, LLC 2017

Notes:

# Chapter Six

# Batch Entering Transactions

QuickBooks has functionality that allows for the convenient batch entry of the most typically used transactions. Transactions can be pasted from Excel or the screen can be used stand alone. The transactions available for batch entry include:

- Checks
- Deposits
- Credit Card Charges and Credits
- Bills and Bill Credits
- Invoices and Credit Memos

The data entry screens can be customized to match the user's Excel spreadsheets so that entire blocks of data can be copied and pasted from Excel into QuickBooks. After pasting or manuually entering data into the input screens, items such as names and account numbers that do not match QuickBooks lists appear in red to indicate a correction needs to be made.

In each of the transaction types, certain fields are mandatory while other fields are optional.

## Two Important Differences Between Batch and Regular Transaction Entry

**No Warnings on Duplicate Reference Numbers** – Unlike the transaction screens in various QuickBooks modules, the Batch Enter Transaction screen does not warn the user that duplicate reference numbers such as check numbers or invoice numbers are being used. For example, the message shown next will be generated in the Banking module if an attempt to record a check with a number that has already been entered is made.

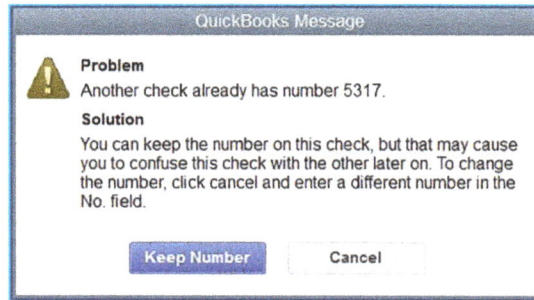

**QuickBooks Message**

⚠ **Problem**
Another check already has number 5317.

**Solution**
You can keep the number on this check, but that may cause you to confuse this check with the other later on. To change the number, click cancel and enter a different number in the No. field.

[ **Keep Number** ]   [ Cancel ]

No such warning message is given in similar circumstances using the Batch Enter Transaction screen.

**Splits functionality not supported** – "Splits" in QuickBooks refers to situations where multiple account codes are used on one transaction. For example, a vendor bill may be "Split" between more than one account, class, and/or job code. The expense side of the vendor bill is split to multiple expense accounts while the payable side appears as one total due the vendor. When using the batch enter transaction screen, multiple lines can be used for part of the same underlying transaction, but these lines will remain separate when recorded. For example, if a Vendor bill is entered into QuickBooks in the batch enter transactions screen with three "splits," three payables will also appear on the Vendor side as well.

# Examples of Batch Transaction Entry from Excel

From the main menu, select Accountant, then Batch Enter Transactions. In this screen, the user can select which type of transaction is desired. In this example, Checks has been chosen.

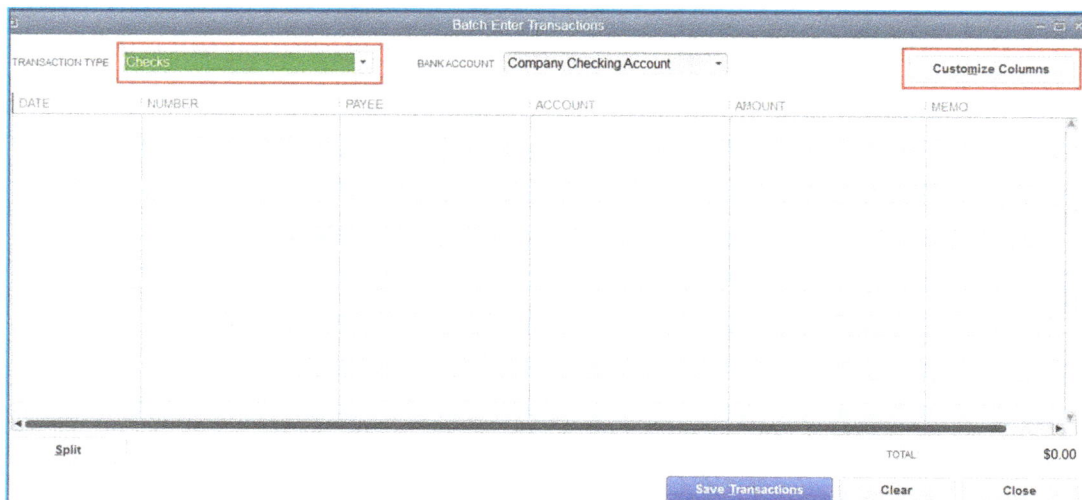

Clicking on the "Customize Columns" tab on the right will bring up the screen shown next for the user to add or remove fields and change the column order to match the layout of the Excel document for more accurate and faster copying and pasting. When this screen initially comes up, the default screen appears.

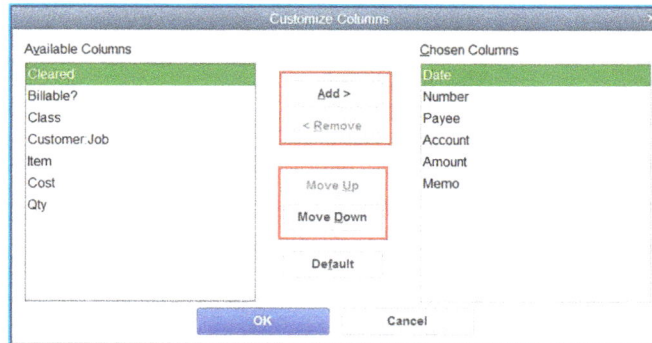

Below is an excel spreadsheet set up to import check information. Note the column header's are in the same sequence as the import screen in the Batch Enter Transactions Screen.

| | A | B | C | D | E |
|---|---|---|---|---|---|
| 1 | | | | | |
| 2 | | | | | |
| 3 | Date | Number | Vendor | Account | Amount |
| 4 | | | | | |
| 5 | 12/22/2019 | 1001 | Vin's Restaurant | Meals and Entertainment | 200 |
| 6 | 12/22/2019 | 1002 | Women's Shelter | Contributions | 300 |
| 7 | 12/22/2019 | 1003 | Mullen Travel | Travel | 325 |
| 8 | 12/22/2019 | 1004 | King, Vicki | Mileage | 155 |
| 9 | 12/22/2019 | 1005 | King, Vicki | Car/Truck Expense:Mileage | 75 |
| 10 | 12/22/2019 | 1006 | King Vicki | Car/Truck Expense:Mileage | 200 |

The area in blue will be imported as follows:

- In QuickBooks, have the Batch Enter Transactions Screen open.
- In Excel, highlight the area to be imported (as shown in the blue area in the example above), then right click and select Copy.
- Toggle over to QuickBooks, put the cursor on the top left part of the data entry area (1st row under date), then right click and select Paste.

The data from Excel is now pasted into QuickBooks and will appear as below:

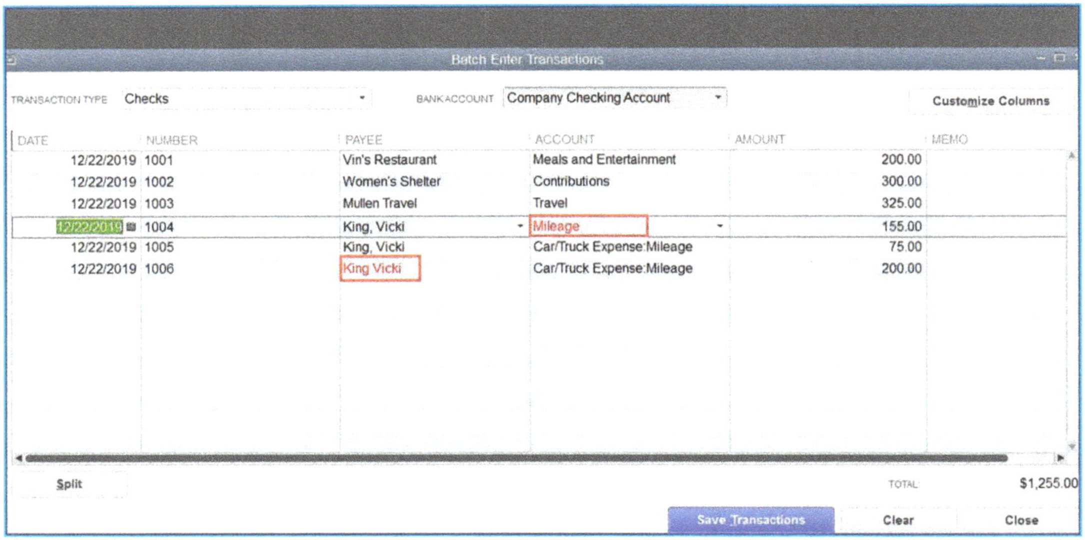

Notice that on check 1004, the Account "Mileage" is in red, and on check 1006, the Payee "King Vicki" is also in red. These codes do not match QuickBooks lists, so would need to be corrected in the Batch Enter Transactions screen (rather than correcting in Excel and starting over) before these transactions could be imported. The corrections can be made with the drop down arrows in the respective column.

Notes:

_____

_____

_____

_____

_____

_____

_____

_____

_____

_____

_____

_____

_____

_____

_____

_____

_____

_____

_____

_____

_____

_____

_____

_____

_____

_____

_____

_____

_____

_____

_____

_____

# Chapter Seven
# Reclassifying Transactions

It's not unusual that whole blocks of transactions need to be reclassified due to a change in how transactions are grouped on financial statements or an ongoing error in data entry. Using this functionality involves first selecting the transactions to be reclassified, then assigning those transactions new account and/or class codes.

As an example, suppose that Vendor Bills for vehicle insurance were coded to Insurance Expense along with other insurance bills, but management has decided that the bills related to auto insurance should be shown in a separate expense category called Insurance-Auto as a sub-account of Car/Truck Expense. Additionally, these expenses were originally coded to the class Administration, but are to be changed to class code Operations.

From the main menu, select Accountant, then Client Data Review, then Reclassify Transactions to bring up the screen shown below.

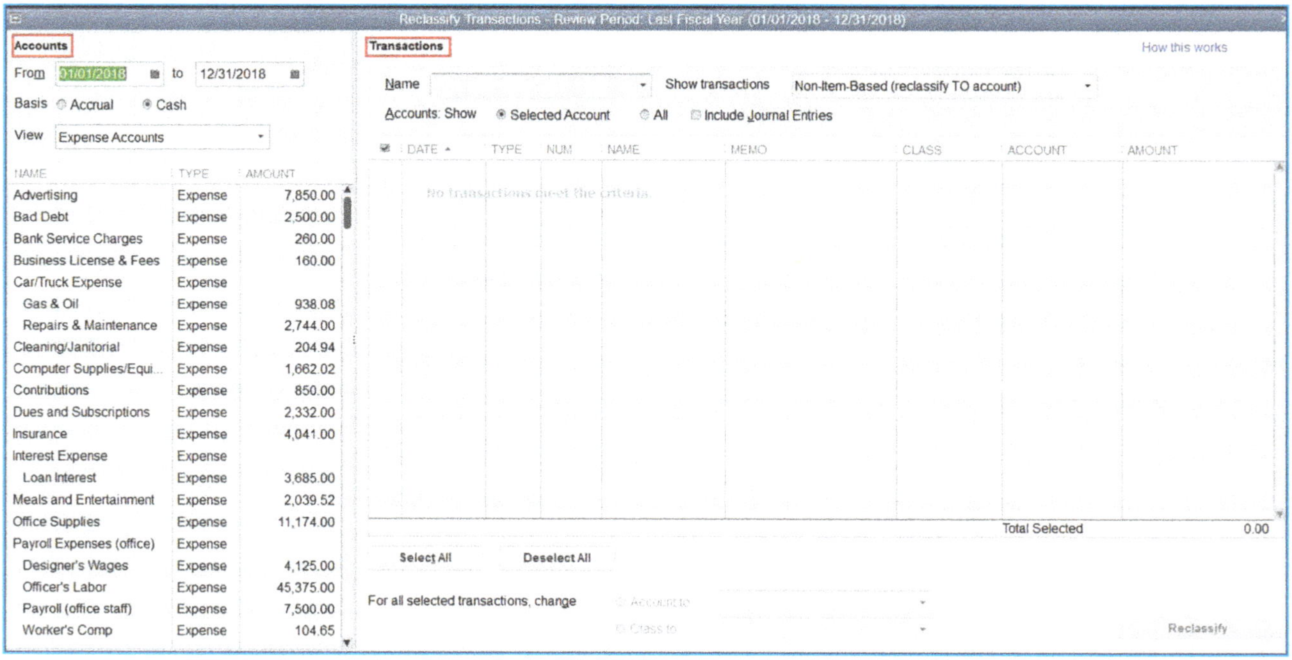

The two major sections of the screen are Accounts on the left side and Transactions on the right.

In the Accounts section top left, there are three selection criteria that when chosen, will change the list of accounts appearing beneath it. The selection criteria is used to zero in on the exact transactions to be reclassified.

- Date range – from and to
- Basis – Accrual or Cash (Transactions such as Vendor Bills that have been entered but not paid yet will only appear if Accrual is chosen.)
- View – there are three options:

  ➢ Expense Accounts – Only accounts with an account type "Expense" will appear.
  ➢ Profit and Loss Accounts – All Profit and Loss accounts will appear.
  ➢ Balance Sheet Accounts – All Balance Sheet accounts will appear.

Below shows the left side of the Reclassify Transactions screen completed in preparation for reclassifying the insurance expenses in the aforementioned example. Clicking on an account in the list on the left side will cause the transactions for that account to appear on the right side as shown for the Insurance Expense account.

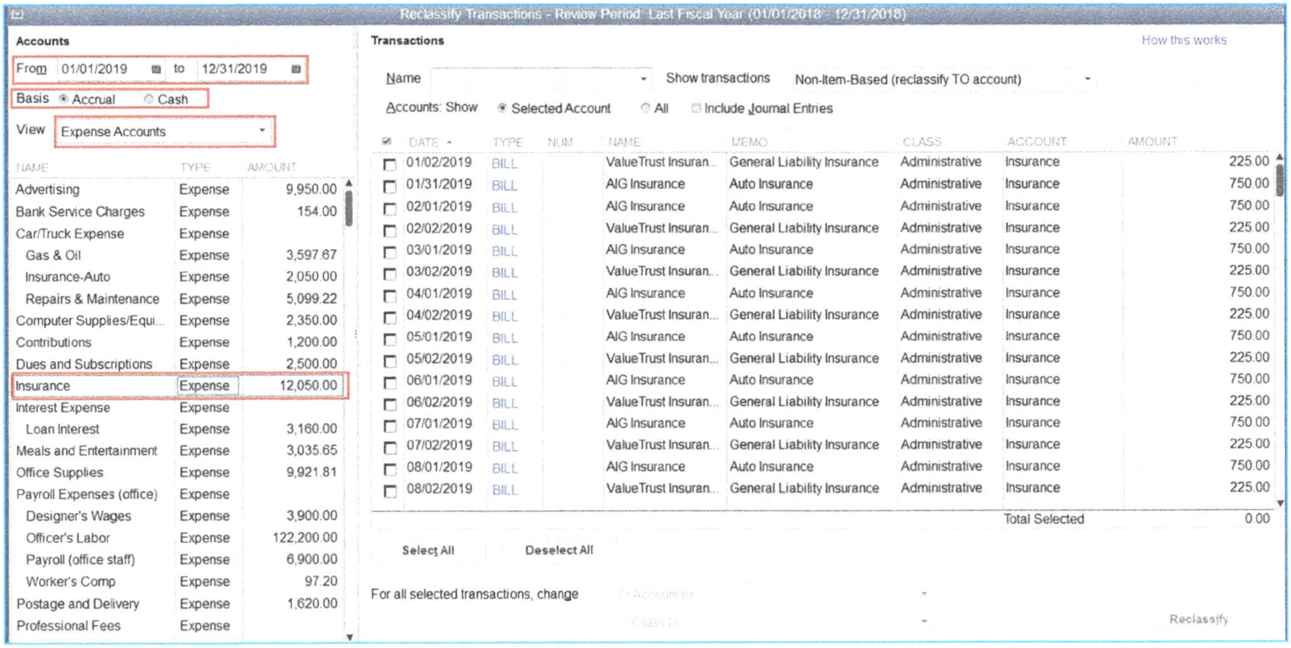

The top section of the Transaction side of the screen offers four additional selection criteria that can be used as follows:

**Name** – The list of transactions to be reclassified can be narrowed down by any name from the lists of names for Vendor, Customer:Job, Employee, or Other Name.

© The CFO Source, LLC 2017

**Show Transactions** – three options are available:

- Non-Item Based will show transactions recorded using accounts. When this criterion is chosen, both accounts and classes can be reclassified.
- Item Based will show transactions recorded using item codes. When using this criterion, only class codes can be reclassified.
- All will show transactions recorded with either accounts or item codes. When using this criterion, accounts will be changed for Non-Item Based transactions only. Classes for all transactions selected will be reclassified.

**Accounts Show** – This option allows you to show either the selected account (from the list of accounts on the left) or all accounts. If All Accounts is selected and a Name is entered, all transactions for that Name will appear regardless of the account. This is useful for selecting all transactions related to a specific Name.

**Include Journal Entries** – When checking off this box, transactions processed with journal entries will be shown in addition to other transactions.

**Selecting Transactions** – Once the list of transactions has been created, the user needs to pick which transactions are to be reclassified. This can be done by either clicking the check box to the left of the date on each row of the list, or if all transactions are desired, by clicking on the Select All box in the lower left of the screen. In the below example, all of the transactions have been selected.

**Choosing Accounts and Classes** – The last step is to check off the Account To and, if desired, Class To boxes in the bottom center of the screen, then using the drop-down menu, select the accounts and classes desired.

Click on the Reclassify box lower right to finalize the process. Below shows the resulting reclassified transactions:

### Transaction Detail By Account
#### January 1 through December 15, 2019

| Type | Date | Num | Name | Memo | Class | Amount | Balance |
|---|---|---|---|---|---|---|---|
| **Car/Truck Expense** | | | | | | | |
| Insurance-Auto | | | | | | | |
| Bill | 01/31/2019 | | AIG Insurance | Auto Insura... | Operations | 750.00 | 750.00 ◄ |
| Bill | 02/01/2019 | | AIG Insurance | Auto Insura... | Operations | 750.00 | 1,500.00 |
| Bill | 03/01/2019 | | AIG Insurance | Auto Insura... | Operations | 750.00 | 2,250.00 |
| Bill | 04/01/2019 | | AIG Insurance | Auto Insura... | Operations | 750.00 | 3,000.00 |
| Bill | 05/01/2019 | | AIG Insurance | Auto Insura... | Operations | 750.00 | 3,750.00 |
| Bill | 06/01/2019 | | AIG Insurance | Auto Insura... | Operations | 750.00 | 4,500.00 |
| Bill | 07/01/2019 | | AIG Insurance | Auto Insura... | Operations | 750.00 | 5,250.00 |
| Bill | 08/01/2019 | | AIG Insurance | Auto Insura... | Operations | 750.00 | 6,000.00 |
| Bill | 09/01/2019 | | AIG Insurance | Auto Insura... | Operations | 750.00 | 6,750.00 |
| Bill | 10/01/2019 | | AIG Insurance | Auto Insura... | Operations | 750.00 | 7,500.00 |
| Bill | 11/01/2019 | | AIG Insurance | Auto Insura... | Operations | 750.00 | 8,250.00 |
| Bill | 12/01/2019 | | AIG Insurance | Auto Insura... | Operations | 750.00 | 9,000.00 |
| Total Insurance-Auto | | | | | | 9,000.00 | 9,000.00 |
| Total Car/Truck Expense | | | | | | 9,000.00 | 9,000.00 |
| **TOTAL** | | | | | | 9,000.00 | 9,000.00 |

Notes:

## Chapter Eight

# Fixing Unapplied Customer Payments and Credits

One of the most important areas accountants are responsible for is the timely collection of receivables. Failure to collect monies due in a timely manner can put a company in serious financial trouble.

The best practice for the use of QuickBooks accounts receivable is up to date reports that only show valid open receivables. However, it is not uncommon that QuickBooks aging reports show the following:

- Customers listed with zeroes in all columns.
- Customers with positive amounts in some columns, negative amounts in other columns, netting to a zero balance.

The cause of these problems are payments and credits recorded at the customer level, but not offset against, or "applied" to, specific open invoices. QuickBooks still treats these transactions as open since they've not been offset and shows the transactions on reports.

Unapplied payments and credits can be brought up individually and applied, but this could take a long time if there are a lot of transactions. The Fix Unapplied Payments and Credits area of the Client Data Review gives the user the ability to apply payments and credits to invoices in bulk, greatly speeding up the process of offsetting these transactions and producing a clean A/R Aging Summary.

As an example, the Aging Summary on the next page shows that ABC company has a net zero balance, but shows positive and negative amounts in various columns of the aging report.

**Quality-Built Construction**
**A/R Aging Summary**
As of October 31, 2017

| | Current | 1 - 30 | 31 - 60 | 61 - 90 | > 90 | TOTAL |
|---|---|---|---|---|---|---|
| ABC Comp... | 0.00 | -6,000.00 | 2,000.00 | -12,000.00 | 16,000.00 ▶ | 0.00 ◀ |
| James Smith | 0.00 | 0.00 | 6,500.00 | 0.00 | 12,500.00 | 19,000.00 |
| Cruz, Albert | 20,000.00 | 0.00 | 0.00 | 0.00 | 0.00 | 20,000.00 |
| Hamby, Sh... | 0.00 | 0.00 | 15,000.00 | 0.00 | 0.00 | 15,000.00 |
| Molotsi, Hu... | 0.00 | 0.00 | 0.00 | 7,500.00 | 0.00 | 7,500.00 |
| TOTAL | 20,000.00 | -6,000.00 | 23,500.00 | -4,500.00 | 28,500.00 | 61,500.00 |

Drilling down on the total shows that the zero balance is made up of the following:

**Quality-Built Construction**
**A/R Aging QuickZoom**
As of October 31, 2017

| Type | Date | Num | Name | Terms | Due Date | Class | Aging | Open Balance |
|---|---|---|---|---|---|---|---|---|
| **ABC Company** | | | | | | | | |
| Invoice | 06/01/2017 | 01115 | ABC Company | | 08/01/2017 | | 91 | 16,000.00 ◀ |
| Payment | 08/04/2017 | | ABC Company | | | | | -2,000.00 |
| Payment | 08/11/2017 | | ABC Company | | | | | -2,000.00 |
| Payment | 08/18/2017 | | ABC Company | | | | | -4,000.00 |
| Payment | 08/24/2017 | | ABC Company | | | | | -2,000.00 |
| Payment | 08/31/2017 | | ABC Company | | | | | -2,000.00 |
| Invoice | 09/23/2017 | 01119 | ABC Company | | 09/23/2017 | | 38 | 2,000.00 |
| Credit Memo | 10/04/2017 | 01121 | ABC Company | | 10/04/2017 | | 27 | -6,000.00 |
| Total ABC Company | | | | | | | | 0.00 |
| **TOTAL** | | | | | | | | 0.00 |

Using the Fix Unapplied Customer Payments and Credits functionality, these transactions can be offset and won't appear on the aging report.

From the main menu, select Accountant, then Client Data Review, then Fix Unapplied Customer Payments and Credits, which brings up the screen shown below:

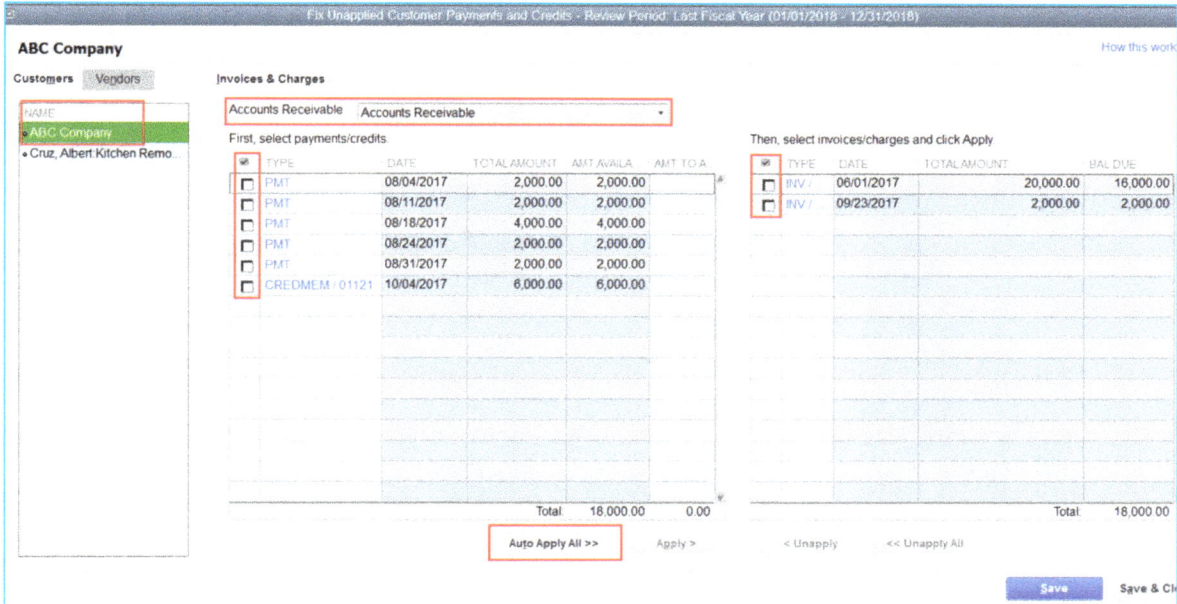

Customers can be selected from the list on the left. If multiple Accounts Receivable accounts are used, these can be selected from the drop-down at the top.

Offsetting payments and credits against invoices can be done two ways. First, individual transactions can be checked off on either side or, if the totals on both sides are the same, the Auto Apply All option can be selected. If individual transactions are selected, the Apply button must be clicked to create the link. Once the transactions have been applied, the transactions will appear grayed out as shown below:

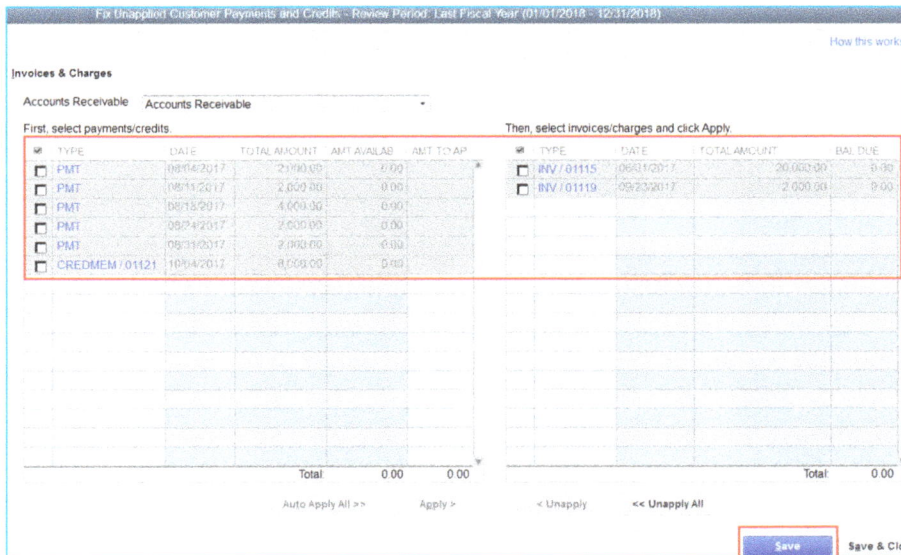

Once the selections have been made and applied, click on the Save button in the lower right to finish the process.

Below is the new A/R Aging Summary after applying all of ABC Company's payments and credits against open invoices. Note that the grand total is still the same and the only difference is that ABC Company no longer appears on the report.

### Quality-Built Construction
### A/R Aging Summary
#### As of October 31, 2017

| | Current | 1 - 30 | 31 - 60 | 61 - 90 | > 90 | TOTAL |
|---|---|---|---|---|---|---|
| James Smith | 0.00 | 0.00 | 6,500.00 | 0.00 | 12,500.00 | 19,000.00 |
| Cruz, Albert | ▶ 20,000.00 ◀ | 0.00 | 0.00 | 0.00 | 0.00 | 20,000.00 |
| Hamby, Sh... | 0.00 | 0.00 | 15,000.00 | 0.00 | 0.00 | 15,000.00 |
| Molotsi, Hu... | 0.00 | 0.00 | 0.00 | 7,500.00 | 0.00 | 7,500.00 |
| TOTAL | 20,000.00 | 0.00 | 21,500.00 | 7,500.00 | 12,500.00 | 61,500.00 |

Notes:

# Chapter Nine

# Researching Voided and Deleted Transactions

The ability to void and delete transactions in QuickBooks streamlines things for bookkeepers and accountants. However, if not used properly, those options can create numerous headaches too. Transactions voided or deleted incorrectly can result in:

- Report balances not matching tax returns and/or issued financial statements.
- Bank reconciliations not matching previously completed reconciliations.
- Accounts Receivable invoices that are not due showing as outstanding, or invoices that are due not being reported.
- Accounts Payable bills that are not due appearing as due, or bills that are due not being reported.

QuickBooks has several reports that can show voided and deleted transactions useful in making needed adjustments.

## Voided/Deleted Transaction Summary and Voided/Deleted Transaction Detail Reports

From the main menu, select Reports, then Accountant & Taxes, then either Voided/Deleted Transactions Summary or Detail to show voided and deleted transactions entered regardless of the date assigned to the transaction. They also show who made each adjustment, which is very valuable information for training purposes. A date range for when the adjustments were made can be selected, making this a useful report for accountants to run each time they review a client's file to see what the client voided or deleted since the last review.

Below is the Summary level report:

**Test Contracting, LLC**
**Voided/Deleted Transactions Summary**
Entered/Last Modified

8:15 PM
08/05/16

| Num | Action | Entered/Last Modified | Date | Name | Memo | Account | Split | Amount |
|---|---|---|---|---|---|---|---|---|
| **Transactions entered or modified by Admin** | | | | | | | | |
| **Bill** | | | | | | | | |
| ▸ | Deleted Transaction | 07/27/2015 17:56:44 | | | | | | 0.00 ◂ |
| | Added Transaction | 07/27/2015 17:52:22 | 07/27/2015 | HMS Insurance | | Accounts Payable | Equipment C… | -5,000.00 |
| **Bill** | | | | | | | | |
| | Deleted Transaction | 07/27/2015 18:36:49 | | | | | | 0.00 |
| | Changed Transact… | 07/27/2015 18:03:16 | 07/27/2015 | Johnson Insurance… | | Accounts Payable | Insurance Ex… | -2,500.00 |
| | Added Transaction | 07/27/2015 17:51:47 | 07/27/2015 | Sunoco | | Accounts Payable | Equipment C… | 0.00 |
| **Bill** | | | | | | | | |
| | Deleted Transaction | 07/27/2015 18:36:34 | | | | | | 0.00 |
| | Added Transaction | 07/27/2015 18:08:34 | 07/27/2015 | Ready Roofers | | Accounts Payable | -SPLIT- | -6,500.00 |
| **Invoice 5** | | | | | | | | |
| 5 | Deleted Transaction | 07/27/2015 17:54:11 | | | | | | 0.00 |
| 5 | Added Transaction | 07/27/2015 17:53:20 | 07/27/2015 | Ajax Corporation:G… | | Accounts Receiva… | Job Income | 5,000.00 |
| **Invoice 6** | | | | | | | | |
| 6 | Deleted Transaction | 07/27/2015 18:36:18 | | | | | | 0.00 |
| 6 | Added Transaction | 07/27/2015 18:10:27 | 07/27/2015 | Ajax Corporation:G… | | Accounts Receiva… | -SPLIT- | 9,000.00 |

Here's the Detail report for the same three bills at the top of the summary report:

**Test Contracting, LLC**
**Voided/Deleted Transactions Detail**
Entered/Last Modified

8:20 PM
08/05/16

| Num | Action | Entered/Last Modified | Date | Name | Memo | Account | Split | Debit | Credit |
|---|---|---|---|---|---|---|---|---|---|
| **Transactions entered or modified by Admin** | | | | | | | | | |
| **Bill** | | | | | | | | | |
| ▸ | Deleted Transaction | 07/27/2015 17:56:44 | | | | | | 0.00 | ◂ |
| | Added Transaction | 07/27/2015 17:52:22 | 07/27/2015 | HMS Insurance | | Accounts Payable | Equipment C… | | 5,000.00 |
| | | | | Ajax Corporation:G… | Builder's Ris… | Equipment Costs:… | Accounts Pa… | 5,000.00 | |
| **Bill** | | | | | | | | | |
| | Deleted Transaction | 07/27/2015 18:36:49 | | | | | | 0.00 | |
| | Changed Transact… | 07/27/2015 18:03:16 | 07/27/2015 | *Johnson Insuran…* | | Accounts Payable | *Insurance E…* | | 2,500.00 |
| | | | | *Ajax Corporation…* | *Builders Ri…* | *Insurance Expense* | Accounts Pa… | 2,500.00 | |
| | Added Transaction | 07/27/2015 17:51:47 | 07/27/2015 | Sunoco | | Accounts Payable | Equipment C… | 0.00 | |
| | | | | Sunoco | | Equipment Costs:… | Accounts Pa… | 0.00 | |
| **Bill** | | | | | | | | | |
| | Deleted Transaction | 07/27/2015 18:36:34 | | | | | | 0.00 | |
| | Added Transaction | 07/27/2015 18:08:34 | 07/27/2015 | Ready Roofers | | Accounts Payable | -SPLIT- | | 6,500.00 |
| | | | | Ajax Corporation:G… | Roof Framing | Professional Fees | Accounts Pa… | 5,000.00 | |
| | | | | Ajax Corporation:G… | Roofing, Fla… | Subcontractors Co… | Accounts Pa… | 1,500.00 | |

**Closing Date Exception Report** – A highly recommended practice is to set a "Closing Date," which requires users to know a special password in order to make adjustments prior to that date. This report shows transactions entered before the Closing Date. The report is run from the Accountant & Taxes section of reports. For a report to be generated, a Closing Date must first be set in the Preferences section. Upon clicking on the report option, the report below will appear, listing all transactions made to a Closed period after the closing date was set as well as show which user made the transaction. Note that there is no selection of dates to be made for this report.

| | | | | | | | | | | | |
|---|---|---|---|---|---|---|---|---|---|---|---|
| | | | | Closing Date Exception Report | | | | | | | — ▢ × |
| Customize Report | Comment on Report | Share Template | Memorize | Print ▼ | E-mail ▼ | Excel ▼ | Hide Header | Refresh | | | |

8:30 PM
08/05/16

**Test Contracting, LLC**
**Closing Date Exception Report**
Books Closed As of June 30, 2015

| Num | Entered/Last Modified | Last modified by | State | Date | Name | Memo | Account | Split | Debit | Credit |
|---|---|---|---|---|---|---|---|---|---|---|

**Closing Date History**
Closing date set to 06/30/2015 on 08/05/2016 20:26:34 by Admin

**Transactions entered or modified by Admin**
General Journal 3

| 3 | 08/05/2016 20:28:09 | Admin | Latest | 05/31/2015 | | record vehic... | Furniture and Equ... | Ford Motor C... | 20,000.00 | |
| | | | | | | record vehic... | Ford Motor Credit ... | Furniture and... | | 20,000.00 |

**Audit Trail** – As detailed in chapter four, this report will show not only voided and deleted transactions, but also transactions that have been changed.

**Reconciliation Discrepancy Report** – As detailed in chapter ten, this report will show transactions that have been changed after the transactions were used to reconcile bank and/or other accounts.

**Correcting Problems Uncovered** – The reports mentioned above should enable the user to find voided, deleted, or changed transactions that need to be corrected. For transactions other than banking transactions (which will be discussed in the next section), the following guidelines apply:

- If voided or deleted transactions are causing problems with prior period reports, those transactions should be re-entered as originally recorded. If the changes that were made are still desired, the adjustment to the transaction should be made in the current period. For example, if an accounts receivable invoice was deleted because it was deemed uncollectible, it should be reentered with the original date and then a credit memo recorded in the current period to write off the balance.
- If a transaction amount was changed, the amount of the transactions should be restored to its original amount. Any change desired should then be recorded in the current period with an additional transaction such as a credit memo or journal entry.

Notes:

# Chapter Ten
# Bank Reconciliations

Bank reconciliations are an important internal control practice for all organizations, and a critical part of the defense against check fraud, identity theft, and embezzlement. Reconciliations need to be done on a timely basis, and the best practice is doing them as soon as bank statements are available. Reconciliations should be performed by persons that are not involved with the day to day recording of cash transactions so that proper segregation of duties is in place. Allowing personnel to handle all aspects of recording cash transactions and having them prepare bank reconciliations should be avoided at all cost.

Whether you are preparing or reviewing bank reconciliations, knowing how the QuickBooks reconciliation process works and understanding the available reports is important. In this chapter, we'll review the functionality for bank reconciliations and provide guidance for resolving issues that can arise.

## Making Full Use of the Bank Reconciliation Function

(and other tips for reconciling your bank account)

QuickBooks bank reconciliation allows the user to match transactions on their bank statement with transactions recorded on the books. Users input the beginning and ending balances from bank statements as the starting point (ending balances are carried forward to be beginning balances in the next month). The reconciliation involves the user checking off transactions in QuickBooks with those found on the bank statement until all transactions are accounted for. The process is critical to assure that there are no missing or duplicate entries and amounts on the books match bank statements. Most users consider the process complete when the "Difference" shown on the bottom right of the bank reconciliation screen is zero (image example shown later in this chapter), although it is recommended that other analysis as described next be undertaken.

To start a bank reconciliation, from the main menu, select Banking, then Reconcile, which will bring up the screen below:

Use the drop-down selection at the top left, next to Account, to select the bank account you wish to reconcile. Input the ending balance of the bank account as shown on the bank statement in the Ending Balance box highlighted in red. The Beginning Balance is carried over from the previous month, and in most cases, need not be entered. (Issues with the beginning balance on this screen not matching the bank statement will be discussed in the "tips" area.) After entering this data, click on Continue to bring up the Reconcile Screen where the matching, or "checking off" of transactions is performed.

# Tips For Using The QuickBooks Bank Reconciliation Screen

Understanding the functionality in the QuickBooks bank reconciliation screen can make the job of matching QB transactions with bank statements go quickly while successfully revealing all the information about errors and missing entries you'll need to make adjustments for.

Please refer to the reconciliation screen example shown below while reviewing the following tips:

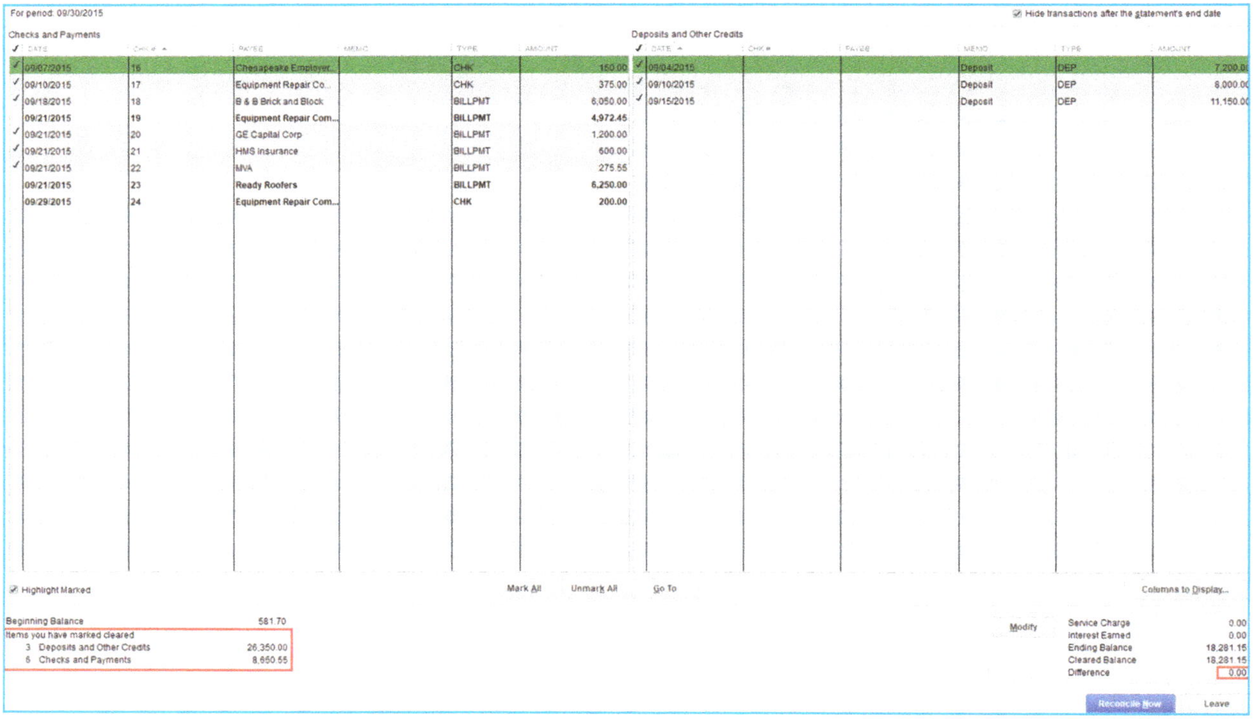

1. The "Hide transactions after the statement's end date" box should be checked to keep future transactions from cluttering the screen.
2. Click the "Columns to Display" Box and check all available columns as some of this information could come in handy.

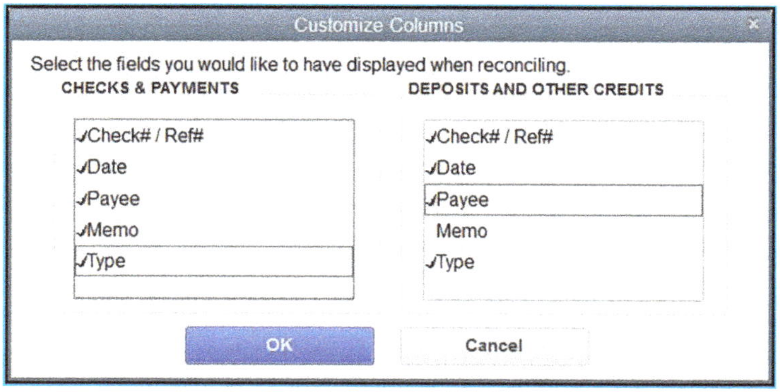

3. Use the sorting functionality – clicking on any of the column headers will sort the data by that column. In the example reconciliation screen, the disbursements are sorted by the "CHK #" column, but could just as well be sorted by dollar amount, date, payee, or memo field. Sorting by check number will allow the user to easily check off QuickBooks checks with the listing of checks from the bank as both lists will be in the same order. Sorting by amount can be helpful when trying to find a specific dollar amount.

4.  Reconcile either Disbursements or Deposits first, then do the other – use the totals in the "Items you have marked cleared" to match the bank statement.

5.  If you need to leave the reconciliation screen to add a transaction, click on the Leave button in the bottom right hand corner. Your work will be saved for use later.

6.  If you need to modify a transaction already showing on the reconciliation, you can either double click on the transaction or, with the cursor on the transaction, click on the Go To button. When you close out of the transaction after making an adjustment, you will be returned to the reconciliation screen.

7.  Even though you have gotten the reconciliation difference to zero, does your reconciliation make sense? If you have any of these situations, some investigation may be warranted:

    ➢ Old outstanding checks – Checks older than three months should be voided and reissued; users should check to see if these are duplicates that just didn't get voided.

    ➢ Outstanding disbursements that are made automatically by your bank or other financial institution – If these are automatic, it's doubtful they're outstanding. These types of outstanding disbursements should be investigated to see if they are duplicates.

    ➢ Outstanding deposits – Other than deposits made on the last day of the month, it's highly unlikely that deposits would be outstanding.

8.  Be sure to check off any zero-dollar items that appear, which may be due to voided transactions.

9.  Evaluate whether transactions can be recorded in such a way as to facilitate reconciliations. For example, non-check disbursements will appear in the list of disbursements along with checks. By assigning uniform descriptions to like transactions, these transactions will be grouped when sorting by check number.

10. In some situations where a significant number of issues exist with a bank reconciliation it may be easier to "undo" a bank reconciliation and start over. This is done in the Begin Reconciliation screen by clicking on the "Undo Last Reconciliation" button This returns any transactions that were cleared to an uncleared status.

# Resolving Bank Reconciliation Issues

It's not uncommon to review bank reconciliations prepared in QuickBooks and find problems either due to human error or untrained preparers. Typical issues include:

* Previous reconciliations no longer match the ending cash balance shown in QuickBooks.
* Transactions that were "cleared" as part of the reconciliation have been voided, deleted, or the amounts changed.
* Deposits recorded in QuickBooks in the middle of the month have not been marked as cleared. While it makes sense that a deposit recorded on the last day of the month may not show as clearing the bank until the next month, a mid-month deposit should show as cleared. It's likely that an uncleared deposit from the middle of the month may be a duplicate transaction and need to be deleted.

- Automated bank disbursements that are not showing as cleared. Some disbursements are set up to be automatically deducted on the same day of the month. If these appear as not having cleared the bank, it warrants an investigation as the disbursement may have been duplicated in QuickBooks and needs to be deleted.

In some cases, there are valid reasons for the differences; in other cases, transactions that have been altered, voided, or deleted could point to training issues that need to be addressed.

There are several reports that can be generated to review and troubleshoot bank reconciliations.

**Previous Reconciliation Report** – accessed in the Banking area of Reports, lets the user review already completed reconciliations. In the event of an issue, it is recommended to select the second option of the report as shown below:

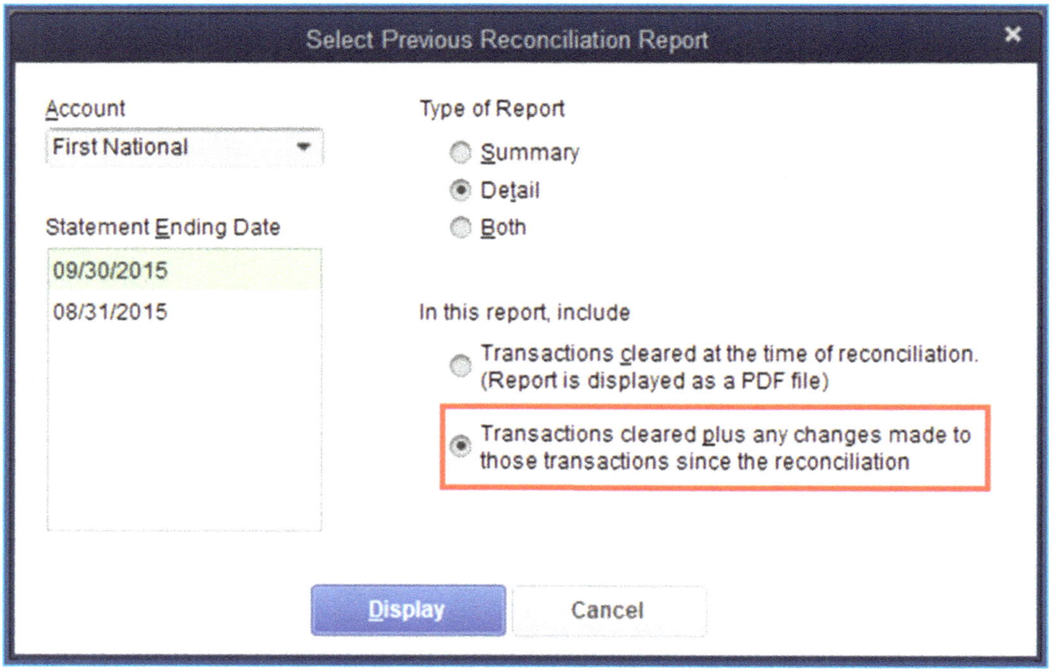

Comparing the second report with the first should highlight any differences. Note that in the Pro Version of QuickBooks, users can only access the most recent reconciliation that was completed. In the Premier and Enterprise versions, users can access all reconciliations that were completed.

**Reconciliation Discrepancy Report** – run from the Banking Section of reports. This report can be very useful in figuring out why bank reconciliations no longer match previously completed ones.

As part of the bank reconciliation process, the user checks off transactions they verify as matching with the

---

bank and QuickBooks marks or tags those transactions as "Cleared." A common problem is that untrained users may void, delete, or alter the dollar amount of transactions that have already been marked as cleared. This renders previously worked bank reconciliations incorrect, assuming that the altered transactions were correct as first recorded.

To illustrate the Reconciliation Discrepancy Report, assume that the below reconciliation has been completed. It shows both cleared transactions with an X in the "CLR" column and un-cleared (or outstanding) transactions as part of the reconciliation.

**Test Contracting, LLC**
**Reconciliation Detail**
First National, Period Ending 09/30/2015

| Type | Date | Num | Name | Clr | Amount | Balance |
|---|---|---|---|---|---|---|
| Beginning Balance | | | | | | 581.70 |
| Cleared Transactions | | | | | | |
| Checks and Payments - 6 items | | | | | | |
| Check | 09/07/2015 | 16 | Chesapeake Emplo... | X | -150.00 | -150.00 |
| Check | 09/10/2015 | 17 | Equipment Repair C... | X | -375.00 | -525.00 |
| Bill Pmt -Check | 09/18/2015 | 18 | B & B Brick and Block | X | -6,050.00 | -6,575.00 |
| Bill Pmt -Check | 09/21/2015 | 20 | GE Capital Corp | X | -1,200.00 | -7,775.00 |
| Bill Pmt -Check | 09/21/2015 | 21 | HMS Insurance | X | -600.00 | -8,375.00 |
| Bill Pmt -Check | 09/21/2015 | 22 | MVA | X | -275.55 | -8,650.55 |
| Total Checks and Payments | | | | | -8,650.55 | -8,650.55 |
| Deposits and Credits - 3 items | | | | | | |
| Deposit | 09/04/2015 | | | X | 7,200.00 | 7,200.00 |
| Deposit | 09/10/2015 | | | X | 8,000.00 | 15,200.00 |
| Deposit | 09/15/2015 | | | X | 11,150.00 | 26,350.00 |
| Total Deposits and Credits | | | | | 26,350.00 | 26,350.00 |
| Total Cleared Transactions | | | | | 17,699.45 | 17,699.45 |
| Cleared Balance | | | | | 17,699.45 | 18,281.15 |
| Uncleared Transactions | | | | | | |
| Checks and Payments - 3 items | | | | | | |
| Bill Pmt -Check | 09/21/2015 | 23 | Ready Roofers | | -6,250.00 | -6,250.00 |
| Bill Pmt -Check | 09/21/2015 | 19 | Equipment Repair C... | | -4,972.45 | -11,222.45 |
| Check | 09/29/2015 | 24 | Equipment Repair C... | | -200.00 | -11,422.45 |
| Total Checks and Payments | | | | | -11,422.45 | -11,422.45 |
| Total Uncleared Transactions | | | | | -11,422.45 | -11,422.45 |
| Register Balance as of 09/30/2015 | | | | | 6,277.00 | 6,858.70 |
| Ending Balance | | | | | 6,277.00 | 6,858.70 |

The short version of the reconciliation would be as follows:

1. Balance per Bank (Cleared balance) is $18,281.15
2. Less Outstanding Checks (Un-cleared Transactions) is $11,422.45
3. Balance per Ledger (Ending Balance) is $6,858.70

To continue the illustration, the following changes will be made:

1. Check 16 in the amount of $150.00 will be voided.
2. Check 17 in the amount of $375.00 will be deleted.
3. The 9/15/2015 deposit for $11,150 will be increased to $11,500.

As a result of the changes, the ending balance in cash of $6,858.70 no longer matches the QuickBooks balance as of the same date:

**Test Contracting, LLC**
**Balance Sheet**
As of September 30, 2015

|  | Sep 30, 15 |
|---|---|
| ▼ **ASSETS** |  |
| ▼ **Current Assets** |  |
| ▼ **Checking/Savings** |  |
| First National | 7,733.70 |
| **Total Checking/Savings** | 7,733.70 |

The difference of $875.00 (7,733.70 – 6,858.70) can be found by running the Previous Reconciliation Discrepancy Report from the Banking Section:

**Test Contracting, LLC**
**Previous Reconciliation Discrepancy Report**
First National

| Type | Date | Entered/Last Modif... | Num | Name | Reconciled Amo... | Type of Change | Effect of Chan... |
|---|---|---|---|---|---|---|---|
| **Statement Date: 09/30/2015** | | | | | | | |
| Deposit | 09/15/2015 | 08/15/2016 20:04:31 | | | 11,150.00 | Amount | 350.00 |
| Check | 09/07/2015 | 08/15/2016 20:03:50 | 16 | Chesapeake Emp... | -150.00 | Amount | 150.00 |
| Check | 09/10/2015 | 08/15/2016 20:04:03 | 17 | Equipment Repair... | -375.00 | Deleted | 375.00 |
| Total 09/30/2015 | | | | | | | 875.00 |
| | | | | | | | 875.00 |

Notes:

# Chapter Eleven

# Troubleshooting the Undeposited Funds Account

Occasionally, when reviewing a client's file, issues are uncovered related to the Undeposited Funds account. Common problems include large balances that build up over time or the account not zeroing out on a regular basis. Of course, if the Undeposited Funds account balance is not correct, it's likely that a related account is out of balance as well. This could include a cash account or accounts receivable. Understanding how it is supposed to function is critical for understanding how to correct issues that can come up.

## Why Using the Undeposited Funds Account is Recommended.

If the Undeposited Funds account is not used, the debit side of recording customer payments is recorded to a cash account with one line per customer appearing in the detail of that account. This makes completing bank reconciliations difficult because the single lump sum deposit that will appear on the bank statement won't match with customer payments that were recorded as individual entries. The user is left with the onerous task of having to match individual customer deposits in QuickBooks to lump sum deposits on the bank statement.

This account is meant to be a "clearing" or "wash" account for customer payments and subsequent deposits. Its primary function is to allow for the grouping of payments from multiple customers into a single bank deposit to facilitate the bank reconciliation process. Typically, payments from multiple customers are grouped on a single deposit ticket and only the amount of the total deposit is shown on a bank statement. QuickBooks allows for this grouping in a two-step process:

- The first step, done in the Customer section, applies payments to customer's accounts. This is done on a customer by customer basis, one customer at a time.

- In the second step, done in the banking section, payments from multiple customers are checked off so that the total of all payments checked off totals to the deposit ticket taken to the bank.

Rather than have customer payments debited directly to a cash account, payments are debited to the Undeposited Funds account first, then transferred to the appropriate cash account as a second step by recording a bank deposit where the grouping takes place.

# How it is Designed to Work

The Undeposited Funds account is turned on or off in the Payments section of Preferences as shown below:

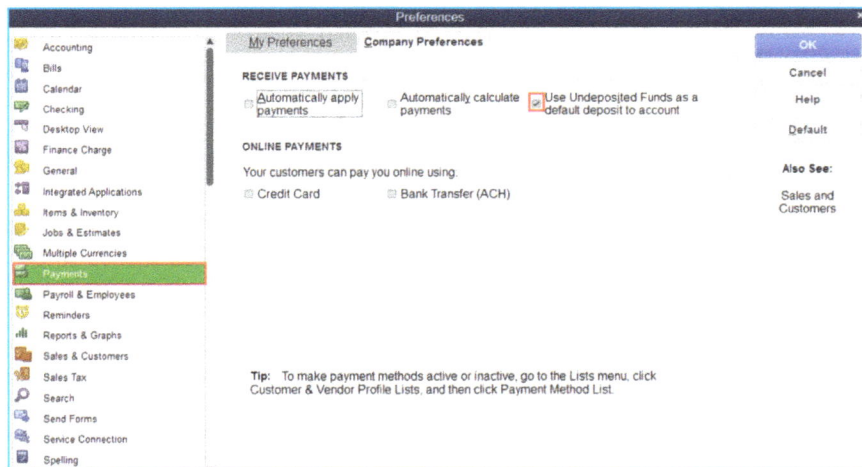

Since this is a "clearing" account, the balance in the account should be zero in most cases. The flow of accounting, the section of QuickBooks where these transactions are recorded, and the transaction types are as follows:

|  | DEBIT | CREDIT |
|---|---|---|
| Accounts Receivable | $500 | |
| Sales | | $500 |

To record credit sales to customers – done in the Customers/Create Invoices screen with a transaction type of "Invoice."

|  | DEBIT | CREDIT |
|---|---|---|
| Undeposited Funds | $500 | |
| Accounts Receivable | | $500 |

To record the receipt of a payment from a customer – done in the Customers/Receive Payments screen with a transaction type of "Payment."

| | DEBIT | CREDIT |
|---|---|---|
| Cash | $500 | |
| Undeposited Funds | | $500 |

To record the deposit of funds and clear the Undeposited Funds account – done in the Banking/Make Deposits screens with a transaction type of "Deposit."

Note that in the above example, both the Accounts Receivable and Undeposited Funds accounts zero out, leaving an increase in both cash and sales.

# Verifying the Balance in the Undeposited Funds Account

Two approaches can be used to see if the balance in the Undeposited Funds account is correct. The example below illustrates the correct use of the account and how to verify the balance.

In the first approach, a balance sheet is run as of a selected date to determine the account balance. As an example, the following asset section of a balance sheet is presented, showing a balance in Undeposited Funds of $18,350:

**Test Contracting, LLC**
**Balance Sheet**
**As of August 31, 2015**

| | Aug 31, 15 |
|---|---|
| ▼ASSETS | |
| ▼ Current Assets | |
| ▼ Checking/Savings | |
| First National | 7,581.70 |
| Total Checking/Savings | 7,581.70 |
| ▼ Accounts Receivable | |
| Accounts Receivable | 22,600.00 |
| Total Accounts Receivable | 22,600.00 |
| ▼ Other Current Assets | |
| Inventory Asset | 43,900.00 |
| Prepaid Insurance | 428.11 |
| Undeposited Funds | 18,350.00 |
| Total Other Current Assets | 62,678.11 |
| Total Current Assets | 92,859.81 |
| ▼ Fixed Assets | |
| Furniture and Equipment | 20,000.00 |
| Total Fixed Assets | 20,000.00 |
| TOTAL ASSETS | 112,859.81 |

Drilling down on the details (double click the line item to open details) shows what makes up the balance:

**Test Contracting, LLC**
**Transactions by Account**
As of August 31, 2015

| Type | Date | Num | Adj | Name | Memo | Class | Clr | Split | Debit | Credit | Balance |
|---|---|---|---|---|---|---|---|---|---|---|---|
| **Undeposited Funds** | | | | | | | | | | | 0.00 |
| Payment | 08/03/2015 | | | ABC, Inc.:Virginia ... | | | ✓ | Accounts Re... | 5,000.00 | | 5,000.00 |
| Payment | 08/03/2015 | | | Ajax Corporation:G... | | | ✓ | Accounts Re... | 8,000.00 | | 13,000.00 |
| Payment | 08/04/2015 | | | XYZ Company:Sta... | | | ✓ | Accounts Re... | 7,500.00 | | 20,500.00 |
| Deposit | 08/05/2015 | | | -MULTIPLE- | Deposit | | ✓ | First National | | 20,500.00 | 0.00 |
| Payment | 08/31/2015 | | | Acme Supermarke... | | | | Accounts Re... | 7,200.00 | | 7,200.00 |
| Payment | 08/31/2015 | | | XYZ Company | | | | Accounts Re... | 11,150.00 | | 18,350.00 |
| Total Undeposited Funds | | | | | | | | | 38,850.00 | 20,500.00 | 18,350.00 |
| **TOTAL** | | | | | | | | | 38,850.00 | 20,500.00 | 18,350.00 |

- The balance as of 8/31/2015 is $18,350, which is made up of two payments dated 8/31/2015 ($7,200 and $11,150). It should be verified that a deposit to clear these payments was made early in the next month.
- The balance in the account started at zero at 8/1/2015, increased as a result of three payments, and then returned to zero on 8/5/2015 when the three payments were "grouped" and recorded as a deposit for $20,500 ($5,000 + $8,000 + $7,500).

It's important to realize that grouping individual payments to match lump sum deposits, which is done in the Banking/Make Deposits area, requires two steps. In the first screen, Payments to Deposit, the user checks off the deposits to be "grouped" on the left. The Payments Subtotal in the lower right of the screen should match the total of the deposit ticket if there are no "non-customer" deposits to record.

**Payments to Deposit**

SELECT VIEW
View payment method type    All types
Sort payments by            Payment Method

What are payment method views?

SELECT PAYMENTS TO DEPOSIT

| ✓ | DATE | TIME | TYPE | NO | PAYMENT METH | NAME | AMOUNT |
|---|---|---|---|---|---|---|---|
| ✓ | 08/03/2015 | | PMT | | Check | ABC, Inc.:Virginia Re... | 5,000.00 |
| ✓ | 08/03/2015 | | PMT | | Check | Ajax Corporation:Gar... | 8,000.00 |
| ✓ | 08/04/2015 | | PMT | | Check | XYZ Company:State ... | 7,500.00 |

3 of 3 payments selected for deposit

Payments Subtotal    20,500.00

Select All    Select None

OK    Cancel    Help

Click on OK to bring up the Make Deposits screen shown next.

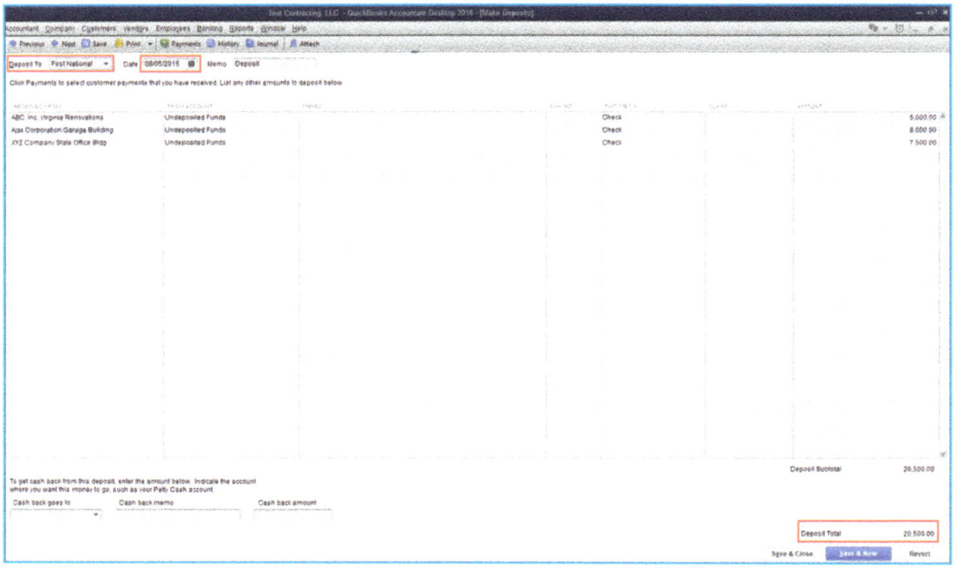

The above screen brings over the customer deposits to be included in the deposit and also allows for the entry of non-customer related deposits. The user must also select the bank and date of the deposit at the top left. The Deposit Total at the bottom right should match the deposit that will be recorded at the bank.

A second approach to see if the balance of $18,350 is correct is to bring up the Payments to Deposit screen, the first screen in the Banking/Make Deposit section, as shown below. Note that the sum of the deposits adds up to $18,350. This approach must be done typically using today's date, meaning that it won't work to verify the balance in undeposited funds from a prior time period as those deposits should have already been recorded and won't show as needing to be deposited.

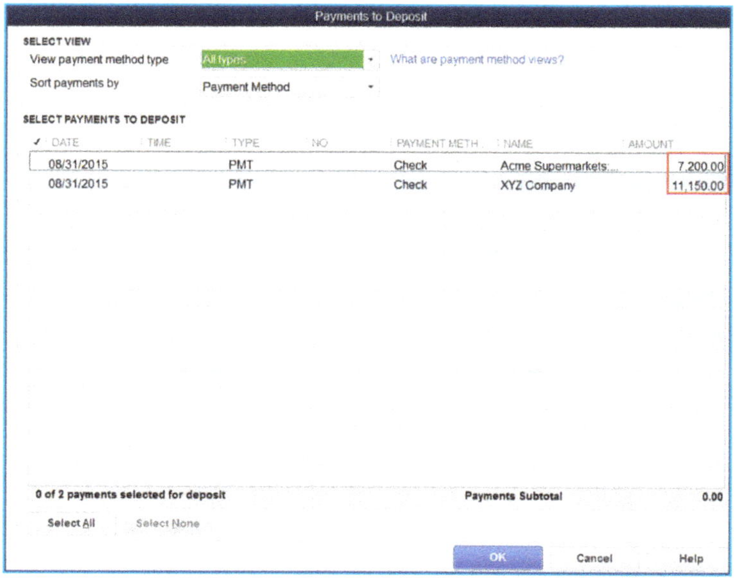

This view will either show deposits are being recorded correctly with the deposits to record matching the balance in undeposited funds or that it's not being done correctly with deposits that have not been recorded.

# Typical Problems and How to Correct Them

Untrained bookkeepers and accountants can record transactions that seemingly make sense to them, but do not correctly record transactions. Incorrectly recorded transactions in one area lead to problems in other areas. If bank reconciliations are not done timely and/or a company's accounting is not reviewed on a regular basis, these problems may go undetected for some time. In this section, several problem areas will be discussed.

**Customer Payments are being recorded in the Customer area, but the second step to make deposits in the Banking area and clear Undeposited Funds is not being done.**

If this is the case, the Payments to Deposit screen shown above will display numerous deposits from dates going back for some time. This scenario results in a large debit balance in Undeposited Funds although the balance and detail in Accounts Receivable will be correct.

If bank deposits for customer payments *are not* being recorded, it's likely that the cash balance in QuickBooks is a large negative number even though reality says otherwise. If in addition, bank reconciliations are behind, it's likely that there is a backlog of bank deposits that need to be recorded. In this case, the Payments to Deposit screen will show a large list of payments to be grouped as deposits. The correction in most cases is to record the deposits by grouping payments, making sure the deposits recorded match bank statements. Having the deposit tickets will take the guess work out of this process.

If there are a large number of deposits spanning several months or even years, the deposits could be cleared with journal entries. In the case of clearing deposits with journal entries, the following entry would be made:

|  | DEBIT | CREDIT |
| --- | --- | --- |
| Cash | $X | |
| Undeposited Funds | | $X |

The credit portion of this entry would be shown in the Payments to Deposit screen and need to be offset against the customer payments.

If deposits for customer payments are being recorded and bank reconciliations are up to date, yet the Undeposited Funds account has a large balance that has grown over time, it must be determined where the credit side of the deposit transactions were recorded.

**There are older customer payments that have not cleared against deposits.**

In this scenario, while the majority of payments are offset, selected payments have not been offset and the balance in Undeposited Funds does not go to zero.

It must first be determined which transaction(s) are causing the problem. Scanning the transaction detail report from a point in time when the balance was zero can usually help to identify the problem transactions. If there are numerous problems, sorting the report by the "CLR" column will group the un-cleared transactions. Below is the transaction detail report sorted in this manner:

Once the problem transactions are identified, each would need to be researched. Possible situations and resolutions include:

- The offsetting deposit was recorded with a journal entry or in the register with the credit amount going to accounts receivable. In this case, the receivable balance for the customer would be understated since the customer's balance was reduced for the same payment twice. Deleting the payment would solve this, although if the payment was in a prior period, a journal entry debiting Accounts Receivable and crediting Undeposited Funds in the current period would be recommended.
- The offsetting deposit was recorded with a journal entry or in the register with the credit amount going to an income account. Income would be over-stated since the invoice to the customer and the journal entry or register entry both recorded the sale. Deleting the payment would not solve this as deleting the payment would just make the receivable appear as due when it had already been paid. A journal entry debiting an Income account and crediting Undeposited Funds in the current period is recommended.
- The payment is a duplicate. While this would be hard to do since the first payment recorded would clear the invoice to be offset with a deposit, it's possible if invoices were entered, deleted, and then re-entered. The payment may need to be deleted if in the current period, or a journal entry if in a prior period.

---

Notes:

# Chapter Twelve

# Accounts Payable One Step/ Two Step Problem

A common problem accountants come across is the incorrect processing of vendor bills and checks using conflicting sections of QuickBooks. QB has two ways to record payments to Vendors, and when the two ways are combined, problems result. These are the symptoms of the One Step/Two Step problem:

- Vendor bills and/or balances appear on the Accounts Payable Aging that the client says have been paid.
- Duplicate expenses. When viewing expense detail, the same amounts are shown twice for the same vendor with dates from about the same time period, one transaction showing a transaction type of Bill and the other as Check.

To correct the problem, an understanding of how things *should* work is needed. The two ways of processing vendor bills and checks are as follows:

**One Step** – Vendor bills are paid by issuing or recording a check in the Banking section. From the main menu, select Banking, then Write Checks. When checks are generated this way, the transaction will show a transaction type of Checks. In the One Step approach, accounts payable is not used and bills are not tracked.

**Two Step** – All transactions are recorded in the Vendor section. Bills are entered and, usually at a later date, a check to pay the bill is issued. This approach provides the tools needed to manage accounts payable. The two steps are:

1. Record the bill from a vendor. From the main menu, select Vendors, then Enter Bills. These transactions will show a transaction type of Bill.
2. Issue a check to the vendor. From the main menu, select Vendors, then Pay Bills. These transactions will show a transaction type of Bill Pmt – Check.

**The Problem**

When a bill is recorded in the Vendor section (step one in the "Two Step" method), but the check for the bill is processed in the Banking section (the only step in the "One Step" method). When a check for a bill is not processed through the Vendor section, the bill will continue to show as open even though the bill has been paid. Additionally, the expense for the bill will be recorded twice—once when the bill was recorded in the Vendor section and again when the check was issued in the Banking section.

**Multiple Ways to Correct the Problem:**

- Delete the Vendor bill – Assuming the bill is in the current period, deleting the bill will remove it from payables and eliminate the duplicate expense.
- Record a Credit Memo – A credit memo could be recorded for the amount of the bill, then offset against the already paid bill. This would also remove it from payables and eliminate the duplicate expense. If the bill is from a prior closed period, the credit memo should be dated in the current period.
- Change the account coding on the check issued through the banking section – Typically, when this "One Step/Two Step" problem occurs, the account assigned to the check issued in the Banking section is an expense account. By changing the account to Accounts Payable, the open bill in Accounts Payable will be offset.

Notes:

## Chapter Thirteen
# Creating and Setting Up New Company Files

Accountants are frequently called upon to set up new company files in QuickBooks. Several situations can create this need:

- A start-up company that needs its accounting set up.
- A new corporation that will be part of a related group of already existing corporations.
- An existing company file that has grown "too large" or has so many errors and issues that the decision to "start over clean" has been made.
- A conversion to QuickBooks from another accounting software package.

Setting up the file is only the first step in getting a company file fully functional. Numerous other tasks must be completed, such as getting Lists set up, inputting company information, setting preferences, defining the chart of accounts, connecting bank and credit accounts, and getting beginning balances correctly entered.

The functionality to create new company files differs depending on the version of QuickBooks being used, though all versions will allow the user to create a new file. Those differences are:

- Only the Accountant's version provides the option to create a new file from an existing file.
- Industry versions, such as the contractor's version, will set up not only a chart of accounts but also item codes geared toward the particular industry.
- The Accountant's version will not set up industry oriented item codes.

Regardless of which version is being used, any new file created will need to be customized beyond the basic set of codes initially generated.

From the File option in the main menu, the New Company option brings up the screen shown below where all of the options for setting up a new company file are available.

The example below was generated from the Accountant's version, and hence shows the Create New File from an Existing File option.

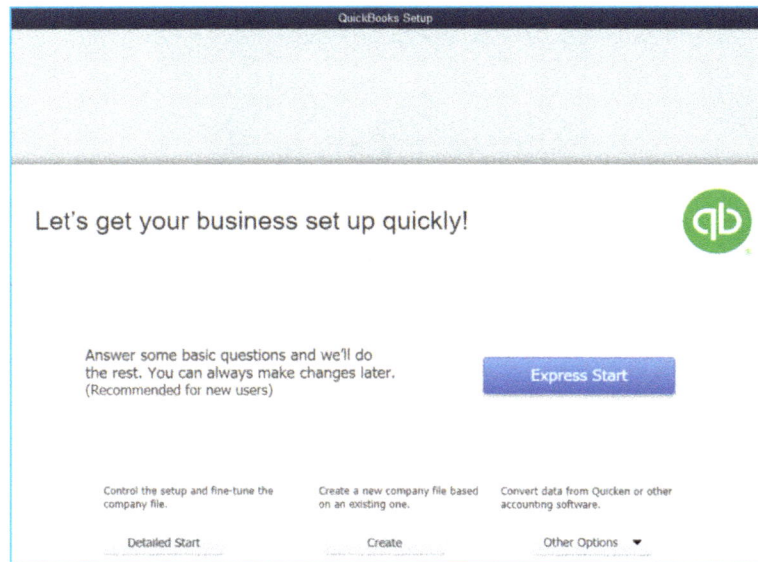

**Express Start**

The fast way to set up a new company. Clicking on the blue "Express Start" tab prompts the user to enter information about the new company.

Clicking on the "Help me choose" link next to the Industry box will bring up the "Select Your Industry" screen. This screen allows the user to select which industry the new company best fits. QuickBooks uses that selection to prefill the Chart of Accounts with codes that "fit" the industry.

While in this screen, the user can click on different industries on the left and QuickBooks will display the chart of accounts that will be set up on the right. These prefilled lists can be helpful and save time in setup, but in most cases, still need to be adjusted.

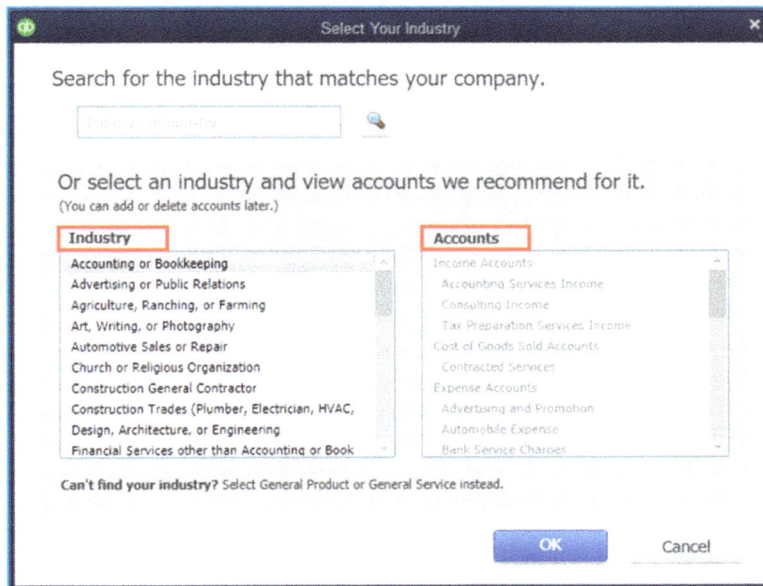

Clicking on the "Help me choose" link next to the Business Type box will bring the "Select Your Company Type" screen shown below where the user can select the type of entity the company is for tax purposes. Clicking on OK returns the user to the Express Start "Glad You're Here" screen.

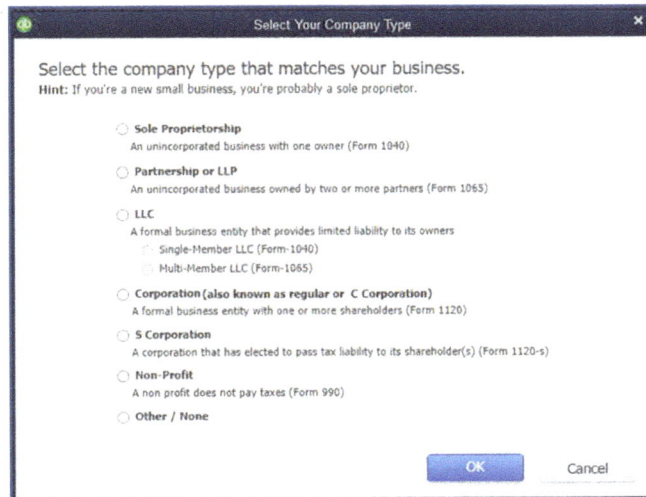

After clicking on the "Create Company" button in the Express Start screen, the new company file will be created. The screen shown next will then appear, allowing the user to enter information about customers, vendors, products and services, and bank accounts. As an alternative, the "Start Working" option can be chosen, which will complete the initial part of the setup, but require the user to enter additional information later.

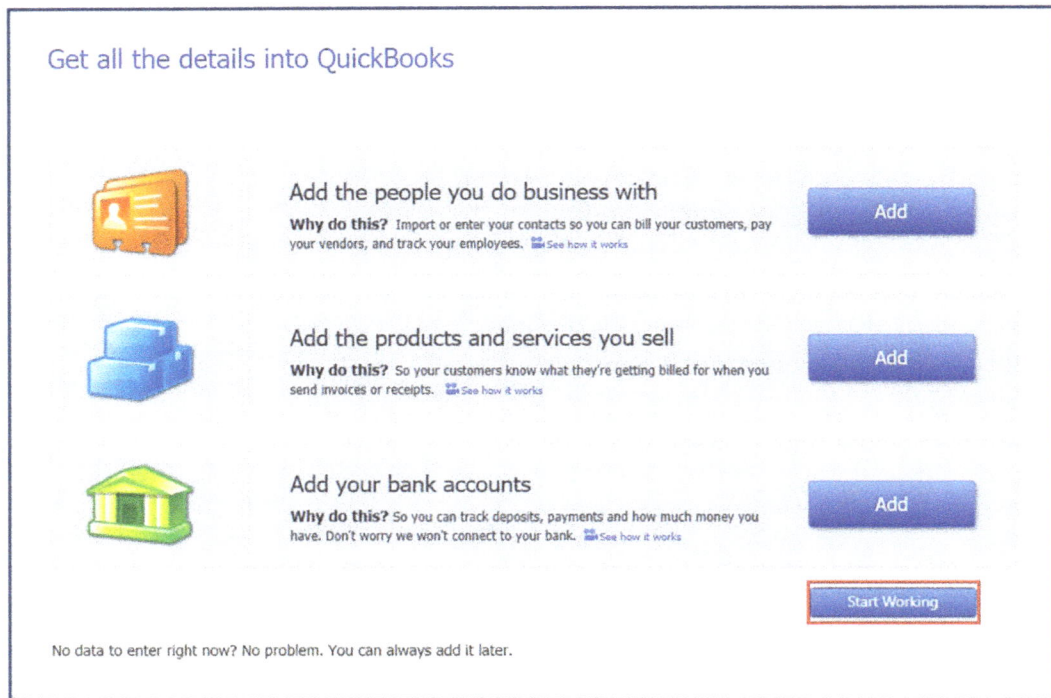

Get all the details into QuickBooks

Add the people you do business with

**Why do this?** Import or enter your contacts so you can bill your customers, pay your vendors, and track your employees. See how it works

Add

Add the products and services you sell

**Why do this?** So your customers know what they're getting billed for when you send invoices or receipts. See how it works

Add

Add your bank accounts

**Why do this?** So you can track deposits, payments and how much money you have. Don't worry we won't connect to your bank. See how it works

Add

Start Working

No data to enter right now? No problem. You can always add it later.

**Detailed Start**

This option for setting up a new company has a much more detailed interview process than the Express Start option, so it does a more thorough job of getting a new file ready to use. While it takes longer to answer all the questions, this option is recommended over the Express Start option because of the time it saves in adjusting things after setup.

Clicking on the "Detailed Start" screen from the QuickBooks Setup menu brings up a series of screens where information can be entered. The answers to the interview questions and selections establish the chart of accounts, create company information, and set various preferences in QuickBooks. Keep in mind that setup information derived from the initial interview can be changed at a later time if desired. The detailed start interview screens allow the user to set up or establish:

- Legal name of the company, address, and FEIN
- Chart of accounts that best fits your company's industry
- Type of entity your company is for tax filing purposes
- First month of your fiscal year
- Administrator password
- Name for the company file and where it will be saved
- Whether services, products, or both are sold
- Whether sales taxes are to be charged

- Use of estimates
- Tracking customer orders
- Sending customers statements
- Whether invoices will be sent to clients
- Whether vendor bills will be tracked
- Usage of inventory
- Tracking of time for employees and billing
- Whether employees and/or 1099 contractors are utilized
- Start date of your QuickBooks

**New Company from Existing Company File**

The first step is to open the company file to be copied. Once the file is open, this option can be accessed from the File part of the menu using the "New Company from Existing Company File" option.

Selecting "New Company from Existing Company File" will bring up the screen below:

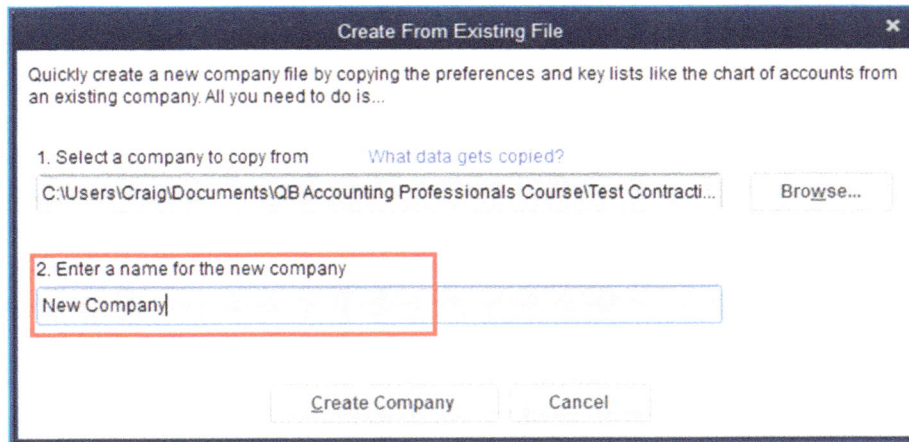

A name for the company must be entered, and then "Create Company" can be clicked to move forward. This brings up the screen below where the file is named and saved:

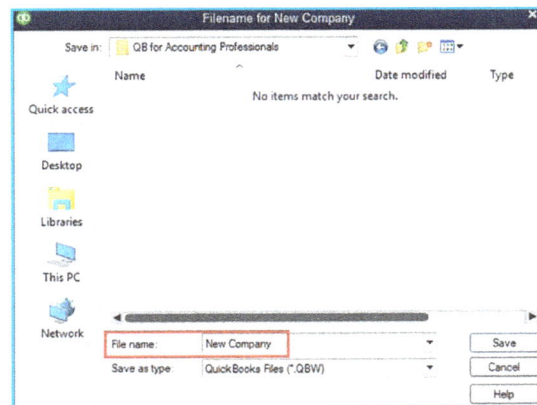

© The CFO Source, LLC 2017

Once complete, the following message is displayed:

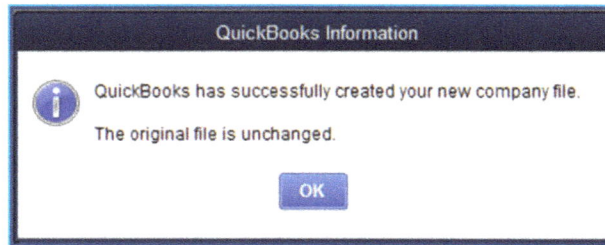

The areas of QuickBooks that get transferred from the old company to the new file are:

- Chart of Accounts (except Cash Accounts)
- Preferences
- Sales Tax Item Codes
- Memorized Reports

# Set Up Vendors, Customers, and Item Codes

For brand new companies, these can be entered individually in the related section of QuickBooks or in the List section under the Add/Edit Multiple List Entries. Entries into this screen can be "cut and pasted" from Excel or manually entered. Unfortunately, this section only allows for the setup of Service and Non-Inventory Part item codes.

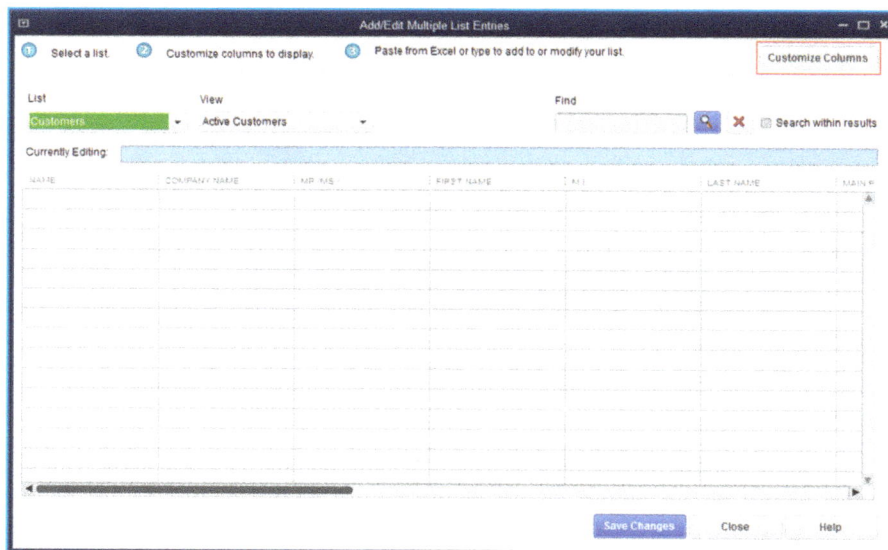

The Customize Columns tab brings up the screen shown next, which allows the user to add or remove fields and arrange the fields on the input screen shown above.

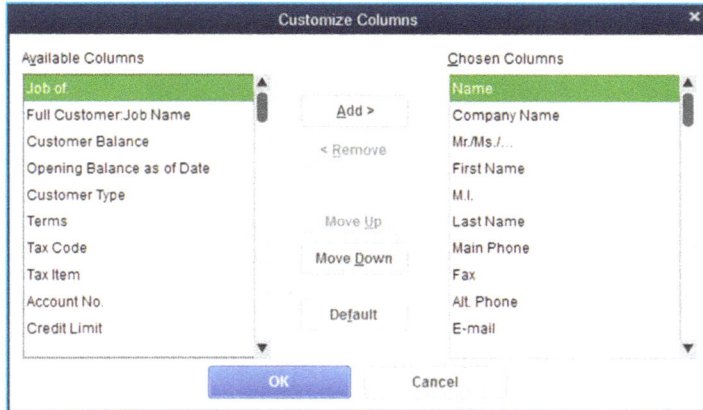

**Transferring Files From Existing Company Files**

While a new company file can be created from an existing company file, the only complete list that gets copied is the chart of accounts. However, using the utilities function, any list can be exported from the old company file and imported into the new file.

To export a list, while in the old company, select File from the main menu, then Utilities, then Export, then Lists to IIF Files. This will bring up the below screen showing all the lists available for export:

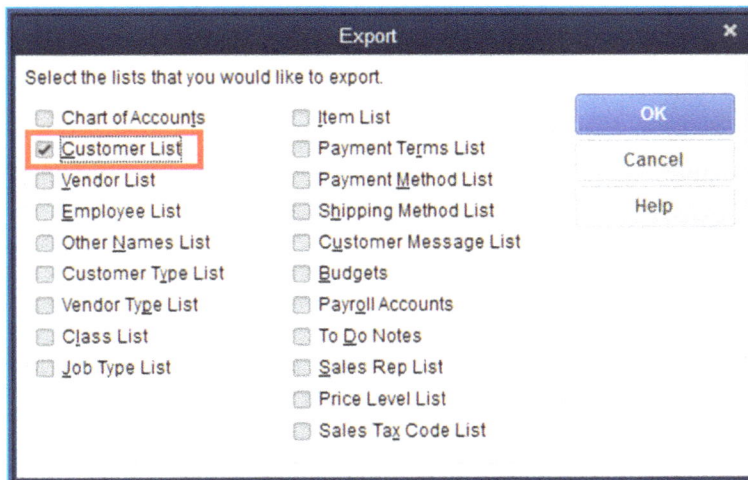

Clicking on OK will prompt the user to name and save the file.

Once the file is created, the new company should be opened and the saved list file can be imported.

To import a list, while in the new company, select File from the main menu, then Utilities, then Import, then IIF Files to select the file for import.

The following message will be displayed once the import is complete:

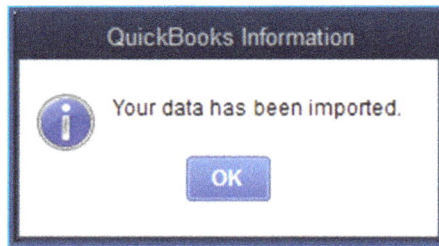

Once imported, the lists should be reviewed to see if any list items should be deleted.

# Recording Beginning Balances

If an existing company is being set up, then account balances and "open" transaction details of the company will need to be set up in the new QuickBooks file. While recording a journal entry of the trial balance as of the selected transfer date might sound appropriate, this approach alone fails to bring over the details needed to process transactions going forward. For example, if the open accounts receivable invoices from the old system are not entered into the new QuickBooks file, then applying payments received from customers against specific invoices will not be possible.

When setting up an existing company, the below approach is recommended to get balances set up so that transactions can be processed:

- Choose a month-end or year-end date and close the books in the old system.
- Enter all of the open accounts receivable invoices as of the transfer date, using the actual date of each transaction. Run an accounts receivable aging in QuickBooks and make sure it agrees with the old system.
- Enter all of the unpaid accounts payable bills as of the transfer date, using the actual date of the transaction. Run an accounts payable aging in QuickBooks and make sure it agrees with the old system.
- Enter all of the un-cleared bank reconciliation items as of the transfer date, using the actual date of the transaction. Typically, this should just be checks that have not cleared the bank as of the transfer date. The disbursements should be coded to the expense account the underlying check relates to, *not* to accounts payable. After this is done, make sure the balance in cash in QuickBooks equals the amount of the outstanding reconciliation items as a credit balance.
- Once all the "open transactions" have been entered into the new QuickBooks file, run a trial balance as of the transfer date from QuickBooks and export the report to Excel.
- Run a trial balance from the old system as of the transfer date and export the report to Excel.

- Prepare a single spreadsheet with the trial balances from the old system and QuickBooks. Create a column for each system, then a third "differences" column, making sure the rows for accounts line up correctly.
- Make a journal entry as of the transfer date for the differences in the trial balance spreadsheet. This will effectively record the balances in accounts with no "open" transactions as of the transfer date.
- After entering the journal entry of differences, run a new trial balance from QuickBooks and make sure it agrees with the trial balance from the old system.

Notes:

# Chapter Fourteen
# Verify and Rebuild Utilities

As with any computer software, QuickBooks may display signs that there are issues with data integrity. These can include messages generated from QuickBooks that pop up at inconvenient times or reports that are "out of balance." For example, the balance sheet may not balance or the total of an accounts receivable or payables aging may not match the balance sheet.

In many cases, QuickBooks Verify and Rebuild utilities can identify and resolve these problems. Before using the utilities, it is recommended that a backup copy of your company file be created. There are two ways to create a backup file, both are found in the File section of the main menu. For the first method, select File, then Create Local Back up. For the second method, select File, then Create Copy, then Backup Copy.

**Verify Data Utility** – from the main menu, select File, then Utilities, then Verify. This utility scans your company file for data issues. The information below was based on running this utility on a "live" file that was in use for over ten years in a large organization, not a sample file:

If no issues are found, the following message will appear:

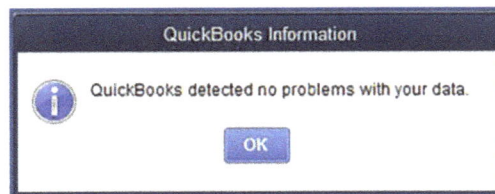

If problems are found, the following message will appear:

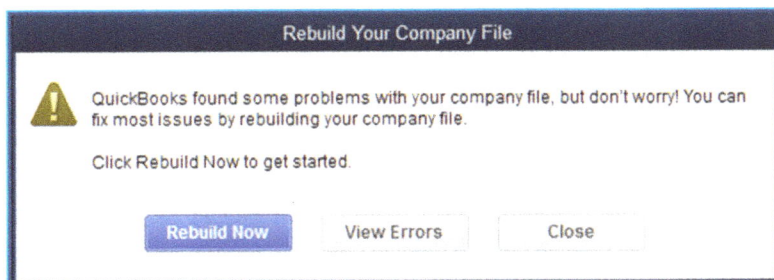

Clicking on the View Errors button will bring up the following screen:

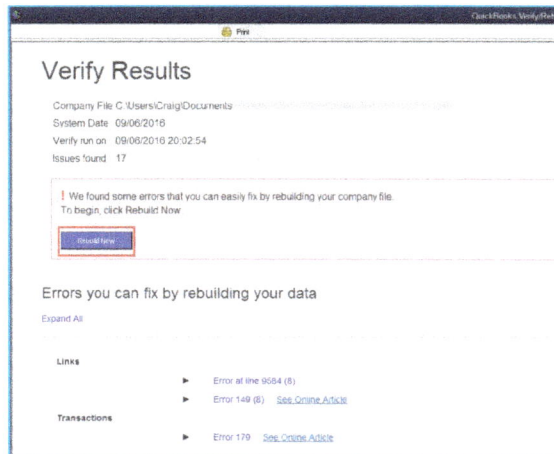

It is suggested to print the above page in the event the rebuild is not successful and further help is needed. Clicking on Rebuild Now will display the message below:

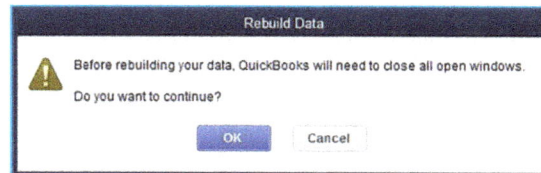

After clicking OK, you will be prompted to create a backup file:

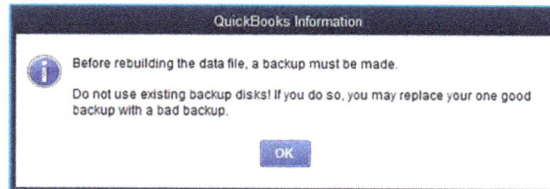

After the backup is complete, the Rebuild will start and the user will get the following message:

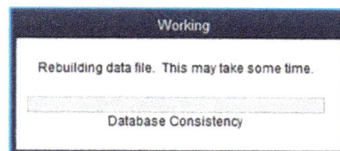

Once the Rebuild is complete, the following message will appear:

It is suggested to click on the View Issues button, which will bring up the following screen:

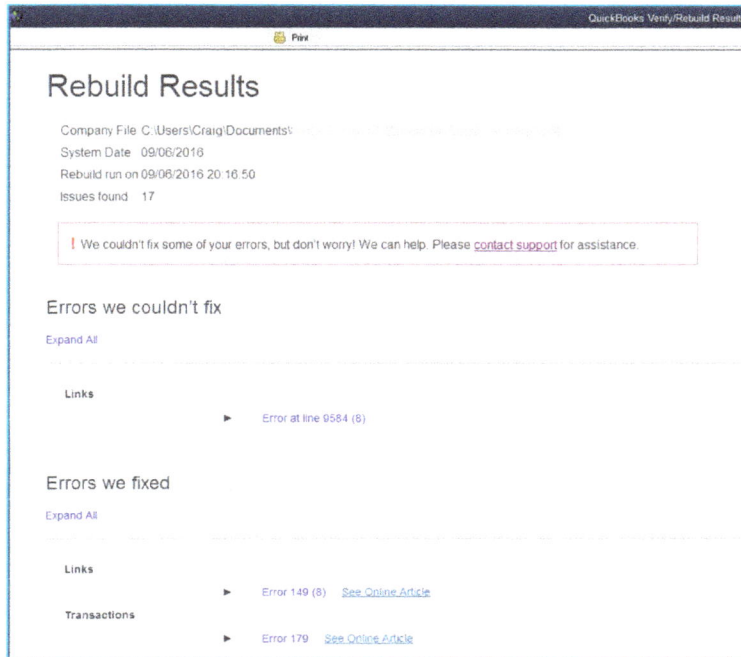

It is suggested that the Expand All option be chosen for Errors that couldn't be fixed, which will detail the errors as follows:

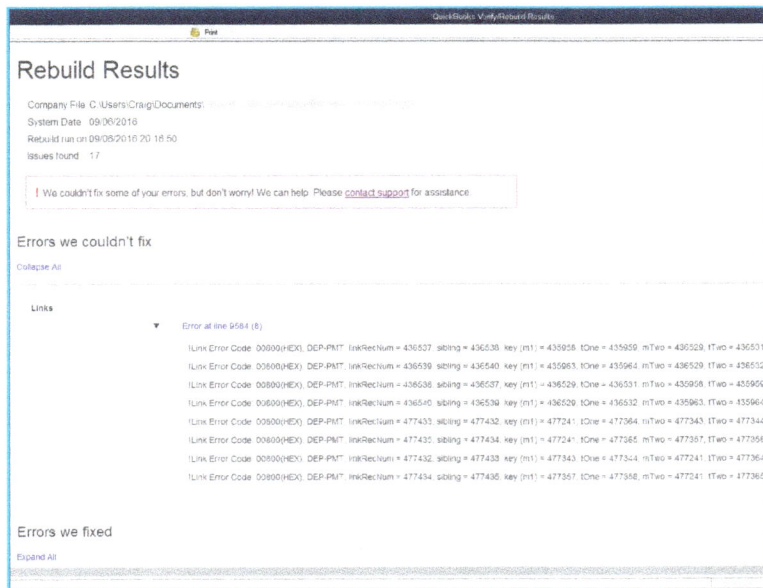

Even though all errors may not have been fixed, the company file may work without experiencing any issues. Additionally, running the Rebuild Utility multiple times may correct all issues. If the issues are believed to be causing serious problems, contact Intuit customer support for help repairing the file.

Notes:

# Chapter Fifteen
# The Condense Utility

Companies with large amounts of data spanning several years may experience a "slowing down" of their QuickBooks file. Slow response times for entering data, running reports, or files taking a long time to load can occur when files grow too large. The Condense Utility shrinks the size of the file by condensing transaction data into summary journal entries and removing unused list names. Condensing data can improve response times by shrinking the size of the file.

The Condense Utility collapses transaction data and eliminates the ability to "drill down" for data before the collapse date. In addition, reports that draw on transaction details such as the Audit Trail will not be accurate. Further, Cash Basis reports from periods before the condense date will not be accurate because Cash Basis reports rely on the individual cash transactions, which will no longer exist.

Users who want to retain all of their detail data while improving QB performance that has degraded due to files growing too large have these options:

- Make a copy of the company file with a different name to preserve details before running the condense utility. With this approach, two company files would exist, one having the transaction detail before the condense date for historical research and the other acting as the current "working file." While QuickBooks makes a copy of the file before starting the condense utility, making this backup copy of the file with a unique name is suggested as an added precaution.
- For those users running QuickBooks Pro or Premier, upgrade to QuickBooks Enterprise for a more robust database that can handle larger volumes of data. This may eliminate the need to condense data altogether.

The decision to condense a QuickBooks data file should be based on how severe performance problems are and the impact these issues are having on user productivity. It would be wise to explore whether an upgrade of computer hardware might resolve performance issues before condensing a QuickBooks file.

Before running the Condense Data utility, it is recommended to run the Verify and, if need be, Rebuild utilities first. The Condense Data utility will not run if data integrity issues exist.

# Using the Condense Data Utility

The user must pick a date for which all transactions occurring prior to are condensed. Using a company's fiscal year end date is recommended, preferably three or four years in the past. Because the Condense Utility cannot be undone, it is recommended to pick a date sufficiently in the past such that there would be little need to refer back to transaction details.

The Condense Utility offers three options as to how QuickBooks treats the transaction data that is condensed. These options are:

- Creation of a single summary journal entry that replaces all transactions before the selected condense date. This is, in essence, a journal entry recording the trial balance on the condense date. A drawback to this option is that the user can no longer run financial statements before the condense date.
- Creation of summary journal entries for each month to replace all detailed transactions before the condense date. Rather than being a journal entry of the trial balance as of the condense date like in the first option, these journal entries are the net change in each account for the month of the entry. This option gives the user the ability to run financial statements before the condense date, and is the recommended option for that reason.
- The removal of all transactions before the condense date without the recording of a journal entry. This option is not recommended.

For illustration purposes, the Condense Data utility was run on a large file in use for over ten years. Prior to running the utility for the example images shown next, the F2 button was pushed to bring up the following information on the file: (Note the file size is 207,616 kilobytes, or 207 megabytes. The average email with an attachment is less than 5 mbs.)

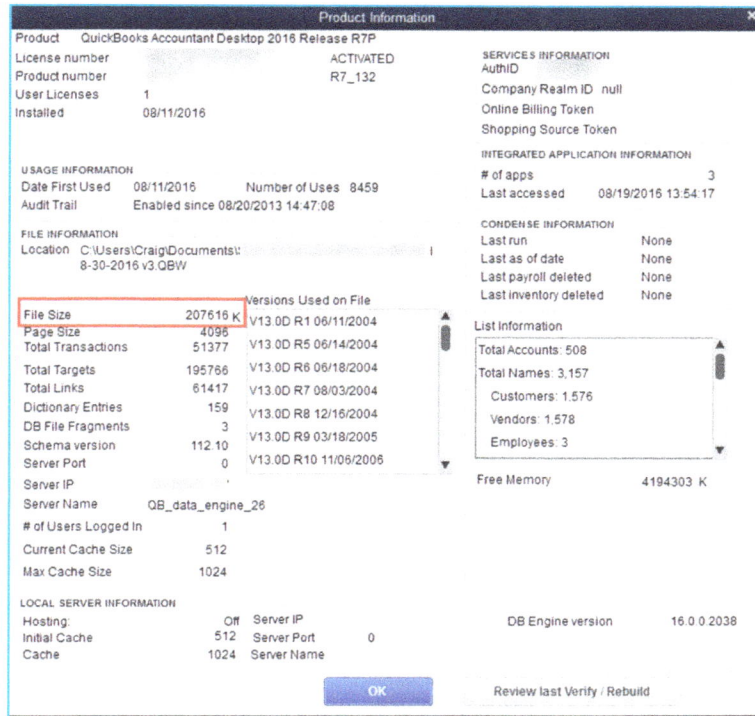

To run the Condense Data utility, from the main menu, select File, then Utilities, then Condense Data, which will bring up the screen below. This example has a June 30th year end, so one day after the fiscal year end was the date chosen. The utility condenses all transactions before the date input.

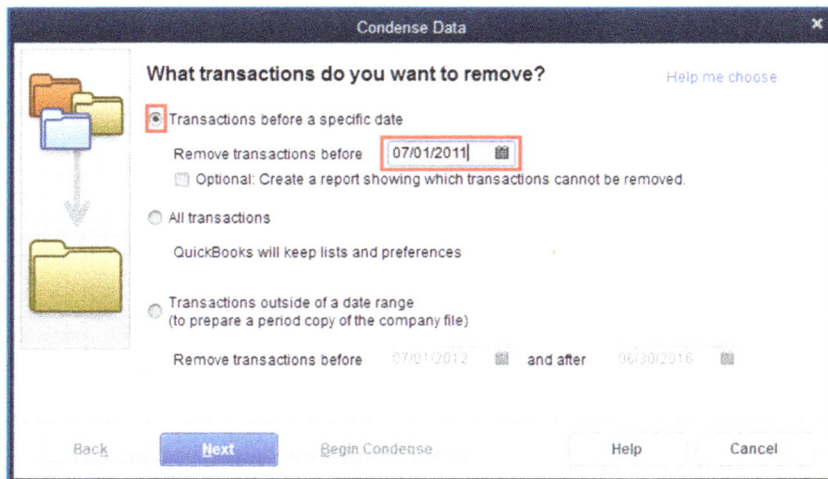

Click Next to select which of the three methods to use for condensing transactions:

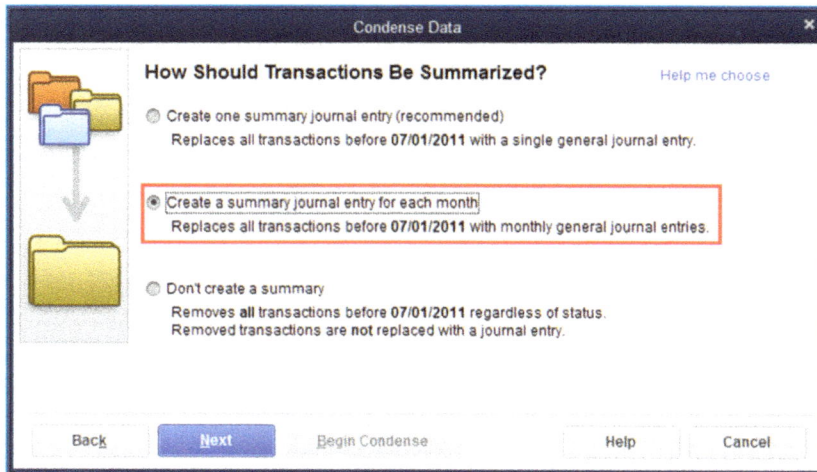

Click Next to bring up the screen below, which only applies if inventory is used:

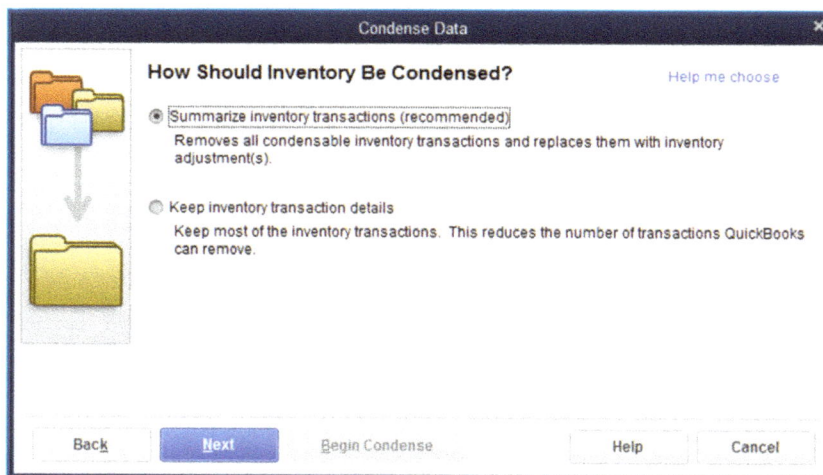

In the next screen, the user can override recommended transactions to be condensed:

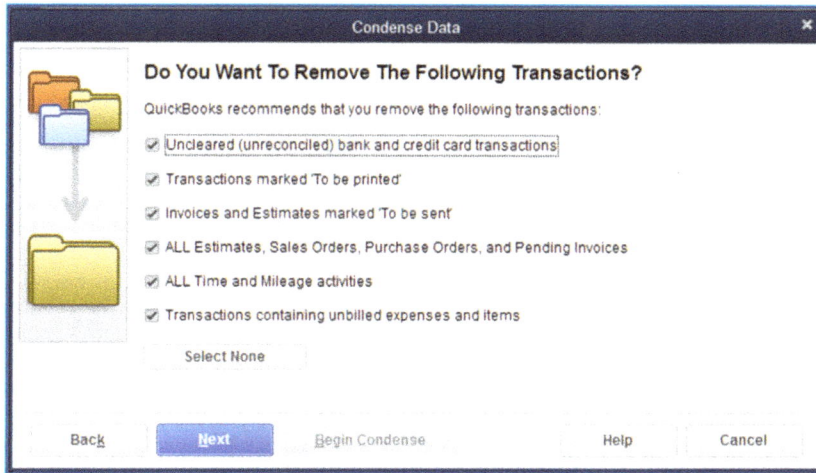

In the next screen, elect whether to remove list entries that have not been used *after* the condense date:

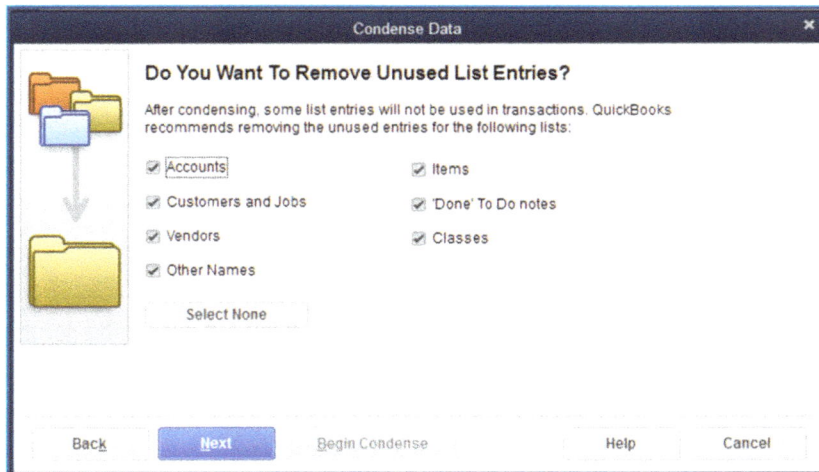

In the final screen, the user tells QuickBooks to begin the condense utility. QuickBooks will make a copy of the company file before removing any data as part of this process.

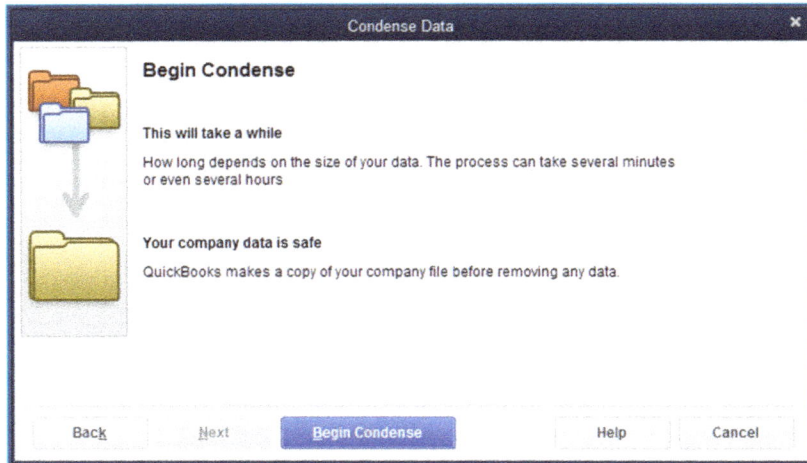

After clicking on Begin Condense, a series of screens will show the steps Quickbooks is taking to condense the data. Upon completion, the following message will indicate the name of the file that was created before the current file was condensed.

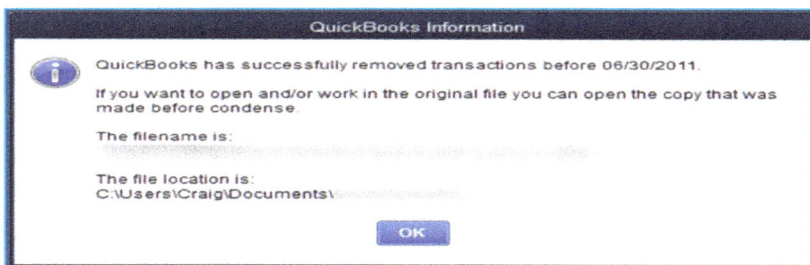

To see how much the file was condensed, hit the F2 button to bring up the screen below. Note the file size that was orginally 207,616 has been reduced to 139,012.

Notes:

# Chapter Sixteen
# Budgeting

Many accountants are called upon to prepare annual budgets and report budget versus actual results as the year progresses. Budgeting can be a powerful tool to control costs and serve as a projection for the upcoming year. Another common use of budgets is to make mid-year adjustments in the event that actual results differ significantly from budget. Most companies budget at the department and/or profit center level and use budgets to hold managers responsible for their area.

QuickBooks supports the tracking of budgets and provides two main reporting tools that can be customized for the necessary reports. Both reports can be run in a traditional P & L format or with classes as the rows. These are:

**Budget versus Actual** – this report displays columns for actual and budget for a selected time period, with variances shown in both dollars and percentages.

**Profit and Loss Budget Performance** – this report displays actual and budget for a selected time period as well as the budget for the entire year.

A company with two retail stores and a corporate office will be presented as an example. Entering the sales budget for one of the stores will be reviewed and the reporting available for individual stores, combined stores, and corporate expenses will be explored.

## Setting up Budgets

Typically, accountants prepare budgets using excel spreadsheets or, in the case of larger companies, specialized software for budgeting and forecasting is used. Once a budget has been completed (typically done outside of QuickBooks), entering the budget into QuickBooks is the next step.

From the main menu, select Company, then Planning & Budgeting, then Set Up Budgets, which will bring up the below screen. The fiscal year for the budget and the type of budget must be chosen. Budgets can be set up for both Profit & Loss Statements as well as Balance Sheets. For this example, a Profit & Loss Budget for 2019 has been chosen.

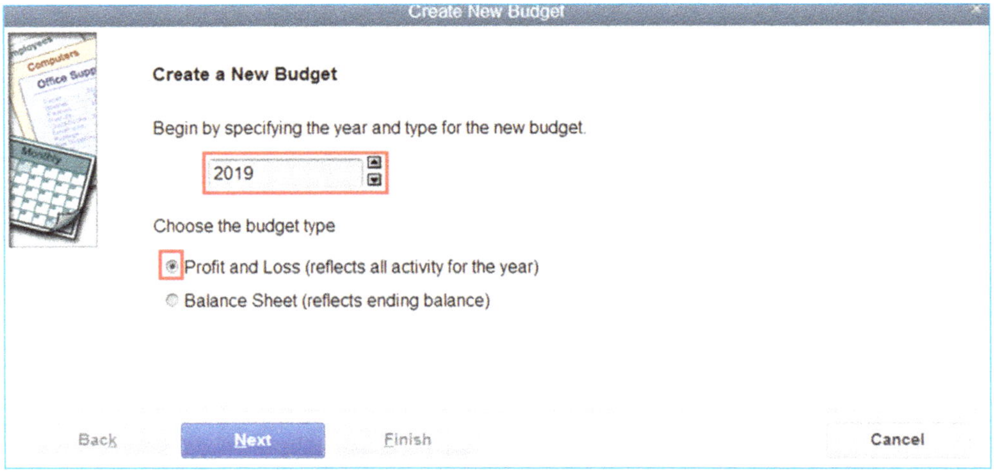

In the next screen, the level of detail for the budget must be selected. Three choices are available:

- No additional criteria – This would be for a company-wide budget with no departments or separate profit centers.
- Customer:Job – This would be for budgeting at the job level.
- Class – This would typically be used for departmental and/or profit center reporting. The preference for class would need to be activated for this option to appear.

In the example below, the class option has been chosen.

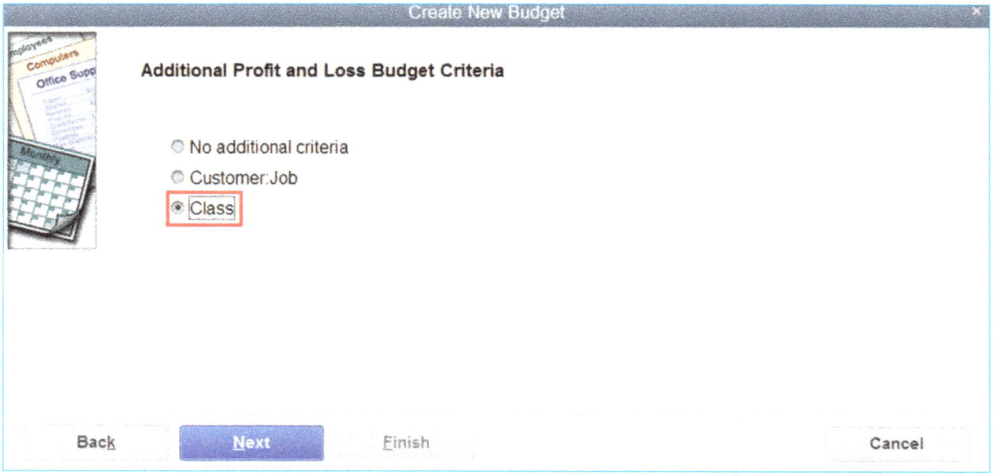

In the next screen, the user is given the option of creating a budget from scratch or using last year's actual figures as the new budget. If the "from Scratch" option is chosen, the user must input each budget line item. If the "actual" option is chosen, the budget will be filled in with prior year figures for each account.

In this example, the "from scratch" option has been chosen.

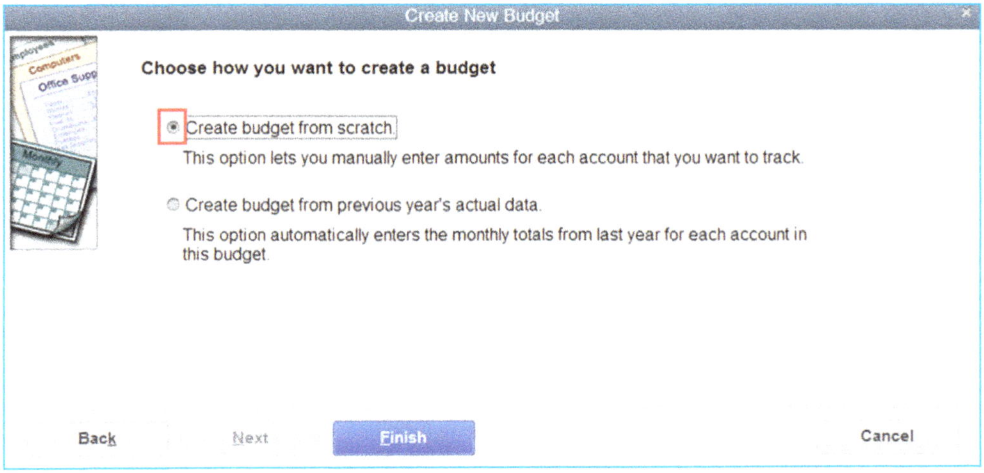

Clicking Next brings up the below screen where the budget can be input. Note that the budget has been given a name, in this example "FY2019 – Profit & Loss by Account and Class." The user cannot change this name; it is driven by budget type and year selected and notes if the class to be budgeted has also been selected.

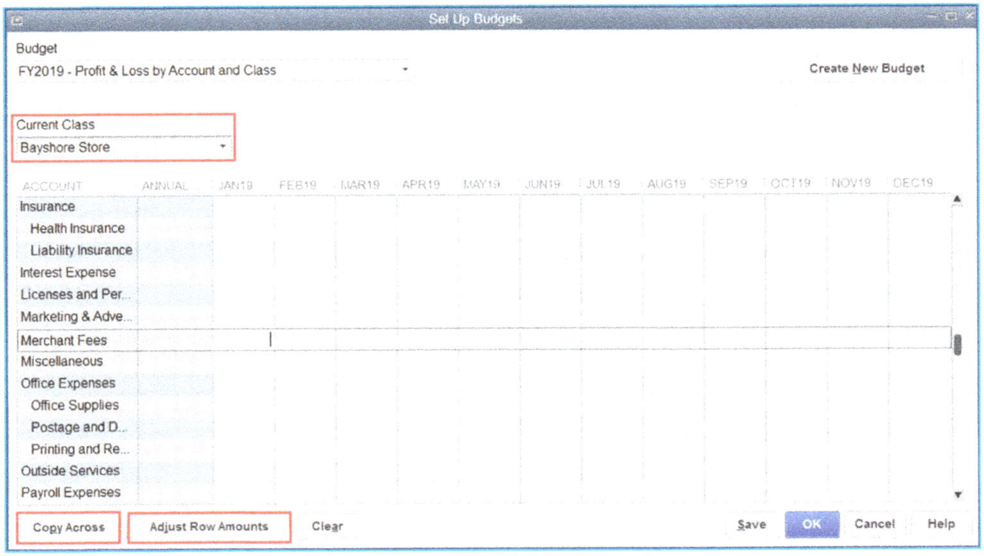

There are two useful tools in this screen that speed up data entry so the budget amounts for each account and each month don't have to be entered.

- Copy Across – If the amount is the same each month, it can be typed in the first month, then do not hit enter but instead click Copy Across to fill in the remaining months with the same figure. The cursor must be in the first month that is to be copied across.
- Adjust Row Amounts – This option is useful if the budget amount is to be increased or decreased each month from a base amount. The change can either be a dollar amount or percentage. The amount can also be compounded. There must first be an amount in each month to be budgeted, which is best done using the "Copy Across" button. The below screen will appear when the "Copy Across" button is clicked:

The user can select when the increase or decrease should start, which can either be the first month of the budget or the currently selected month. In the example above, the budget will be increased 5% on a compounded basis.

Each account is entered independent of other accounts; there is no functionality to budget one account as a percentage of another account.

Making changes to the budget is done by entering new figures into the desired accounts. The "Clear" button in the data entry screen will delete all entries to the page of the budget being worked on.

Below is the first page of the budget screen for the Bayshore Store.

**Entering Budget Data from Excel**

For those who have large budgets with multiple departments, entering budgets as outlined above into QuickBooks can be time consuming. Fortunately, information from Excel spreadsheets can be imported into QuickBooks.

Importing budget data is a done using the QuickBooks file type .IIF, and the information entered must be in a specific format. As with any transfer of data from one software package to another, there must be an exact match of codes or the desired results will not be attained. Because QuickBooks is looking for an import file in an exact format, it is recommended that a budget for a single class be created in QuickBooks first and exported to an Excel file that will show the required layout of rows and columns. Once created, the budget data to be imported can be added to the file, preferably by pasting from the user's excel budget files. The following steps are recommended:

**Step 1:** Create a budget as outlined above, making sure that all the desired accounts in the new budget have a line item.

This will create a file with the correct account names. If there are multiple classes to be budgeted, only a budget for one class need be created. The remaining classes can be added to the import file and the accounts for the remaining classes can be copied. The goal in this step is to get all the accounts that are to be used in the export file so that the account names are an exact match. If they don't match exactly, QuickBooks will create new ones to accommodate the data when it is uploaded.

**Step 2:** Create the export file.

From the main menu, select File, then Utilities, then Export, then List to IIF files, which will bring up the below screen.

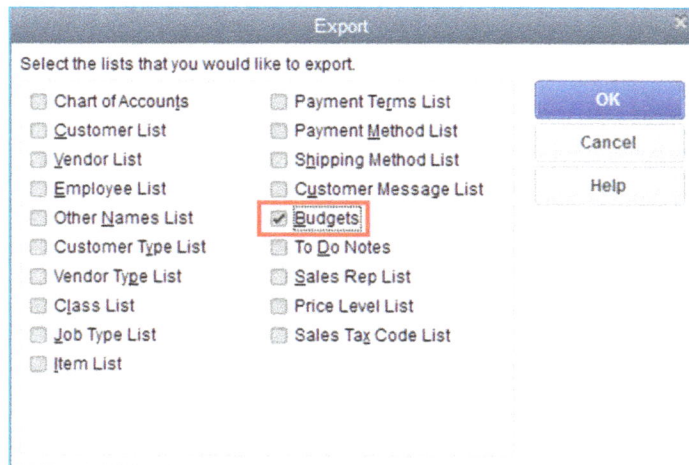

Check the Budgets option, then click OK. This will bring up a screen prompting the user to name the file and select a location where it should be saved. As shown below, the file has been saved as "Budget.IIF":

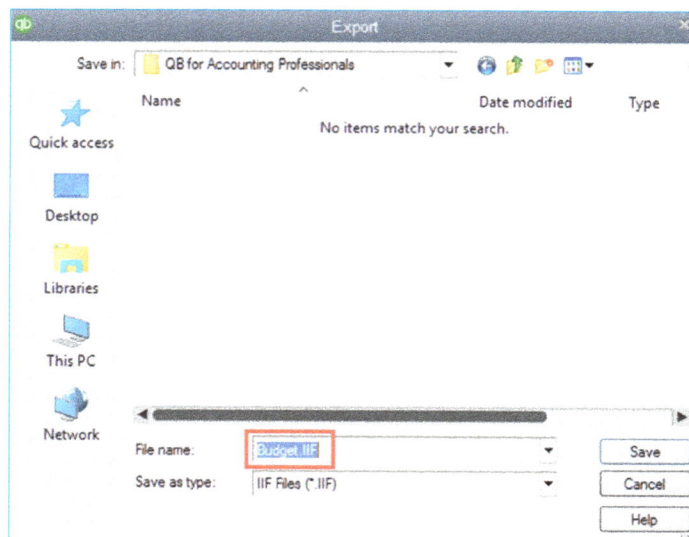

After clicking on Save, you should get the following message:

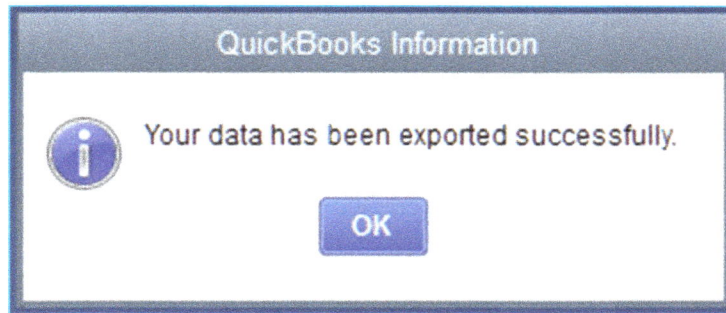

**Step 3:** After exporting the file from QuickBooks, it should then be opened in Excel. Make sure to change the file type in the lower right of the screen shown below to "All Files" when searching for and opening the file.

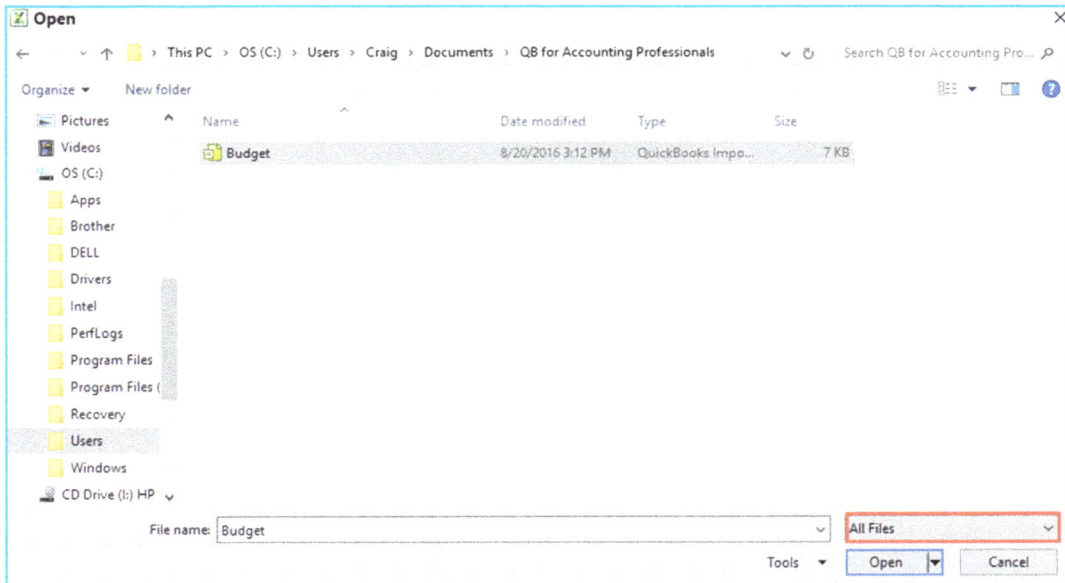

Because an .IIF file is not an Excel file, when the file is opened the Text Import Wizard will be started to convert the file to an Excel format.

Shown below is the first screen. Make sure the "Delimited" option is checked off and then click Next.

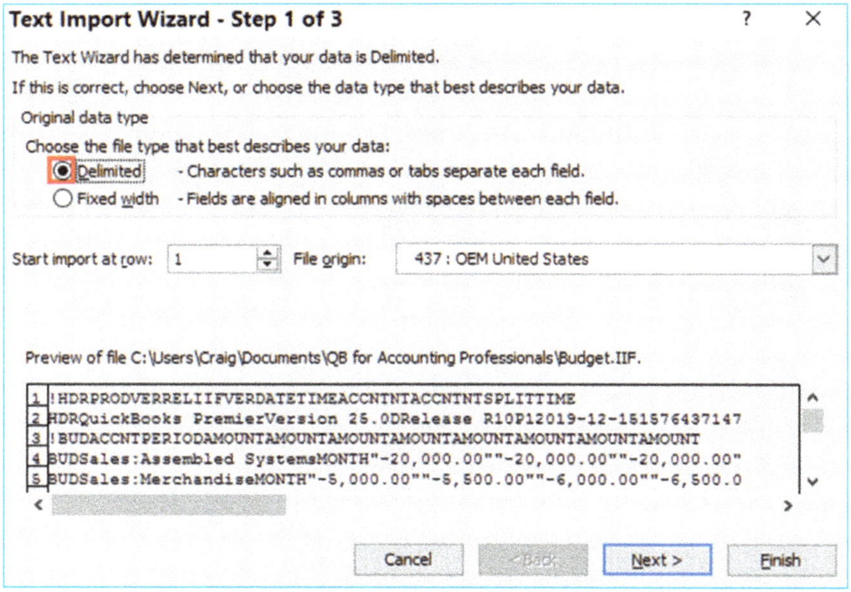

**Text Import Wizard - Step 1 of 3**

The Text Wizard has determined that your data is Delimited.

If this is correct, choose Next, or choose the data type that best describes your data.

Original data type

Choose the file type that best describes your data:

- ○ Delimited   - Characters such as commas or tabs separate each field.
- ○ Fixed width  - Fields are aligned in columns with spaces between each field.

Start import at row: 1    File origin: 437 : OEM United States

Preview of file C:\Users\Craig\Documents\QB for Accounting Professionals\Budget.IIF.

```
1 !HDRPRODVERRELIIFVERDATETIMEACCNTNTACCNTNTSPLITTIME
2 HDRQuickBooks PremierVersion 25.0DRelease R10P12019-12-151576437147
3 !BUDACCNTPERIODAMOUNTAMOUNTAMOUNTAMOUNTAMOUNTAMOUNTAMOUNTAMOUNT
4 BUDSales:Assembled SystemsMONTH"-20,000.00""-20,000.00""-20,000.00"
5 BUDSales:MerchandiseMONTH"-5,000.00""-5,500.00""-6,000.00""-6,500.0
```

Cancel    < Back    Next >    Finish

In the second screen, make sure the Delimiters selection is set to "Tab" and click Next.

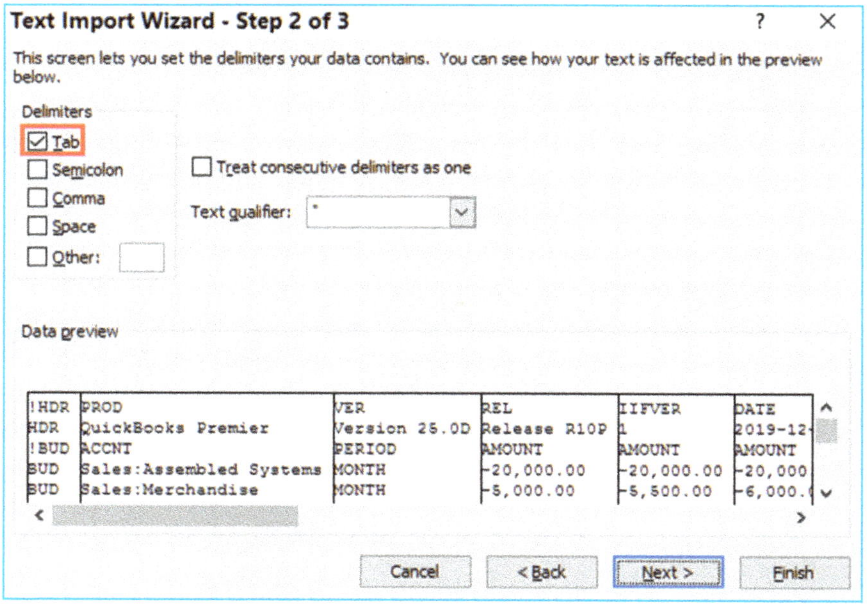

**Text Import Wizard - Step 2 of 3**

This screen lets you set the delimiters your data contains. You can see how your text is affected in the preview below.

Delimiters

- ☑ Tab
- ☐ Semicolon       ☐ Treat consecutive delimiters as one
- ☐ Comma          Text qualifier: "
- ☐ Space
- ☐ Other:

Data preview

| !HDR | PROD | VER | REL | IIFVER | DATE |
|------|------|-----|-----|--------|------|
| HDR | QuickBooks Premier | Version 25.0D | Release R10P | 1 | 2019-12- |
| !BUD | ACCNT | PERIOD | AMOUNT | AMOUNT | AMOUNT |
| BUD | Sales:Assembled Systems | MONTH | -20,000.00 | -20,000.00 | -20,000 |
| BUD | Sales:Merchandise | MONTH | -5,000.00 | -5,500.00 | -6,000.( |

Cancel    < Back    Next >    Finish

In the third screen, make sure the Column Data Format is set to "General" and click Finish.

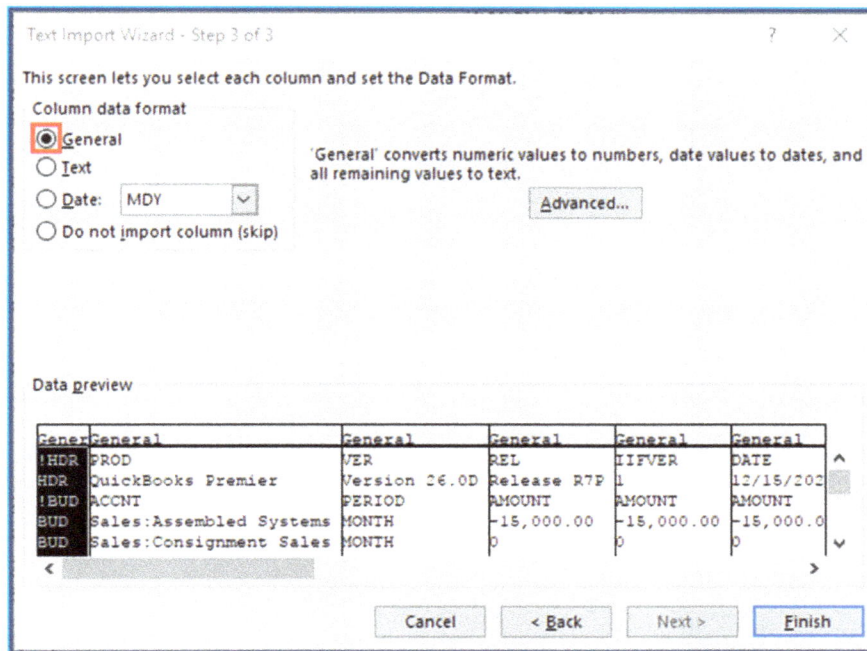

**Step 4:** Use the spreadsheet shown on the next page to enter additional budget items.

Notes on using the spreadsheet for inputting your total budget are as follows:

- The first three rows of the spreadsheet (shown in blue) should not be altered in any way.
- The notations in column A (shown as "BUD") and column C (shown as "MONTH") should be copied to all new rows added to the file. This identifies to QuickBooks in the .IIF file that this is budget data.
- The date shown in column P should be copied to all new rows added to the file.
- To add new rows for budget data, also copy the appropriate account names from column B and class codes from Column Q to include those data points for each new row. If additional class codes are to be added, make sure to input those exactly as they appear in QuickBooks Class List.
- Rather than being flagged as errors, any Account or Class Codes on the import spreadsheet that are not exact matches to already existing codes will be set up in QuickBooks as new codes when the spreadsheet is imported.
- The twelve columns D through O are for monthly budget amounts.
- When copying amounts into the import spreadsheet from budget spreadsheets, make sure to copy the data as values and not the formulas that may have been used to create the budget. Decimals are optional.
- Revenues should be entered as negatives and expenses/costs entered as positives. Like many accounting software packages, QuickBooks uses negatives to denote credit transactions and positives for debit transactions. Accordingly, revenues that are "credit" transactions need to be entered in the budget screen as negative amounts and expense transactions that are "debit" transactions as positives.
- Column R for Customer is used only if you are budgeting at the job level.

© The CFO Source, LLC 2017

| A (HDR) | B (PROD) | C (VER) | D (REL) | E (IIFVER) | F (DATE) | G (TIME) | H (ACCNT) | I (ACCNTNSPLITTIME) |
|---|---|---|---|---|---|---|---|---|
| HDR | QuickBooks Premier | Version 25.0 Release R10P | 1 | | 12/15/2019 | 1576437147 | N | 0 |

| BUD | ACCNT | PERIOD | AMOUNT | AMOUNT | AMOUNT | AMOUNT | AMOUNT | AMOUNT | AMOUNT | AMOUNT | AMOUNT | AMOUNT | AMOUNT | AMOUNT | STARTDATE | CLASS | CUSTOMER |
|---|---|---|---|---|---|---|---|---|---|---|---|---|---|---|---|---|---|---|
| BUD | Sales:Merchandise | MONTH | -5,000.00 | -5,500.00 | -6,000.00 | -6,500.00 | -7,000.00 | -7,500.00 | -8,000.00 | -8,500.00 | -9,000.00 | -9,500.00 | -10,000.00 | -10,500.00 | 1/1/2019 | Bayshore Store | |
| BUD | Sales:Merchandise | MONTH | -2,500.00 | -2,500.00 | -2,500.00 | -2,500.00 | -2,500.00 | -2,500.00 | -2,500.00 | -2,500.00 | -2,500.00 | -2,500.00 | -2,500.00 | -2,500.00 | 1/1/2019 | San Tomas Store | |
| BUD | Cost of Goods Sold | MONTH | 15,000.00 | 15,500.00 | 16,000.00 | 16,500.00 | 17,000.00 | 17,500.00 | 18,000.00 | 18,500.00 | 19,000.00 | 19,500.00 | 20,000.00 | 20,500.00 | 1/1/2019 | Bayshore Store | |
| BUD | Cost of Goods Sold | MONTH | 4,250.00 | 4,250.00 | 4,250.00 | 4,250.00 | 4,250.00 | 4,250.00 | 4,250.00 | 4,250.00 | 4,250.00 | 4,250.00 | 4,250.00 | 4,250.00 | 1/1/2019 | San Tomas Store | |
| BUD | Professional Fees:Accounting | MONTH | 500 | 500 | 500 | 500 | 500 | 500 | 500 | 500 | 500 | 500 | 500 | 500 | 1/1/2019 | Corporate | |
| BUD | Office Expenses | MONTH | 250 | 250 | 250 | 250 | 250 | 250 | 250 | 250 | 250 | 250 | 250 | 250 | 1/1/2019 | Corporate | |
| BUD | Marketing & Advertising | MONTH | 1,500.00 | 1,500.00 | 1,500.00 | 1,500.00 | 1,500.00 | 1,500.00 | 1,500.00 | 1,500.00 | 1,500.00 | 1,500.00 | 1,500.00 | 1,500.00 | 1/1/2019 | Bayshore Store | |
| BUD | Automobile Expense | MONTH | 200 | 200 | 200 | 200 | 200 | 200 | 200 | 200 | 200 | 200 | 200 | 200 | 1/1/2019 | Bayshore Store | |
| BUD | Bank Service Charges | MONTH | 15 | 15 | 15 | 15 | 15 | 15 | 15 | 15 | 15 | 15 | 15 | 15 | 1/1/2019 | Corporate | |
| BUD | Equipment Rental | MONTH | 50 | 50 | 50 | 50 | 50 | 50 | 50 | 50 | 50 | 50 | 50 | 50 | 1/1/2019 | Bayshore Store | |
| BUD | Rent | MONTH | 1,525.00 | 1,525.00 | 1,525.00 | 1,525.00 | 1,525.00 | 1,525.00 | 1,525.00 | 1,525.00 | 1,525.00 | 1,525.00 | 1,525.00 | 1,525.00 | 1/1/2019 | Bayshore Store | |
| BUD | Rent | MONTH | 2,025.00 | 2,025.00 | 2,025.00 | 2,025.00 | 2,025.00 | 2,025.00 | 2,025.00 | 2,025.00 | 2,025.00 | 2,025.00 | 2,025.00 | 2,025.00 | 1/1/2019 | San Tomas Store | |
| BUD | Telephone | MONTH | 275 | 275 | 275 | 275 | 275 | 275 | 275 | 275 | 275 | 275 | 275 | 275 | 1/1/2019 | Bayshore Store | |
| BUD | Telephone | MONTH | 550 | 550 | 550 | 550 | 550 | 550 | 550 | 550 | 550 | 550 | 550 | 550 | 1/1/2019 | San Tomas Store | |
| BUD | Utilities | MONTH | 500 | 500 | 500 | 500 | 500 | 500 | 500 | 500 | 500 | 500 | 500 | 500 | 1/1/2019 | Bayshore Store | |
| BUD | Utilities | MONTH | 350 | 350 | 350 | 350 | 350 | 350 | 350 | 350 | 350 | 350 | 350 | 350 | 1/1/2019 | San Tomas Store | |
| BUD | Merchant Fees | MONTH | 400 | 400 | 400 | 400 | 400 | 400 | 400 | 400 | 400 | 400 | 400 | 400 | 1/1/2019 | San Tomas Store | |
| BUD | Merchant Fees | MONTH | 1,100.00 | 1,100.00 | 1,100.00 | 1,100.00 | 1,100.00 | 1,100.00 | 1,100.00 | 1,100.00 | 1,100.00 | 1,100.00 | 1,100.00 | 1,100.00 | 1/1/2019 | San Tomas Store | |
| BUD | Sales:Assembled Systems | MONTH | -15,000.00 | -15,000.00 | -15,000.00 | -15,000.00 | -15,000.00 | -15,000.00 | -15,000.00 | -15,000.00 | -15,000.00 | -15,000.00 | -15,000.00 | -15,000.00 | 1/1/2019 | Bayshore Store | |
| BUD | Sales:Assembled Systems | MONTH | -4,000.00 | -4,000.00 | -4,000.00 | -4,000.00 | -4,000.00 | -4,000.00 | -4,000.00 | -4,000.00 | -4,000.00 | -4,000.00 | -4,000.00 | -4,000.00 | 1/1/2019 | San Tomas Store | |
| BUD | Sales:Service | MONTH | -12,000.00 | -12,600.00 | -13,230.00 | -13,891.50 | -14,586.08 | -15,315.38 | -16,081.15 | -16,885.21 | -17,729.47 | -18,615.94 | -19,546.74 | -20,524.08 | 1/1/2019 | Bayshore Store | |
| BUD | Sales:Service | MONTH | -6,000.00 | -6,000.00 | -6,000.00 | -6,000.00 | -6,000.00 | -6,000.00 | -6,000.00 | -6,000.00 | -6,000.00 | -6,000.00 | -6,000.00 | -6,000.00 | 1/1/2019 | San Tomas Store | |
| BUD | Payroll Expenses:Gross Wages | MONTH | 1,000.00 | 1,000.00 | 1,000.00 | 1,000.00 | 1,000.00 | 1,000.00 | 1,000.00 | 1,000.00 | 1,000.00 | 1,000.00 | 1,000.00 | 1,000.00 | 1/1/2019 | Bayshore Store | |
| BUD | Payroll Expenses:Gross Wages | MONTH | 3,000.00 | 3,000.00 | 3,000.00 | 3,000.00 | 3,000.00 | 3,000.00 | 3,000.00 | 3,000.00 | 3,000.00 | 3,000.00 | 3,000.00 | 3,000.00 | 1/1/2019 | San Tomas Store | |
| BUD | Payroll Expenses:PR Tax Expense | MONTH | 85 | 85 | 85 | 85 | 85 | 85 | 85 | 85 | 85 | 85 | 85 | 85 | 1/1/2019 | Bayshore Store | |
| BUD | Payroll Expenses:PR Tax Expense | MONTH | 350 | 350 | 350 | 350 | 350 | 350 | 350 | 350 | 350 | 350 | 350 | 350 | 1/1/2019 | San Tomas Store | |
| BUD | Payroll Expenses:PR Tax Expense | MONTH | 4,250.00 | 4,250.00 | 4,250.00 | 4,250.00 | 4,250.00 | 4,250.00 | 4,250.00 | 4,250.00 | 4,250.00 | 4,250.00 | 4,250.00 | 4,250.00 | 1/1/2019 | Bayshore Store | |
| BUD | Payroll Expenses:Officer's Compensation | MONTH | 5,500.00 | 5,500.00 | 5,500.00 | 5,500.00 | 5,500.00 | 5,500.00 | 5,500.00 | 5,500.00 | 5,500.00 | 5,500.00 | 5,500.00 | 5,500.00 | 1/1/2019 | Corporate | |
| BUD | Sales:Consignment Sales | MONTH | 0 | 0 | 0 | 0 | -1,000.00 | -1,050.00 | -1,102.50 | -1,157.63 | -1,215.51 | -1,276.29 | -1,340.10 | -1,407.11 | 1/1/2019 | Bayshore Store | |
| BUD | Outside Services | MONTH | 100 | 100 | 100 | 100 | 100 | 100 | 100 | 100 | 100 | 100 | 100 | 100 | 1/1/2019 | Bayshore Store | |
| BUD | Outside Services | MONTH | 150 | 150 | 150 | 150 | 150 | 150 | 150 | 150 | 150 | 150 | 150 | 150 | 1/1/2019 | San Tomas Store | |

Once additions to the spreadsheet have been completed, the spreadsheet should be saved as an .IIF file with a "Text (Tab delimited)" file type as shown below:

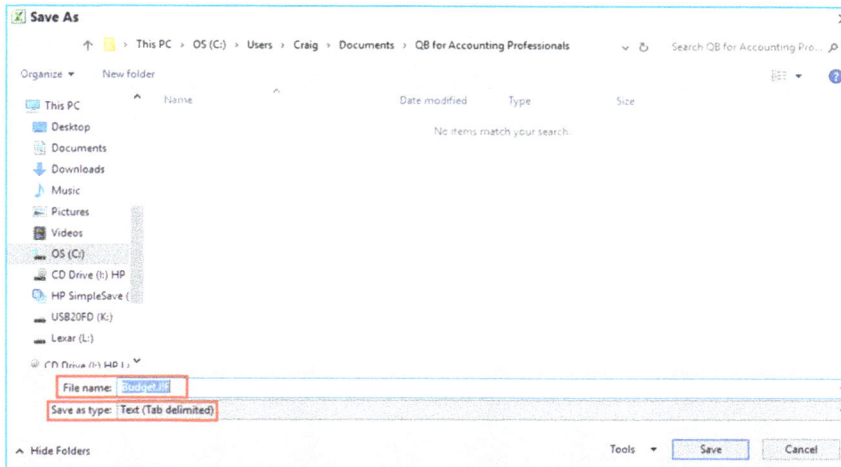

After clicking on Save, you will get the following message. Click Yes to keep the workbook in the desired format.

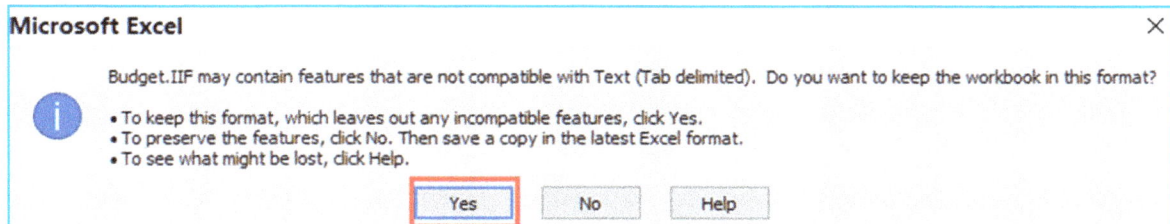

**Importing the Budget Spreadsheet** – from the main menu, select File, then Utilities, then Import, then IIF Files, which will bring up the screen below:

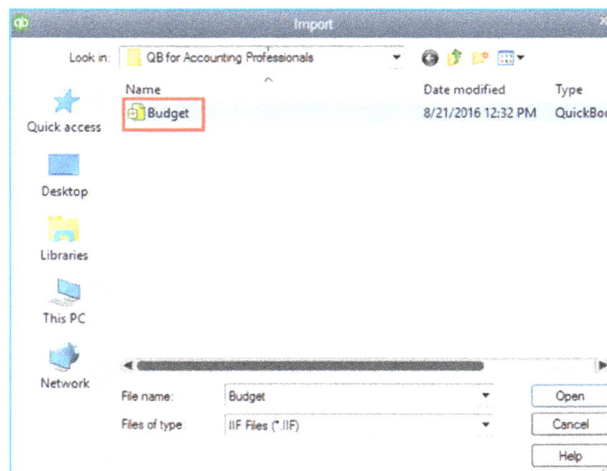

Double click on the file name and the file will be imported, bringing up the below message:

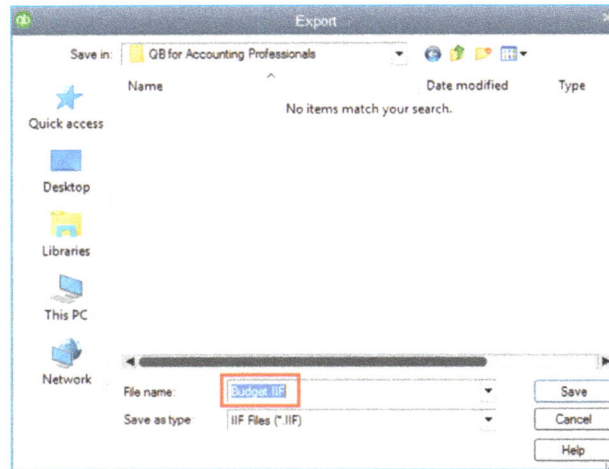

# Validating Budget Entry

It is suggested that once the data entry for a budget is complete, a Budget Overview report (either a Profit & Loss or Balance Sheet) be compared with the source budget to make sure all amounts agree.

QuickBooks produces reports at the total, class, and job level, and they can be customized for each company in the format desired. The reports are accessed from the Budgets & Forecasts section of Reports.

From the main menu, select Reports, then Budgets & Forecasts, then Budget Overview. The user will then need to select the budget that is to be displayed and desired report layout. Options for the layouts are:

- Account by Month
- Account by Class
- Class by Month

Below is an example report:

| | Jun 19 | Jul 19 | Aug 19 | Sep 19 | Oct 19 | Nov 19 | Dec 19 | TOTAL Jan - Dec 19 |
|---|---|---|---|---|---|---|---|---|
| **Income** | | | | | | | | |
| Sales | | | | | | | | |
| Assembled Systems | 19,000.00 | 19,000.00 | 19,000.00 | 19,000.00 | 19,000.00 | 19,000.00 | 19,000.00 | 228,000.00 |
| Consignment Sales | 1,050.00 | 1,102.50 | 1,157.63 | 1,215.51 | 1,276.29 | 1,340.10 | 1,407.11 | 9,549.14 |
| Merchandise | 10,000.00 | 10,500.00 | 11,000.00 | 11,500.00 | 12,000.00 | 12,500.00 | 13,000.00 | 123,000.00 |
| Service | 21,315.38 | 22,081.15 | 22,885.21 | 23,729.47 | 24,615.94 | 25,546.74 | 26,524.08 | 263,005.55 |
| **Total Sales** | 51,365.38 | 52,683.65 | 54,042.84 | 55,444.98 | 56,892.23 | 58,386.84 | 59,931.19 | 623,554.69 |
| **Total Income** | 51,365.38 | 52,683.65 | 54,042.84 | 55,444.98 | 56,892.23 | 58,386.84 | 59,931.19 | 623,554.69 |

Report header:

AM
19
al Basis

Carl's Computer Shop
Profit & Loss Budget Overview
January through December 2019

While QuickBooks generates a budget report by class, it can be a very wide report if there are several classes. For companies that budget at the department and/or profit center level, a separate report for each class code and possibly combinations of classes is suggested for distribution to management. The sample reports below are for one of the retail stores in the example referenced earlier in this chapter. The reports were filtered for one class and the report header customized to show the name of the store. (For details on modifying reports please refer to chapter three.)

# Budget vs Actual Reports

In this report, a selected time period can be chosen. The report will show the actual results and the budget for the same time period. From the main menu, select Reports, then Budgets & Forecasts, then Budget vs. Actual. This will bring up a screen for the user to select which year's budget the report should be created from as shown below:

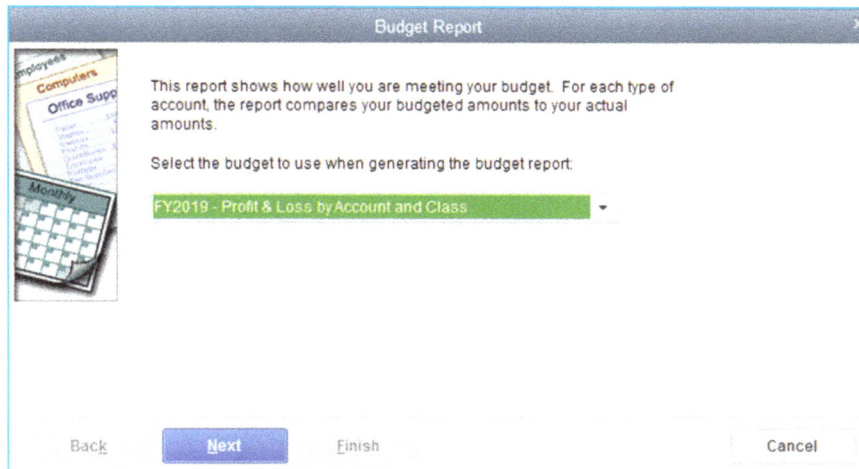

After selecting the desired year's budget, click Next to bring up the layout options. Three options are available:

- Account by Month
- Account by Class
- Class by Month

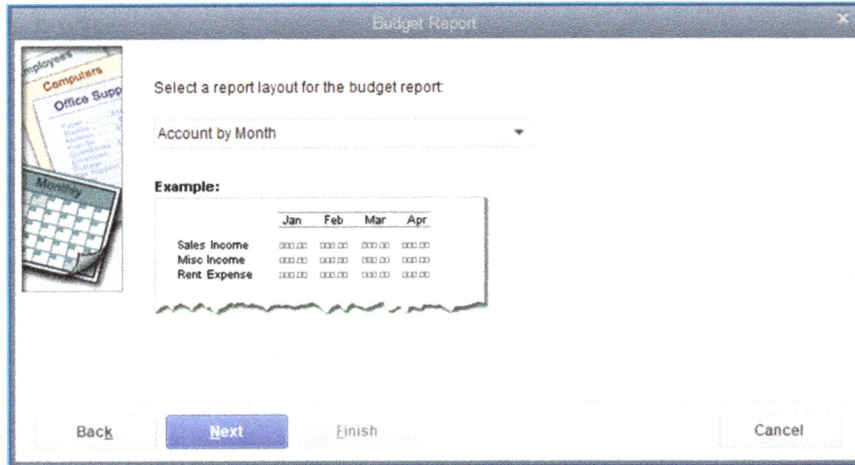

In the below example, the "Account by Month" option was chosen.

**Carl's Computer Shop**
**Bayshore Store - Profit & Loss Budget vs. Actual**
October 2019

| | Oct 19 | Budget | $ Over Budget | % of Budget |
|---|---|---|---|---|
| ▼ Ordinary Income/Expense | | | | |
| ▼ Income | | | | |
| ▼ Sales | | | | |
| Assembled Systems ▶ | 28,325.00 ◀ | 15,000.00 | 13,325.00 | 188.8% |
| Consignment Sales | 0.00 | 1,276.29 | -1,276.29 | 0.0% |
| Merchandise | 3,577.00 | 9,500.00 | -5,923.00 | 37.7% |
| Service | 18,988.00 | 18,615.94 | 372.06 | 102% |
| Total Sales | 50,890.00 | 44,392.23 | 6,497.77 | 114.6% |
| Total Income | 50,890.00 | 44,392.23 | 6,497.77 | 114.6% |
| ▼ Cost of Goods Sold | | | | |
| Cost of Goods Sold | 15,874.00 | 19,500.00 | -3,626.00 | 81.4% |
| Total COGS | 15,874.00 | 19,500.00 | -3,626.00 | 81.4% |
| Gross Profit | 35,016.00 | 24,892.23 | 10,123.77 | 140.7% |
| ▼ Expense | | | | |
| Automobile Expense | 186.00 | 200.00 | -14.00 | 93.0% |
| Equipment Rental | 0.00 | 50.00 | -50.00 | 0.0% |
| Marketing & Adverti... | 2,562.00 | 1,500.00 | 1,062.00 | 170.8% |
| Merchant Fees | 996.28 | 400.00 | 596.28 | 249.1% |
| Office Expenses | 244.00 | 250.00 | -6.00 | 97.6% |
| Outside Services | 0.00 | 100.00 | -100.00 | 0.0% |
| ▼ Payroll Expenses | | | | |
| Gross Wages | 0.00 | 1,000.00 | -1,000.00 | 0.0% |
| PR Tax Expense | 0.00 | 85.00 | -85.00 | 0.0% |
| Total Payroll Expens... | 0.00 | 1,085.00 | -1,085.00 | 0.0% |
| Rent | 1,530.00 | 1,525.00 | 5.00 | 100.3% |
| Telephone | 266.00 | 275.00 | -9.00 | 96.7% |
| Utilities | 511.00 | 500.00 | 11.00 | 102.2% |
| Total Expense | 6,295.28 | 5,885.00 | 410.28 | 107% |
| Net Ordinary Income | 28,720.72 | 19,007.23 | 9,713.49 | 151.1% |
| Net Income | 28,720.72 | 19,007.23 | 9,713.49 | 151.1% |

# Profit & Loss Budget Performance Report

This report is more comprehensive on actual versus budget performance. It includes current period and year to date comparisons, and shows the total annual budget.

From the main menu, select Reports, then Budgets & Forecasts, then Profit & Loss Budget Performance. After selecting which year's budget to be reported, the user will have two report options:

- Account by Month
- Account by Class

In the below example, the "Account by Month" option was chosen and the option to show Dollars ($) and Percentage (%) of budget were selected in the report customization screen.

| | Oct 19 | Budget | $ Over Budget | % of Budget | Jan - Oct 19 | YTD Budget | $ Over Budget | % of Budget | Annual Budget |
|---|---|---|---|---|---|---|---|---|---|
| **Ordinary Income/Expense** | | | | | | | | | |
| ▼ Income | | | | | | | | | |
| ▼ Sales | | | | | | | | | |
| Assembled Systems ▶ | 28,325.00 ◀ | 15,000.00 | 13,325.00 | 188.8% | 136,175.00 | 150,000.00 | -13,825.00 | 90.8% | 180,000.00 |
| Consignment Sales | 0.00 | 1,276.29 | -1,276.29 | 0.0% | 0.00 | 6,801.93 | -6,801.93 | 0.0% | 9,549.14 |
| Merchandise | 3,577.00 | 9,500.00 | -5,923.00 | 37.7% | 37,804.98 | 72,500.00 | -34,695.02 | 52.1% | 93,000.00 |
| Service | 18,988.00 | 18,615.94 | 372.06 | 102% | 115,654.00 | 150,934.73 | -35,280.73 | 76.6% | 191,005.55 |
| Total Sales | 50,890.00 | 44,392.23 | 6,497.77 | 114.6% | 289,633.98 | 380,236.66 | -90,602.68 | 76.2% | 473,554.69 |
| Total Income | 50,890.00 | 44,392.23 | 6,497.77 | 114.6% | 289,633.98 | 380,236.66 | -90,602.68 | 76.2% | 473,554.69 |
| ▼ Cost of Goods Sold | | | | | | | | | |
| Cost of Goods Sold | 15,874.00 | 19,500.00 | -3,626.00 | 81.4% | 93,094.00 | 172,500.00 | -79,406.00 | 54% | 213,000.00 |
| Total COGS | 15,874.00 | 19,500.00 | -3,626.00 | 81.4% | 93,094.00 | 172,500.00 | -79,406.00 | 54% | 213,000.00 |
| Gross Profit | 35,016.00 | 24,892.23 | 10,123.77 | 140.7% | 196,539.98 | 207,736.66 | -11,196.68 | 94.6% | 260,554.69 |
| ▼ Expense | | | | | | | | | |
| Automobile Expense | 186.00 | 200.00 | -14.00 | 93.0% | 1,860.00 | 2,000.00 | -140.00 | 93.0% | 2,400.00 |
| Equipment Rental | 0.00 | 50.00 | -50.00 | 0.0% | 0.00 | 500.00 | -500.00 | 0.0% | 600.00 |
| Marketing & Adverti... | 2,562.00 | 1,500.00 | 1,062.00 | 170.8% | 15,802.00 | 15,000.00 | 802.00 | 105.3% | 18,000.00 |
| Merchant Fees | 996.28 | 400.00 | 596.28 | 249.1% | 3,613.86 | 4,000.00 | -386.14 | 90.3% | 4,800.00 |
| Office Expenses | 244.00 | 250.00 | -6.00 | 97.6% | 2,440.00 | 2,500.00 | -60.00 | 97.6% | 3,000.00 |
| Outside Services | 0.00 | 100.00 | -100.00 | 0.0% | 0.00 | 1,000.00 | -1,000.00 | 0.0% | 1,200.00 |
| ▼ Payroll Expenses | | | | | | | | | |
| Gross Wages | 0.00 | 1,000.00 | -1,000.00 | 0.0% | 7,776.00 | 10,000.00 | -2,224.00 | 77.8% | 12,000.00 |
| PR Tax Expense | 0.00 | 85.00 | -85.00 | 0.0% | 979.73 | 850.00 | 129.73 | 115.3% | 1,020.00 |
| Total Payroll Expens... | 0.00 | 1,085.00 | -1,085.00 | 0.0% | 8,755.73 | 10,850.00 | -2,094.27 | 80.7% | 13,020.00 |
| Rent | 1,530.00 | 1,525.00 | 5.00 | 100.3% | 15,300.00 | 15,250.00 | 50.00 | 100.3% | 18,300.00 |
| Telephone | 266.00 | 275.00 | -9.00 | 96.7% | 2,660.00 | 2,750.00 | -90.00 | 96.7% | 3,300.00 |
| Utilities | 511.00 | 500.00 | 11.00 | 102.2% | 5,110.00 | 5,000.00 | 110.00 | 102.2% | 6,000.00 |
| Total Expense | 6,295.28 | 5,885.00 | 410.28 | 107% | 55,541.59 | 58,850.00 | -3,308.41 | 94.4% | 70,620.00 |
| Net Ordinary Income | 28,720.72 | 19,007.23 | 9,713.49 | 151.1% | 140,998.39 | 148,886.66 | -7,888.27 | 94.7% | 189,934.69 |
| Net Income | 28,720.72 | 19,007.23 | 9,713.49 | 151.1% | 140,998.39 | 148,886.66 | -7,888.27 | 94.7% | 189,934.69 |

*Carl's Computer Shop — Bayshore Store - Profit & Loss Budget Performance — October 2019 — Accrual Basis*

Note that the first report shows the store's total income at 114.6% of budget for the month of October, while the second report shows the store's year to date performance for income at only 76.2%. Using the Budget Performance Report allows the reader to look at month and year to date performance, a useful tool in gauging performance.

The Profit & Loss Budget Performance Report can be configured to report performance by class and generated for total net income or for subsets of revenue or expense accounts. The following report was filtered for just income accounts:

| | Oct 19 | Budget | $ Over Budget | % of Budget | Jan - Oct 19 | YTD Budget | $ Over Budget | % of Budget | Annual Budget |
|---|---|---|---|---|---|---|---|---|---|
| Bayshore Store ▶ | 50,890.00 ◀ | 44,392.23 | 6,497.77 | 114.6% | 289,633.98 | 380,236.66 | -90,602.68 | 76.2% | 473,554.69 |
| San Tomas S... | 21,219.00 | 12,500.00 | 8,719.00 | 169.8% | 93,588.00 | 125,000.00 | -31,412.00 | 74.9% | 150,000.00 |
| TOTAL | 72,109.00 | 56,892.23 | 15,216.77 | 126.7% | 383,221.98 | 505,236.66 | -122,014.68 | 75.8% | 623,554.69 |

*Carl's Computer Shop — Store Sales Budget Performance — October 2019 — Accrual Basis*

© The CFO Source, LLC 2017

Notes:

# Chapter Seventeen
# 1099s

Every January accountants are called upon to prepare and file 1099 tax forms for their clients. QuickBooks users have the following options available for the issuance and filing of 1099s:

- "Paper" 1099-Misc forms and the summary 1096 form can be generated with the purchase of pre-printed forms.
- The program provides a link to the Intuit website where, for additional fees, the electronic filing of 1099s can be generated. This includes 1099-Misc, 1099-Int, 1099-Div, 1099-K, and other 1099 forms.

This chapter will focus on the creation of paper 1099-Misc forms and the accompanying 1096.

Because 1099 and 1096 forms show information about the entity issuing them, it's critical for that information to be correct. It's also a good business practice to use this annual event as a checkpoint for correcting any company information that may have changed since the last tax preparation period. QuickBooks draws this information from the Company Information section.

From the main menu, select Company, then My Company, which will bring up the screen below. The information that will appear on either the 1099s or 1096 are shown boxed in red. If this information is not correct, it should be edited prior to generating any forms by clicking on the editing pencil button in the upper right of the screen.

# Setting Up QuickBooks to Handle 1099s

QuickBooks provides a Wizard that walks the user through the steps for properly generating 1099-Misc forms and the summary 1096. Key steps are:

- Turning on the Preference for 1099s
- Selecting which vendors are to receive a 1099
- Assigning each 1099 vendor its tax identification number
- Mapping expense accounts to categories on the 1099-Misc
- Review of 1099s and 1096s before printing on official forms
- Selecting the year for filing
- Printing forms for filing

**Turning on the Preference for 1099s**

The first step in using QuickBooks to generate 1099s is to turn on the functionality in the Preferences section. From the main menu, select Edit, then Preferences, then the Tax:1099 tab, and select Company Preferences (there are no My Preferences for 1099s). The question "Do you file 1099-Misc forms?" should be answered "Yes" as shown below:

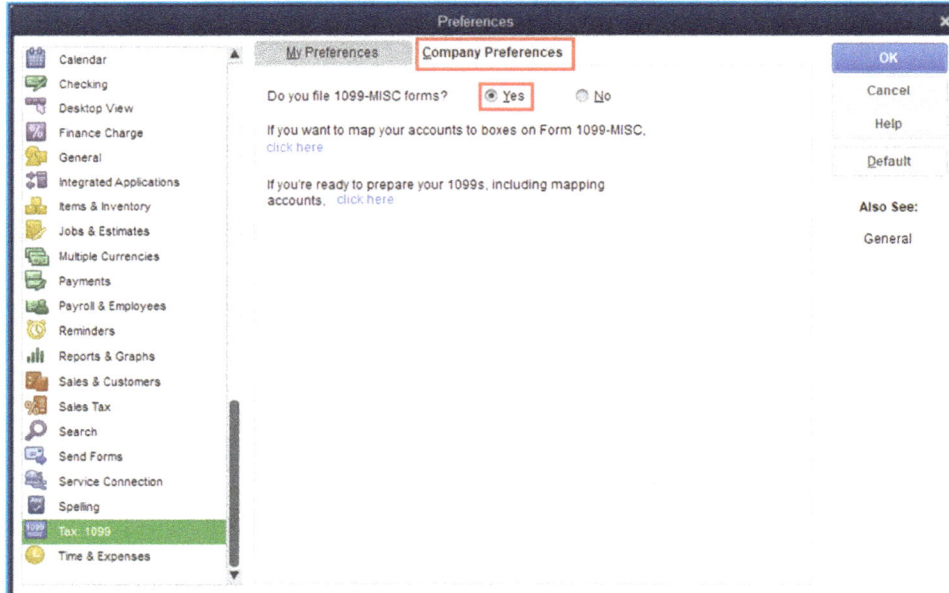

**Using the 1099 Wizard**

The printing of 1099 forms and the associated 1096 must be done using the 1099 wizard. There are two ways to start the wizard.

Method 1: From the 1099 Preference screen, click on the second "click here" section indicating you are ready to prepare your 1099s as shown below:

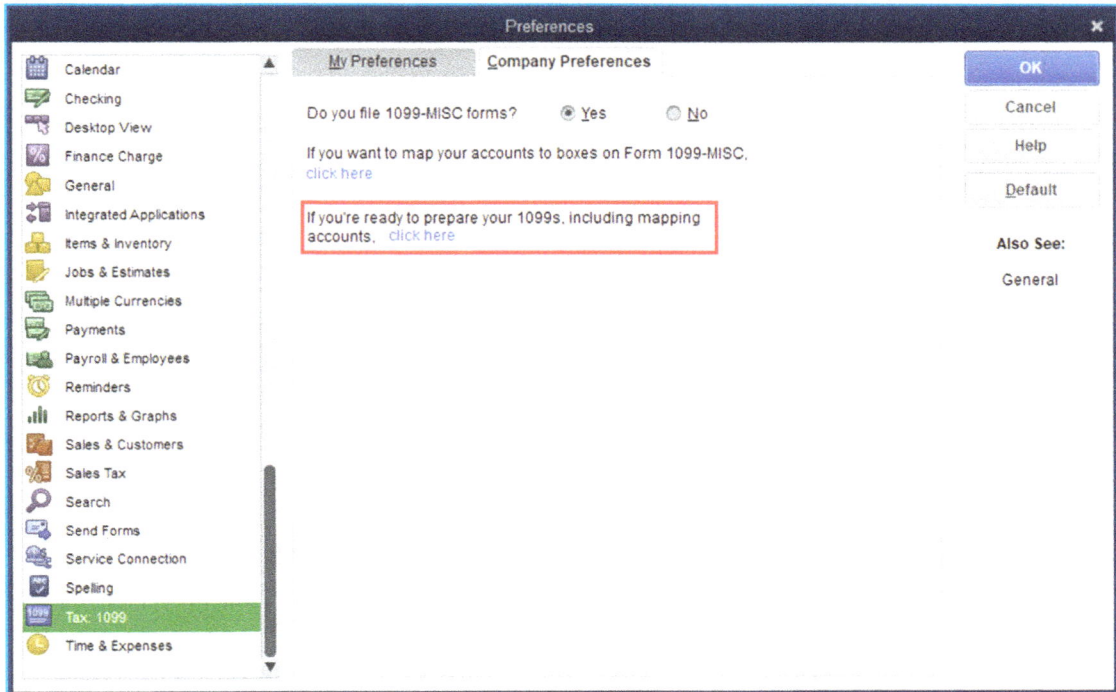

Method 2: From the Vendor section of the main menu, select Print/E-file 1099s, then 1099 Wizard.

Either of those methods will bring up the QuickBooks 1099 Wizard as shown below. Click on Get Started to begin.

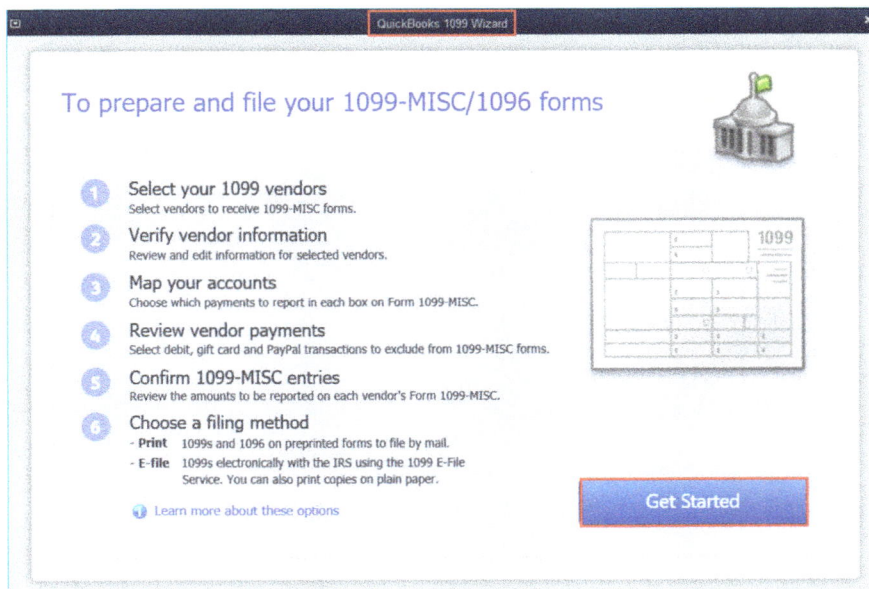

© The CFO Source, LLC 2017

In the first screen of the wizard, Select Your 1099 Vendors, the user can select which vendors are to be issued 1099s by clicking on the box in the column labeled "Create Form 1099-Misc" to the left of the Vendor Name column as shown in the next example.

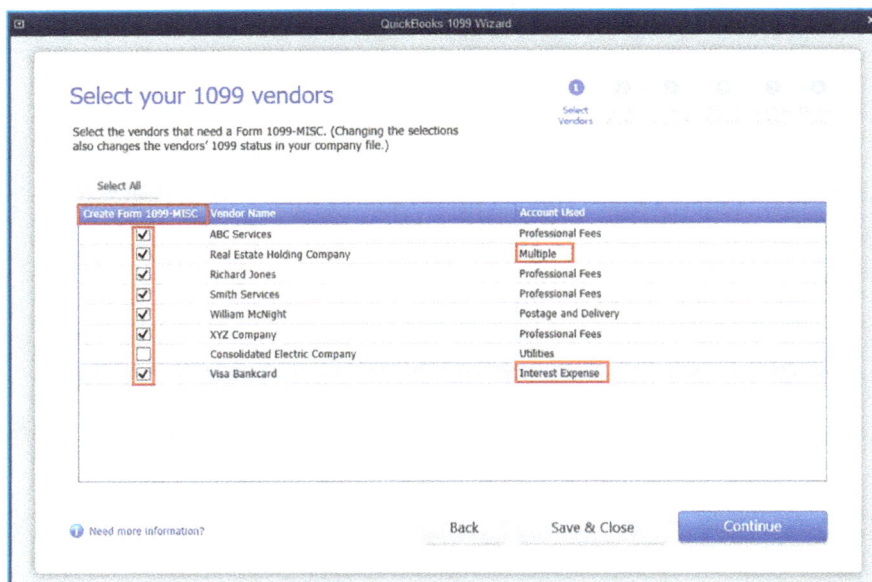

The account(s) used in transactions for each vendor are shown so the user can determine if it is appropriate to issue a 1099. In the example above, VISA Bankcard was selected even though the account used for this vendor is shown as Interest Expense and therefore it would not be appropriate to issue a 1099-Misc. This is corrected by unchecking the box next to that vendor's name. If payments made to a vendor are charged to more than one account, the account use will show "Multiple."

> **PRO TIP** – It is strongly suggested that when new vendors are entered into QuickBooks, a determination be made then as to whether the vendor should be issued a 1099. If a vendor should receive a 1099, that selection should be made in the Tax Settings of their Vendor record when they are initially added. New vendors deemed eligible for 1099s should be requested to provide a W-9 (Request for Taxpayer Identification Number and Certification) *prior to any payments being made to the vendor*. These procedures can eliminate a last-minute scramble to get this information when preparing 1099s and prevent not having the proper paperwork in the event of vendor relationships ending for whatever reason.

In the second screen of the wizard, Verify Your 1099 Vendors' Information, the user can review and make any needed corrections and that will also serve to update the vendor's information in the Vendor section.

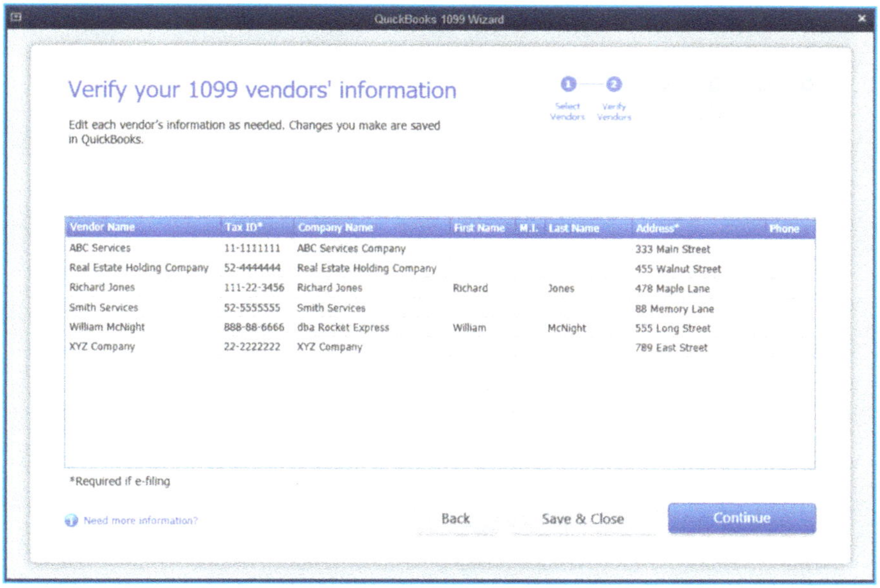

In the third screen of the wizard, Map Vendor Payment Accounts, the accounts used to record payments to the vendors are "mapped" to the appropriate reporting boxes on the 1099 form.

Important to understand is that for vendor payments to appear on a 1099, two setup criteria must align. The vendor must be selected to receive a 1099 AND the account(s) to which payments to the vendor are recorded must be selected in the below "Mapping" screen. If a vendor is selected to receive a 1099 but their payments were recorded to an account that is not mapped, then a 1099 will NOT be issued to that vendor. In addition, if an account is mapped but a vendor is not selected to receive the 1099, a 1099 will not be generated for that vendor.

To "map" an account to a 1099 box, use the drop-down arrows on the right for each account to indicate which box on the 1099 payments should be reported. As shown next, Postage and Delivery and Professional Fees have been mapped to Box 7: Nonemployee Compensation. Additionally, Rent Expense has been mapped to Box 1: Rent. All other accounts shown are not mapped to a 1099 box and payments to those accounts will not appear on the 1099.

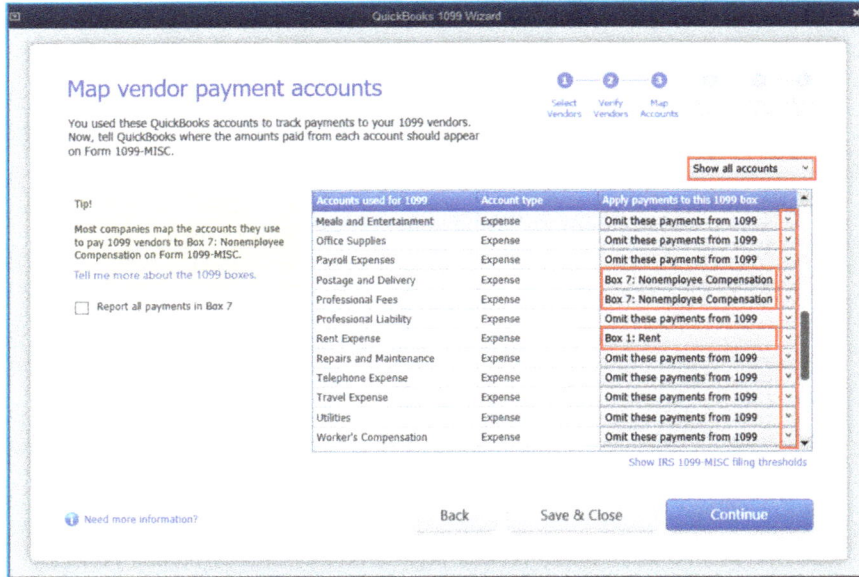

The user can toggle between seeing all accounts, as shown above, to seeing only 1099 accounts, as shown in the example on the next page. When the "Show 1099 accounts" option is chosen, all payments for vendors selected for 1099s will display, allowing for the selection of some accounts but exclusion of others. Note that the account Security Deposit Receivable is shown even though it has not been mapped to receive a 1099.

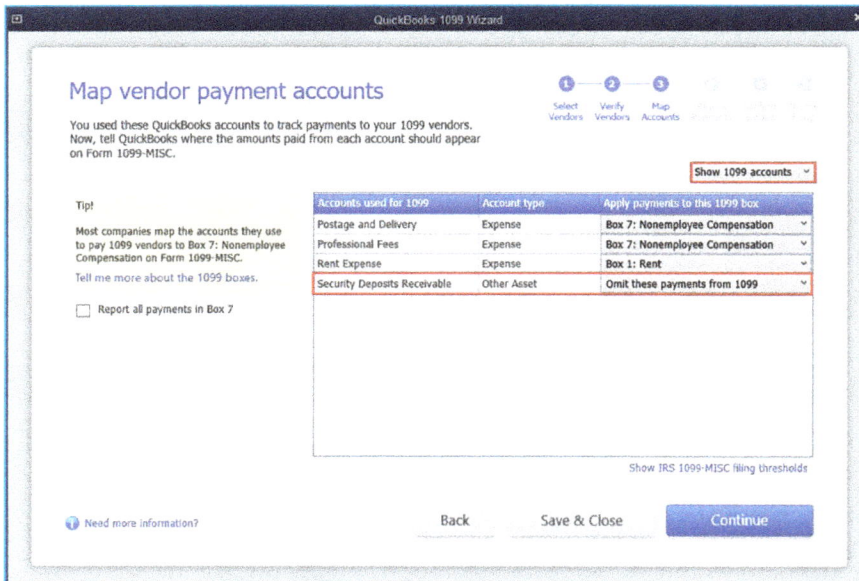

The criteria that BOTH situations must align also creates the ability to include some payment transactions on the 1099 while excluding other payments made to the same vendor. This will be demonstrated as instructions for using the wizard moves forward through the screens.

Note on the first screen of the wizard, Select Your 1099 Vendors, that for Real Estate Holding Company, the account is shown as "Multiple," indicating the vendor received payments coded to two or more accounts. The first was a rent payment for which it is desired that a 1099 be issued. As shown in the above Map Vendor Payments Accounts screen, Rent expense is mapped to Box 1:Rent on the 1099. The second payment was for a security deposit for which a 1099 should not be issued. The account Security Deposits Receivable is set to be omitted from 1099s.

In the fourth screen of the 1099 wizard, Review Payments for Exclusions, the user can review payments that should be excluded from the 1099-Misc form. As indicated in the screen, certain types of transactions should NOT be included, such as payments made with credit cards, debit cards, gift cards, or PayPal. Those payment methods are reported differently as of 2011, so including them in the 1099-Misc form would duplicate the reporting, increasing recipients tax liability incorrectly.

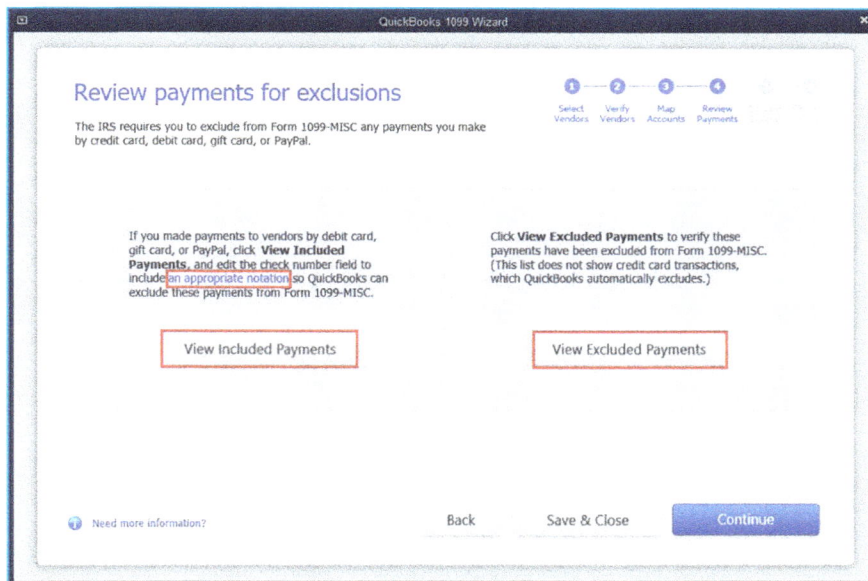

© The CFO Source, LLC 2017

Clicking on the phrase shown in blue, "an appropriate notation," will provide a list indicating the notations to be entered for transactions that are to be excluded.

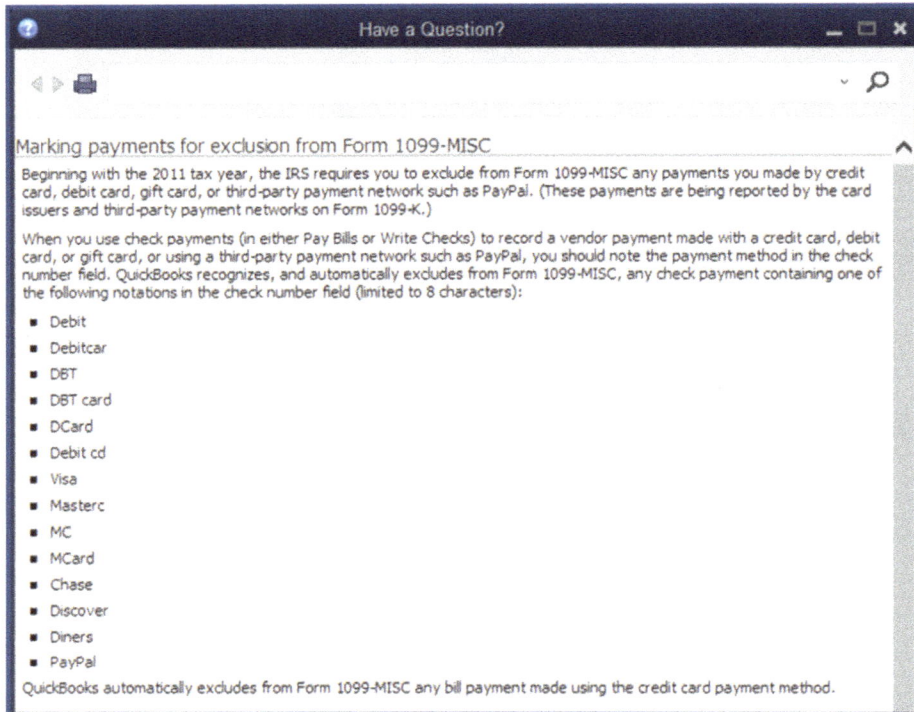

Clicking on the View Included Payments button in the fourth screen of the wizard will bring up the following screen of payments where, if desired, the check number field can be edited to reflect the appropriate notations.

In the fifth screen of the wizard, Confirm Your 1099 Entries, the user can review a summary of what will be reported on the 1099s as well as what has been excluded for those vendors. The report defaults to the latest year.

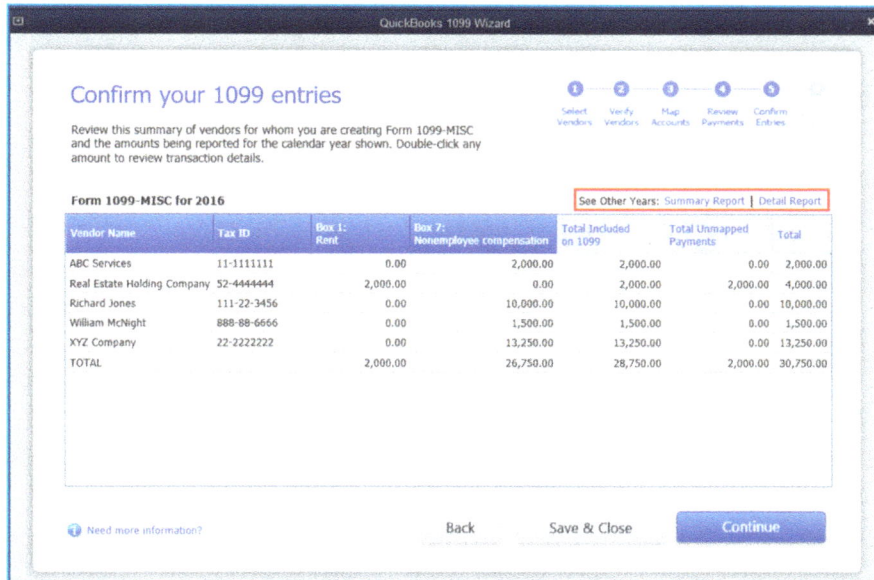

To view other years and/or details of the current year, select either the Summary or Detail Report options on the right of the screen. Both options allow the user to select the from and to dates of the reports. These can also be accessed from the Vendor section of the main menu by selecting Vendor, then Print/E-file 1099s, then either 1099 Summary or Detail Report.

**Summary Report:**

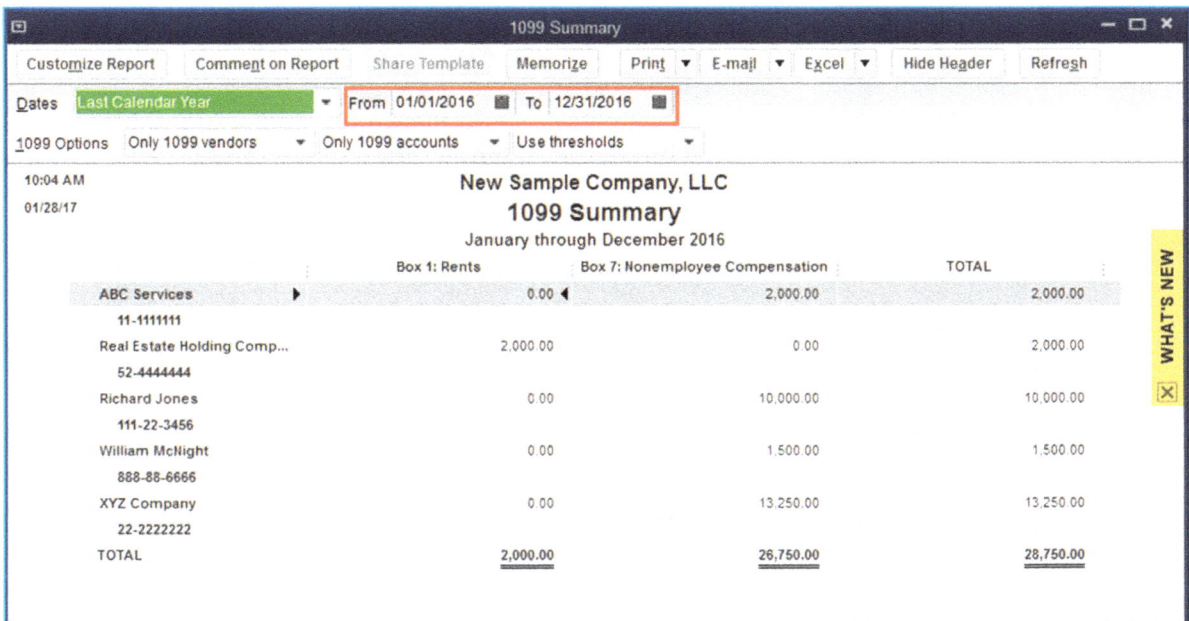

© The CFO Source, LLC 2017

**Detail Report:**

New Sample Company, LLC
1099 Detail
January through December 2016

| Type | Date | Num | Memo | Account | Clr | Split | Original Amount | Paid Amount | Balance |
|---|---|---|---|---|---|---|---|---|---|
| ABC Services | | | | | | | | | |
| 11-1111111 | | | | | | | | | |
| General Journal | 12/31/2016 | 1 | | Professional Fees | | -SPLIT- | 2,000.00 | 2,000.00 | 2,000.00 |
| Total ABC Services | | | | | | | | 2,000.00 | 2,000.00 |
| Real Estate Holding Company | | | | | | | | | |
| 52-4444444 | | | | | | | | | |
| Check | 12/31/2016 | 1002 | | Rent Expense | | First Bank of ... | 2,000.00 | 2,000.00 | 2,000.00 |
| Total Real Estate Holding Company | | | | | | | | 2,000.00 | 2,000.00 |
| Richard Jones | | | | | | | | | |
| 111-22-3456 | | | | | | | | | |
| Bill | 12/29/2016 | | | Professional Fees | | Accounts Pa... | 10,000.00 | 10,000.00 | 10,000.00 |
| Total Richard Jones | | | | | | | | 10,000.00 | 10,000.00 |
| William McNight | | | | | | | | | |
| 888-88-6666 | | | | | | | | | |
| Bill | 12/13/2016 | | | Postage and Delive... | | Accounts Pa... | 1,500.00 | 1,500.00 | 1,500.00 |
| Total William McNight | | | | | | | | 1,500.00 | 1,500.00 |
| XYZ Company | | | | | | | | | |
| 22-2222222 | | | | | | | | | |
| Bill | 12/20/2016 | | | Professional Fees | | Accounts Pa... | 10,000.00 | 1,750.00 | 1,750.00 |
| Credit | 12/20/2016 | cr me... | | Professional Fees | | Accounts Pa... | -1,750.00 | -1,750.00 | 0.00 |
| Bill | 12/28/2016 | | | Professional Fees | | Accounts Pa... | 10,000.00 | 8,250.00 | 8,250.00 |
| General Journal | 12/31/2016 | 1 | | Professional Fees | | Professional... | 5,000.00 | 5,000.00 | 13,250.00 |
| Total XYZ Company | | | | | | | | 13,250.00 | 13,250.00 |
| TOTAL | | | | | | | | 28,750.00 | 28,750.00 |

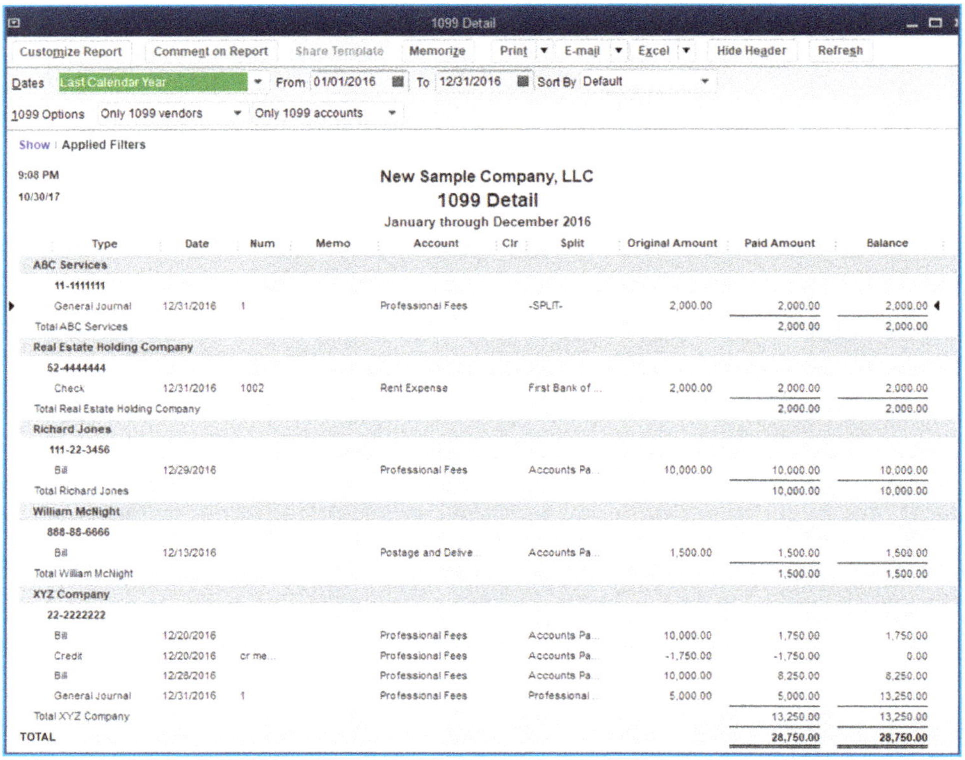

In the sixth (and final) screen of the wizard, Choose a Filing Method, the user can choose whether to Print 1099s for mailing or to use Intuit's E-file service.

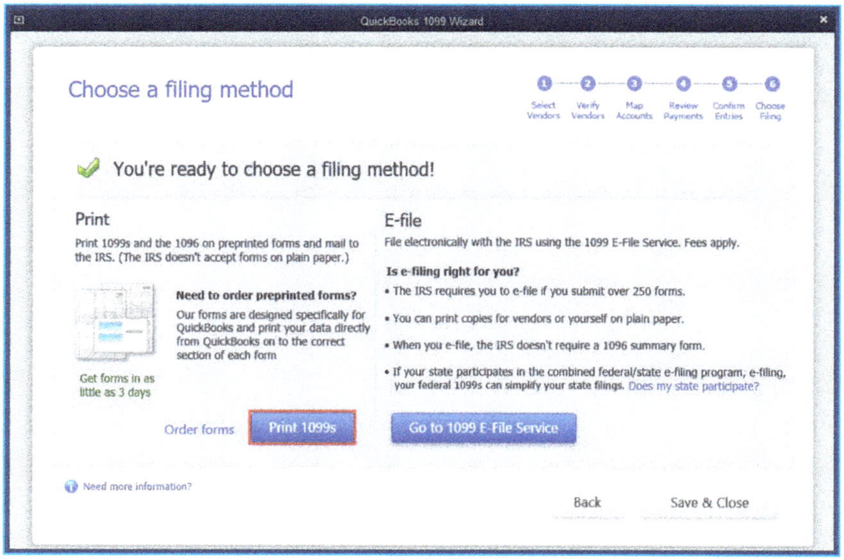

**The Print Option**

Selecting the "Print 1099s" option will prompt the user to select the filing period as shown on the next page. This allows printing for both current year and prior year forms.

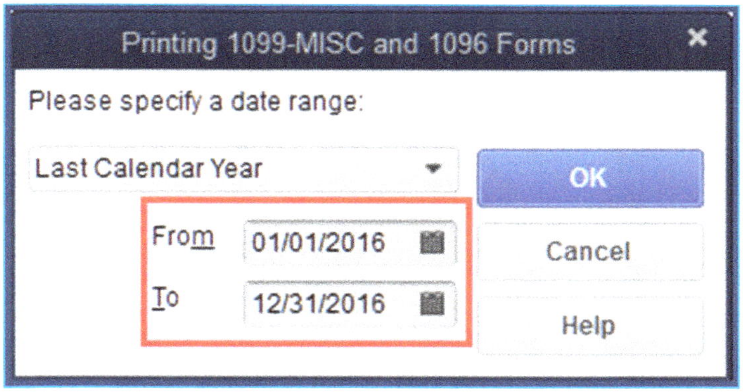

In the next screen, the user can select to preview the 1099s for a final review, which will display the information to be printed but not show the actual form. Some or all of the 1099s can be selected for printing as well as the summary 1096. Pre-printed forms will need to be used, and these are typically available at office supply stores.

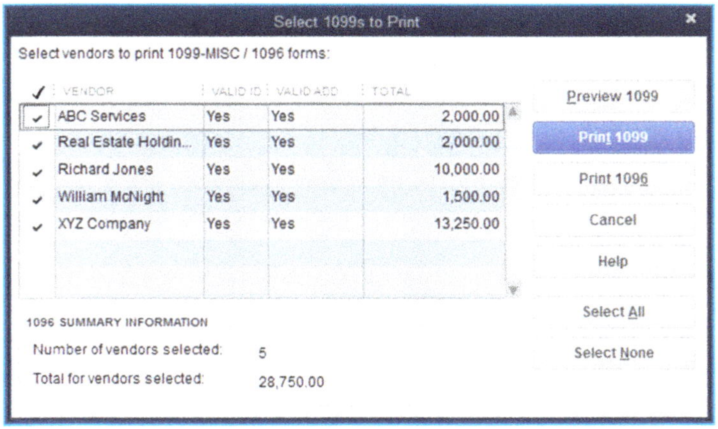

Below is the preview displayed for the first 1099 in the sample company:

```
New Sample Company, LLC
8438 Evergreen Street
Baltimore, MD 21111
888-888-8888




11-1234567          11-1111111

ABC Services Company
                                        2000.00

333 Main Street

Richmond VA 22222
```

Once it's been determined that all of the information is correct, the user can print the 1099s and accompanying 1096. When clicking on Print 1096, the user will be prompted to input the Contact Name that will be printed on the form and, if desired, indicate that a final return is being issued. The final return box is only for companies that want to inform the IRS they will no longer be issuing 1099s in the future.

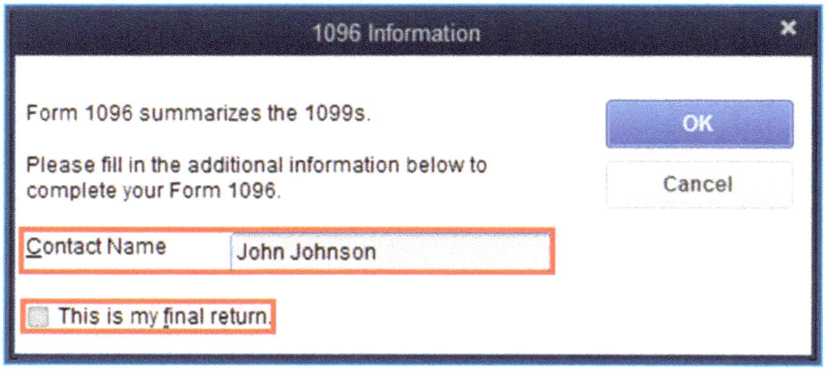

In both the Print 1099 and Print 1096 options, the user will be prompted to select the printer to use as shown next. Make sure the pre-printed forms are loaded correctly before you print.

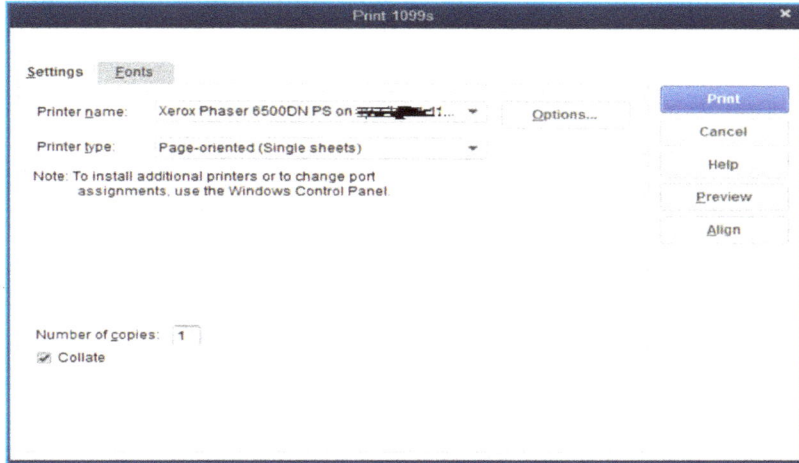

# Which Transactions Won't Appear on 1099s?

- Users can select from four "Name" types when creating a name in QuickBooks, but Payments must be made to Vendors to appear in 1099 data. Payments to Customers, Employees, or Other "Name" types will not generate 1099s.

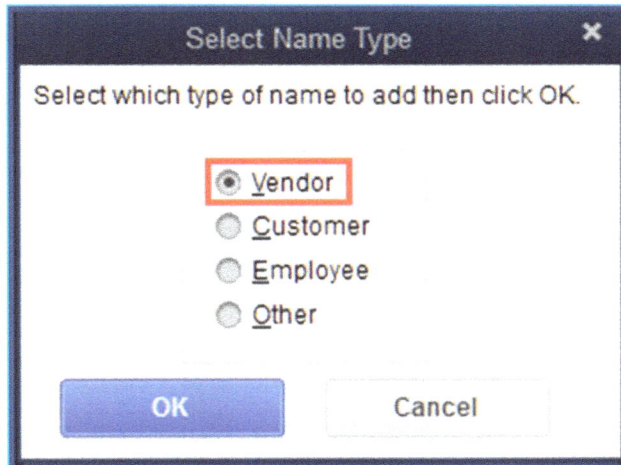

- As mentioned above, payments made with credit or debit cards will not appear on 1099s.
- Payments recorded with journal entries will appear on 1099s if the Vendor name is recorded in the debit side of the transaction. Below is an example of a journal entry that would generate a 1099:

Notes:

# Chapter Eighteen
# Sales Taxes

Companies that sell products or rent/lease equipment are generally required to bill sales taxes to their customers and remit the taxes collected to state and local governments. Certain types of services are also subject to sales taxes in some states. Sales tax laws differ in every state, and in some states, there are also county, city, and/or local sales taxes as well. It is not unusual for one sale to be subject to multiple layers of sales tax. Yet another complexity is that sales of different types of products or services in one jurisdiction can be subject to different sales tax rates.

In addition to requirements to collect and remit sales taxes, companies are also required to report on the amount of sales in various ways. Each state's reporting requirements are different. Some states require only a breakdown of sales by the category or type of sale, typically corresponding to sales with different tax rates. In other states, the reporting must be broken down to show the region, county, and/or city where the sales were made. Yet other states require breakdowns of sales to non-profits or resellers.

Invoicing customers uses item codes for each line of billing. Sales Tax Item Codes indicate the sales tax to apply on invoices just like a product item code displays the product and amount to bill.

This chapter will show how to set up QuickBooks to handle sales tax requirements, but it is outside the scope of this book to provide detailed advice on sales tax rates, subjectivity, and laws in every state. Examples will be shown for several scenarios to give the reader an understanding of how to customize QuickBooks to fit their needs, and it is encouraged that readers determine what the sales tax requirements are for their specific state, county, and/or city.

## Getting Set Up for Sales Taxes

The first step in using QuickBooks to handle sales taxes is to turn on the functionality in the Preferences section. From the main menu, select Edit, then Preferences, then Sales Tax. This will bring up the screen shown next for setting Company Preferences (there are no My Preferences for Sales Taxes).

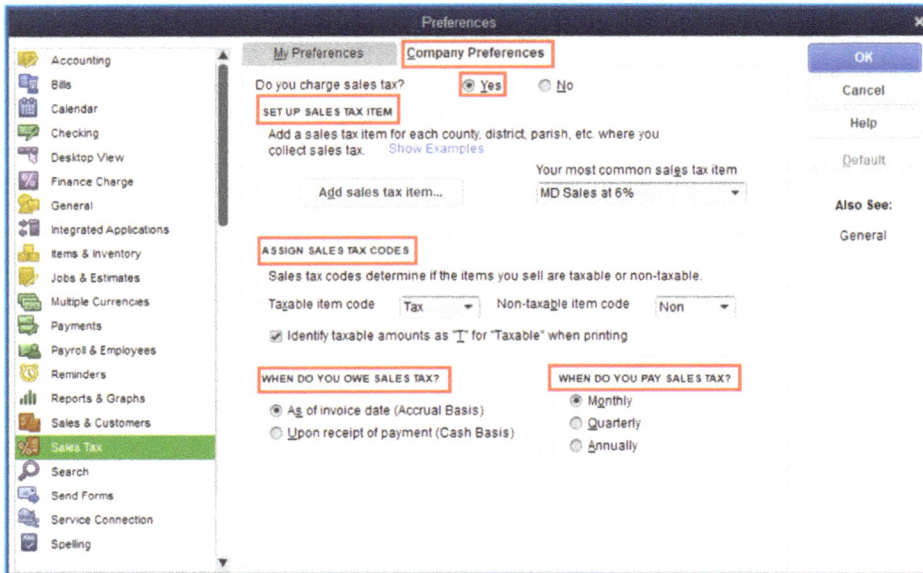

There are several things that must be set up or selected to customize QuickBooks for a company's sale tax collection and remittance requirements. These are:

- Select Yes to turn on the functionality.
- Set up sales tax item codes.
- Assign sales tax codes and set up new ones where appropriate.
- Whether sales taxes are to be paid on an Accrual Basis or a Cash Basis will drive what information appears on sales tax liability reports.
- Determine whether sales taxes are to be paid monthly, quarterly, or annually.

# Setting Up Jurisdictions

Each jurisdiction for which sales taxes are to be remitted must be set up as a vendor in the Vendor section. These vendors will be used as the payees when recording the remittance of sales taxes.

# Sales Tax Codes

These codes are separate from sales tax item codes, which are covered below. These codes are used on each line of an invoice to indicate whether that line is subject or not subject to sales taxes. QuickBooks sets up two codes automatically to indicate whether an invoice line is taxable, "Tax," or not taxable, "Non."

Additional codes can be set up to track categories of taxable or non-taxable sales if needed. From the main menu, select Lists, then Sales Tax Code List, which will bring up the Sales Tax Code List as shown below. Note that only the first code, Tax, is noted as being taxable by the check mark on the far right of the Taxable column. In the example, two additional codes have been added to track Non-Profit and Sales for Resale transactions.

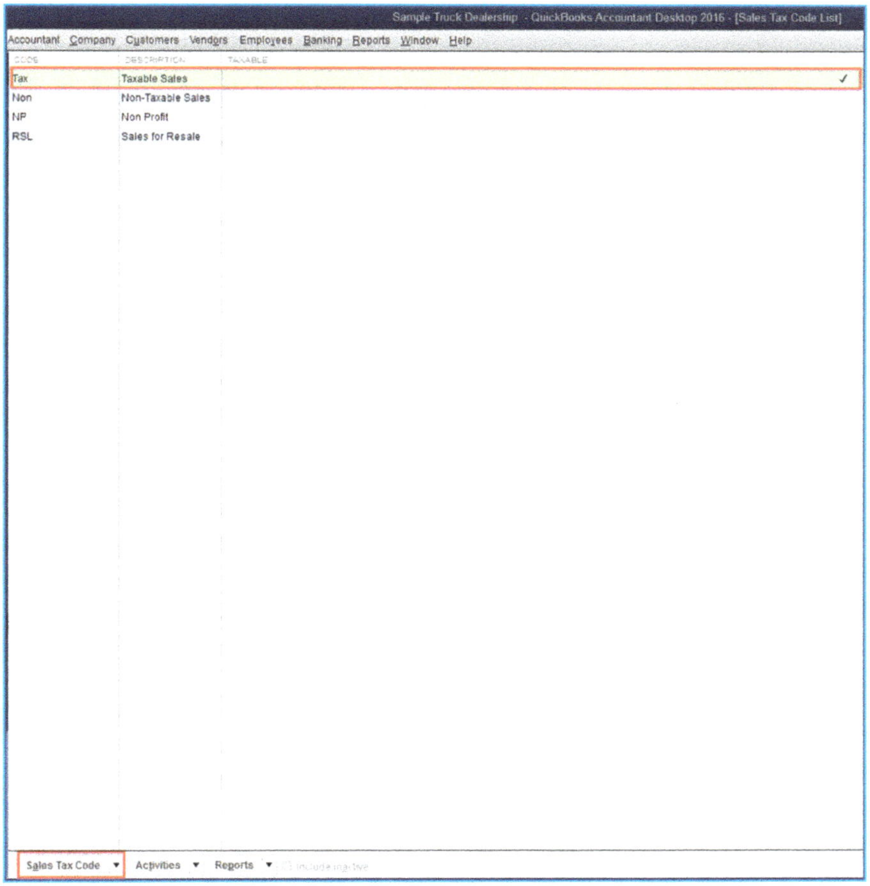

Once in this screen, using the drop-down arrow in the Sales Tax Code box in the lower left, select New to bring up the New Sales Tax. Below shows the Sales Tax code screen set up for a Non-Profit Sales Tax Code, set up as Non-Taxable.

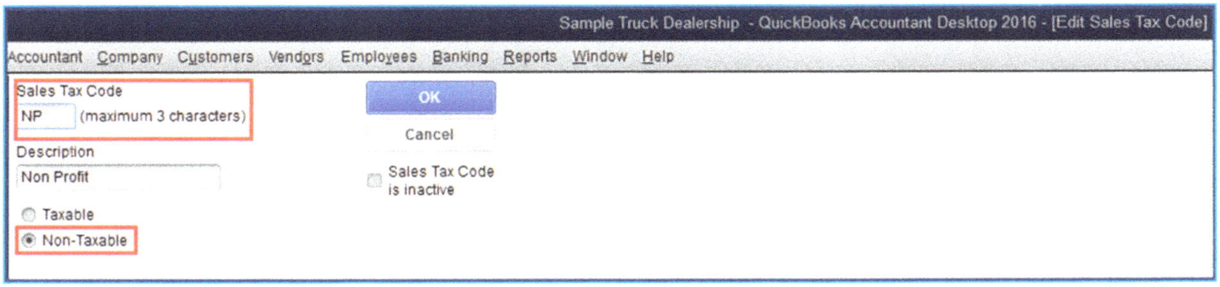

# Overview of Sales Tax Item and Group Item Codes

These two item code types drive functionality in QuickBooks for billing, remittance, and sales reporting of sale taxes.

Sales tax item codes should be set up for:

- each separate jurisdiction where a company is required to collect and remit sales taxes,
- each jurisdiction a company is required to report sales for (which may or may not be the same as the jurisdiction sales taxes are remitted to), and
- each rate of tax.

Sales Tax Group Item codes are used when sales taxes for multiple jurisdictions are required to be billed on one invoice. These codes serve to group individual sales tax item codes.

Guidelines are as follows:

- Sales tax item codes determine the amount of tax to be billed, with set up including a rate/percentage of tax.
- Sales tax item codes determine the jurisdiction that is to be paid the sales tax.
- Sales reporting for sale taxes is driven by sales tax item codes, making it important that each separate jurisdictions' taxes and sales be set up as separate sales tax items for each different rate. For example, if some sales are subject to a 6% rate and other sales are subject to an 8% rate, then two sales tax item codes should be set up. Billing would be done with the respective sales tax item code (see examples in the Invoicing section).
- If sales are subject to multiple levels of sales tax as is the case when required to bill state, county, and/or local sales taxes, then a separate sales tax item code should be set up for each separate sales tax.
- When sales taxes for multiple jurisdictions are to be billed on one invoice, the individual sales tax item codes can be combined using a sales tax group code. This allows for billing to the customer to show as one line for all taxes, but payment and reporting of each jurisdiction's sales and sales taxes to be itemized separately also.

## Sales Tax Item Code Setup

Sales tax item codes are set up in the list area of QuickBooks. From the main menu, select Lists, then Item List.

© The CFO Source, LLC 2017

Once in this screen, use the drop-down arrow in the Item box in the lower left to select New, bringing up the New Item screen. In the example shown below, the sales tax item codes have been set up for Maryland Sales Taxes that are to be billed at 6%.

Sales tax item codes should follow these guidelines:

- The item code type for sales taxes is "Sales Tax Item."
- The name and description of the code should clearly identify when it is to be used.
- The state or local taxing authority where sales taxes are to be remitted is input in the Tax Agency box using the drop-down arrow. These must be set up in the Vendor section first to appear in the drop-down options.
- The Tax Rate is entered as a percent.
- Note in the item list above that the sales tax item codes show an account of Sales Tax Payable. This is a default account in QuickBooks, automatically set up when the preference for sales taxes is turned on. Separate accounts for individual jurisdictions cannot be set up, but breakdowns of sales tax liabilities for individual jurisdictions can be derived from the Sales Tax Liability report (as described below).

**Sales Tax Group Item Code Setup**

To group multiple jurisdictions' sales taxes on a single invoice as a combined sales tax, Sales Tax Group Codes must be used. These are set up in the List area, in a similar fashion to Sales Tax Item codes except that the item code type is Sales Tax Group instead of Sales Tax Item. The individual codes that will be part of the group need to be set up before the group code can be created.

To illustrate the set-up of a Sales Tax Group Code, the example of sales tax billing in Fairfax City, Virginia will be used. In this jurisdiction, there are three levels of sales tax that must be charged to customers for general sales:

1. A Virginia state wide sales tax of 4.3%
2. A local tax of 1%
3. A Northern Virginia Regional tax of .7%

Companies doing business in the city of Fairfax are required to bill customers for each tax, remit all three taxes to the state, and report on the amount of sales for each category of tax. Invoices to customers must be billed a "combined" 6% sales tax.

Below shows the set-up screen for the combined Sales Tax Group for Fairfax City:

Note that there is no provision when setting up a Sales Tax Group code to indicate a Tax Agency. In some states, all payments must be remitted to the state, and in other states, each individual tax jurisdiction may need to be paid. Correct settings for individual tax item codes and accurate vendor records for each jurisdiction will ensure proper reporting and payment while group codes summarize tax fees for billing.

If reporting sales for multiple jurisdictions is needed, then separate sales tax item codes may need to be set up and then grouped. For example, if a company operates in multiple Virginia cities, then each city would need to be set up separately and there would need to be multiple city groups as well. This would enable the sales reporting for each city's respective sales.

# Setting up Item Codes for Sales Tax Billing

Invoicing to customers uses item codes for each line of the billing. The setup of an item code includes the selection of a default "Sales Tax Code" for the item to indicate which Sales Tax Code will apply. This can be helpful in cases where some types of sales are taxable and other types are not. For example, in some states, the sale of parts related to the repair of equipment is taxable while the labor portion is not.

The next image shows an example of the item code used for Long Term Rental billing that has been set up as taxable. Note that QuickBooks has abbreviated the Sales Tax Code to only the notation "Tax Code." These codes will appear on invoices as a default when the item code is used, but can be overridden. Overriding the default code would be needed for sales to organizations such as non-profits that are exempt from sales tax.

# Customer Sales Tax Settings

Sales Tax Codes can be set as a default for each customer to streamline and ensure the consistency of billing. This is done by editing a customer's Sales Tax Settings in the Customer Center. There is also a field to enter a customer's Resale (exemption) number if applicable. For example, a non-profit that is exempt from sales tax can be set up with a Sales Tax Code indicating that the customer is not subject to sales tax billing. When the customer's invoice is created, the Sales Tax code will override the default sales tax code that was assigned to the item code used for billing.

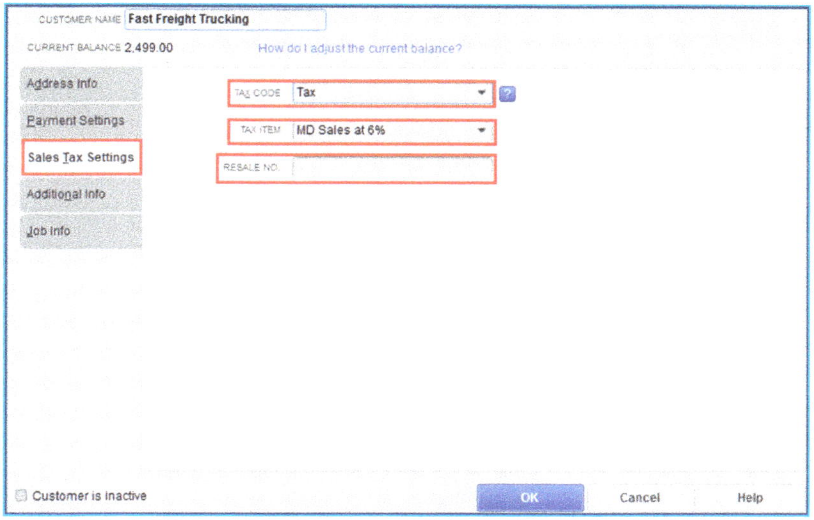

# Invoicing Examples

**Invoicing with Single Tax**

The simplest example is where there is only one taxing jurisdiction and only one type of sale with a single tax rate. Shown below is an invoice for a sale in Maryland with a taxable lease component and a non-taxable labor repair component as two separate lines on the invoice.

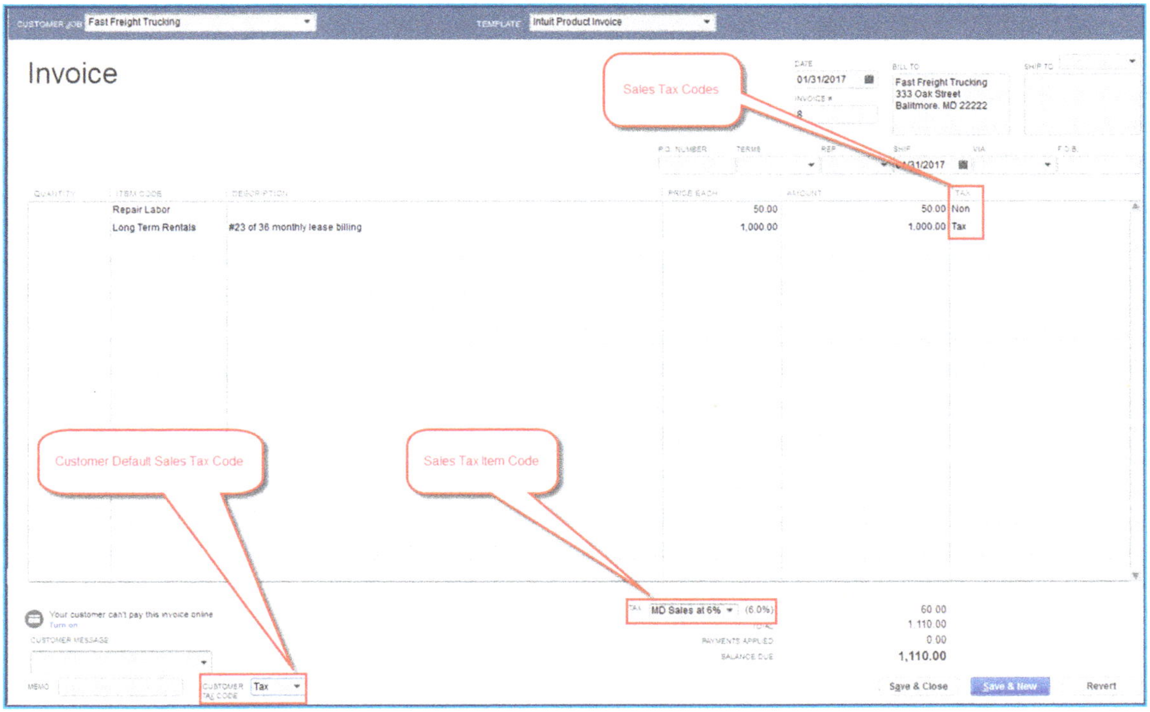

- Repair Labor, the first line of the invoice, is shown with the sales tax code "Non" to the right of the $50.00 billing. No sales tax will be computed for this line.
- The next line for $1,000 in Long Term Rentals shows a Sales Tax Code of "Tax," and the appropriate tax rate will be computed for this line.
- The applicable tax rate is shown as "MD Sales at 6%," which is based on the Sales Tax Item code previously set up. On invoices, QuickBooks abbreviates the Sales Tax Item code to "Tax."
- The sales tax billing is $60, computed as the taxable Long-Term Rental of $1,000 multiplied by a rate of 6%.
- The Customer Tax Code (the default Sales Tax Code assigned to the customer) is shown as "Tax," indicating that this customer is subject to sales tax.
- The Sales Tax Code on each line of the invoice, the Sales Tax Item Code, and the Customer Tax Codes can be changed from default settings to different settings if desired.

**Invoicing to Non-Profit With No Sales Tax**

For customers who are not subject to sales taxes (such as non-profit organizations), invoices can be generated so that no sales tax is billed and the sales to these types of entities can be reported separately on reports to taxing authorities. Below is a billing to a church with no sales tax:

- The customer was set up with a default Sales Tax Code of "NP" as shown on the Sales Tax Code list earlier in this chapter, indicating that no sales tax is to be billed.

- The default Sales Tax Code for the customer overrides the Sales Tax Code for the item code used for billing. Even though the Sales Tax Item code is shown as "MD Sales at 6%," no sales tax is billed.

**Invoicing Sales and/or Taxes for Multiple Jurisdictions**

When the sales and taxes on an invoice are attributable to more than one taxing jurisdiction, a Group Sales tax item code must be used. This allows for multiple scenarios:

- In some states, all payments must be made to the state even though there are separate sales taxes attributable to counties, cities, or regions with different rates. In these situations, the amount of sales and corresponding sales taxes collected within each jurisdiction must be reported while the Tax Agency for all of those sales tax item codes would be the same for remitting the tax payment.
- In some states, payments must be made to multiple jurisdictions. For example, the state would receive state-wide sales tax while individual counties or cities would receive their separate tax. In these situations, the Tax Agency for each county and/or city would need to be associated with the respective sales tax item code.

Below shows an invoice for billing to a customer with "VA Combined – Fairfax City," the Group Sales Tax code previously set up. Note that the individual components of the group are not shown to the customer, but because that group code is compiled of individual codes, reporting and payment remittance requirements can be met.

© The CFO Source, LLC 2017

**Invoicing Different Sales Taxes Rates**

In most states, the sales tax rate is not the same for all goods and services. For example, in Maryland the general sales tax rate is 6% and short-term truck rentals are subject to an 8% rate.

QuickBooks invoices are set up to bill at *one* rate, either using the rate of an individual Sales Tax Item code or the total of the rates comprising the Sales Tax Group code. This code is shown near the bottom of the invoice screen when creating an invoice as shown above. The chosen rate is applied to all items that are tagged with a Sales Tax code indicating the sale as taxable.

Because QuickBooks does not allow for multiple Sales Tax Item Codes or Sales Tax Group Codes to be used on an invoice, goods or services that are to be billed at different sales taxes rates must be billed with separate invoices. Simply put, a customer with sales at different sales tax rates would need to receive multiple invoices.

# Sales Tax Reports

QuickBooks provides two standard reports for sales taxes, which are:

**Sales Tax Revenue Summary** – shows sales for a selected period of time, organized first by the taxing or "remit to" agency and then for the Sales Tax Item codes and/or Sales Tax Group codes used for invoicing. The columns on the report show sales amounts for each Sales Tax Code used. Below is a sample using the three invoice examples shown previously. Note the negative amount of sales for "Multiple taxes for Virginia," which is related to the Group Sales Tax code used and serves to provide a "net" or total sales attributable to the taxing agency. This report is very useful when completing sales and use tax returns.

| Sample Truck Dealership<br>Sales Tax Revenue Summary<br>January 2017 | | | | |
|---|---|---|---|---|
| | Taxable Sales | Non-Taxable Sales | Non Profit | TOTAL |
| ▼ Comptroller of Maryland | | | | |
| MD Sales at 6% | 1,000.00 | 50.00 ▶ | 500.00 ◀ | 1,550.00 |
| Total Comptroller of Maryland | 1,000.00 | 50.00 | 500.00 | 1,550.00 |
| ▼ Virginia Department of Taxation | | | | |
| VA Local Tax - Fairfax City | 800.00 | 0.00 | 0.00 | 800.00 |
| VA North Region - Fairfax City | 800.00 | 0.00 | 0.00 | 800.00 |
| VA State Sales Tax | 800.00 | 0.00 | 0.00 | 800.00 |
| Multiple taxes for Virginia Department of Taxa... | -1,600.00 | 0.00 | 0.00 | -1,600.00 |
| Total Virginia Department of Taxation | 800.00 | 0.00 | 0.00 | 800.00 |
| TOTAL | 1,800.00 | 50.00 | 500.00 | 2,350.00 |

**Sales Tax Liability** – organized in a similar fashion as the Sales Tax Revenue Summary, but adds the tax rate, tax collected, and sales tax payable as of the last day of the report for each Sales Tax Item code. Below is the report using the same information as the prior report. Note that all non-taxable sales are collapsed into one line on this report. The sales tax payable amount will show the cumulative sales tax payable amount, not just the amount due related to the sales shown on the report. For example, if sales taxes have not been paid for a period of time, the Sales Tax Payable Column on the far right will reflect that.

### Sample Truck Dealership
### Sales Tax Liability
#### January 2017

| | Total Sales | Non-Taxable Sales | Taxable Sales | Tax Rate | Tax Collected | Sales Tax Payable As of Jan 31, 17 |
|---|---|---|---|---|---|---|
| **Comptroller of Maryland** | | | | | | |
| MD Sales at 6% | 1,550.00 | 550.00 | 1,000.00 | 6.0% | 60.00 | 60.00 |
| Comptroller of Maryland - Other | 0.00 | 0.00 | 0.00 | | 0.00 | -0.72 |
| Total Comptroller of Maryland | 1,550.00 | 550.00 | 1,000.00 | | 60.00 | 59.28 |
| **Virginia Department of Taxation** | | | | | | |
| VA Local Tax - Fairfax City | 800.00 | 0.00 | 800.00 | 1.0% | 8.00 | 8.00 |
| VA North Region - Fairfax City | 800.00 | 0.00 | 800.00 | 0.7% | 5.60 | 5.60 |
| VA State Sales Tax | 800.00 | 0.00 | 800.00 | 4.3% | 34.40 | 34.40 |
| Multiple taxes for Virginia Department of Taxa... | -1,600.00 | 0.00 | -1,600.00 | | 0.00 | 0.00 |
| Total Virginia Department of Taxation | 800.00 | 0.00 | 800.00 | | 48.00 | 48.00 |
| TOTAL | 2,350.00 | 550.00 | 1,800.00 | | 108.00 | 107.28 |

The report above shows an amount of – $.72 on the row labeled "Comptroller of Maryland – Other." This is for a sales tax discount discussed in the next section.

# Sales Tax Payments – Overview

Preparing checks for sales tax liabilities and/or recording the ACH payment of sales taxes must be done in the Sales Tax area of the Vendor section to ensure payments are properly reflected on sales tax liability reports. Payments recorded this way will show a Transaction Type Code of Sales Tax Payment. Checks processed or ACH transactions recorded outside of the Sales Tax area of the Vendor section will not be reflected properly on the sales tax liability report.

QuickBooks will generate the warning shown below when the user attempts to record a transaction affecting Sales Tax Payable outside of the Sales Tax area of the Vendor section.

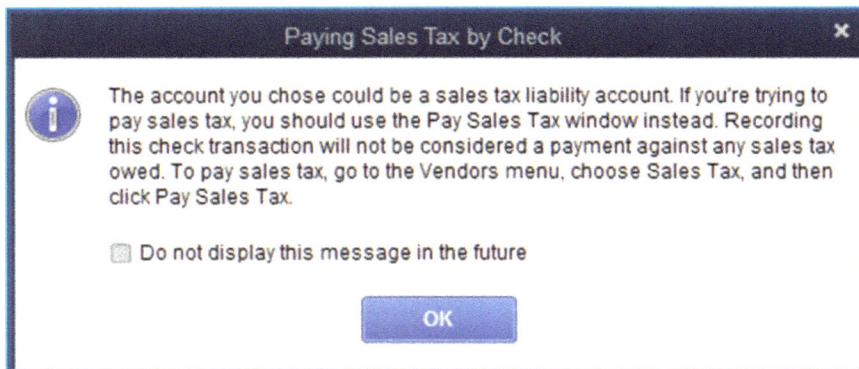

**Recording Sales Tax Discounts, Penalties, and Interest**

Prior to issuing a check or recording an ACH for sales tax payments, any adjustments to the amount due should be recorded. In many cases, an adjustment to the total amount collected in sales taxes is needed to match the payment made. This can be due to:

- a reduction in the amount due because of a discount for timely payment, or
- an increase in the amount due because of penalties and interest for late payment.

To make adjustments to sales tax liabilities, from the main menu, go to Vendors, then Sales Tax, then Adjust Sales Tax Due, which will bring up the Sales Tax Adjustment Screen as shown below:

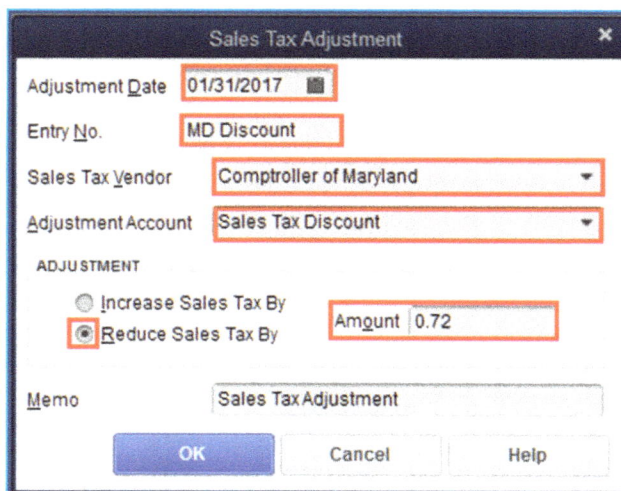

In the above example, a discount is being recorded for the prompt payment of the Maryland sales tax. The discount is 1.2% of the $60.00 sales tax collected, or $.72.

The following fields should be filled in:

- Adjustment Date – the last day of the reporting period is suggested.
- Entry No. – this is a free form field.
- Sales Tax Vendor – the taxing agency the payment relates to.
- Adjustment Account – the account the adjustment is to be posted to with the other side of the entry either a debit or credit to Sales Tax Payable.
- Adjustment – indicate whether the sales tax liability should be increased or decreased, and the amount desired.

Clicking on OK records the adjustment as a journal entry. In the case of the sales tax discount example above, the below entry will be made. Note that in the name field on the line for Sales Tax Payable, the Sales Tax Vendor selected appears.

Only one account can be selected in the Sales Tax Adjustment screen. This would require that two entries be made in the event both a late payment penalty and an interest charge would need to be recorded.

**Issuing Checks or Recording ACH Transactions for Sales Tax Payments**

As mentioned above, these activities *must* be done in the Vendor/Sales Tax area of QuickBooks for the payment to be properly reflected on Sales Tax reports.

From the main menu, select Vendors, then Sales Tax, then Pay Sales Tax, which will bring up the Pay Sales Tax screen as shown next. Select the bank account for the disbursement, the check or ACH Date for the transaction, and the taxes to be paid. In the next example, both the Maryland tax of $60.00 and the discount of $.72 are chosen for a net check of $59.28.

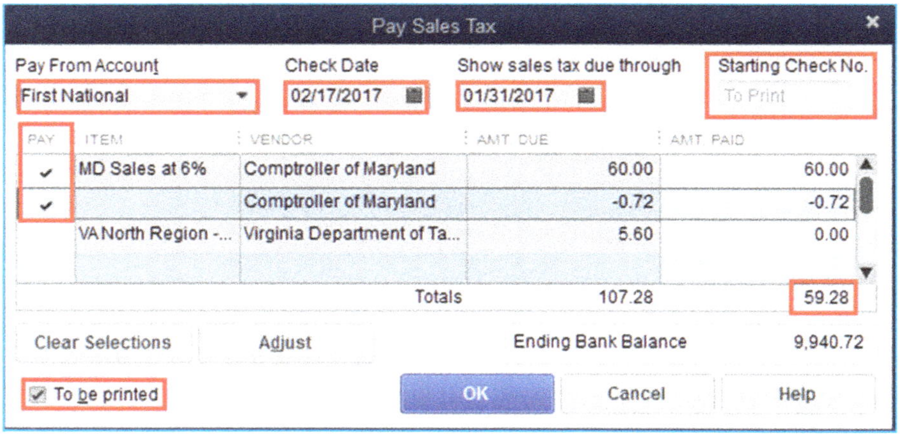

When the "To be Printed" box is checked off, the user cannot input a starting check number until reaching the actual print check screen. To print the check, go to File from the Main menu, then Print Forms, then Checks, which will bring up the screen below:

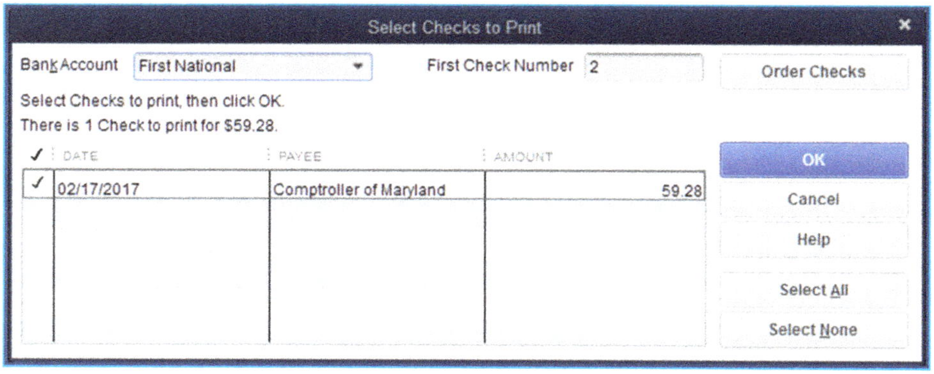

To record an ACH or other type of automatic payment, leave the "To be printed" box on the lower left unchecked, which will allow for a notation in the Starting Check Number field to be input as shown below. Clicking on OK will record the transaction.

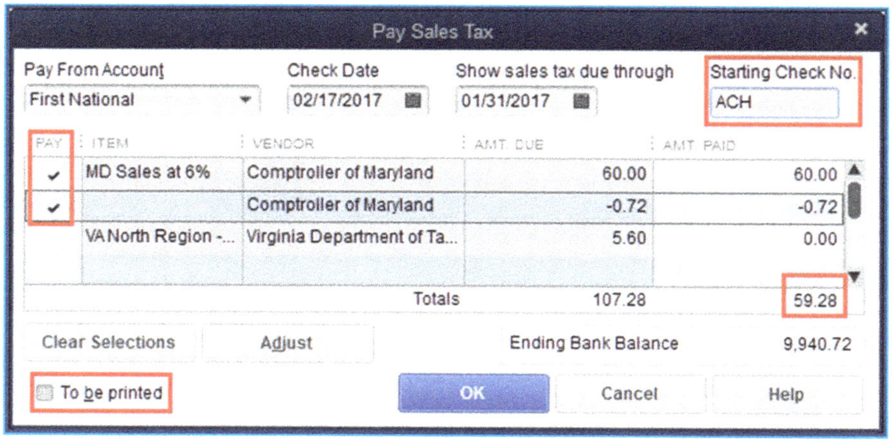

The entry to record the disbursement is shown below, which is done automatically by QuickBooks.

**Sample Truck Dealership**
**Transaction Journal**
All Transactions

| Trans # | Type | Date | Num | Name | Memo | Item | Item Description | Account | Class | Sales Price | Debit | Credit |
|---------|------|------|-----|------|------|------|-----------------|---------|-------|-------------|-------|--------|
| 58 | Sales Tax Paym.. | 02/17/2017 | ACH | Comptroller of Mar.. | | | | First National | | | | 59.28 |
| | | | | Comptroller of Mar.. | | MD Sale.. | MD SalesTax at 6% | Sales Tax Payable | | | 60.00 | |
| | | | | Comptroller of Mar.. | | | | Sales Tax Payable | | | | 0.72 |
| | | | | | | | | | | | 60.00 | 60.00 |
| **TOTAL** | | | | | | | | | | | **60.00** | **60.00** |

# Reconciling Sales Tax Liability Account With General Ledger

If the sales tax functionality is being used correctly, the amount shown on the Sales Tax Liability report in the Sales Tax Payable column (far right) should match the balance in the Sales Tax Payable account on the Balance Sheet or Trial Balance using the same "as of date." Using the above invoice example, below shows the Sales Tax Liability report with Sales Tax Payable of $107.28 as of 1/31/2017. The report below reflects the $.72 discount recorded for timely payment of Maryland sales taxes on a separate line with the notation "-other."

Sales Tax Liability

Customize Report | Comment on Report | Share Template | Memorize | Print ▾ | E-mail ▾ | Excel ▾ | Hide Header | Collapse | Refresh

Dates Custom ▾ From 01/01/2017 To 01/31/2017 Sort By Default ▾

10:28 AM
03/05/17
Accrual Basis

**Sample Truck Dealership**
**Sales Tax Liability**
January 2017

| | Total Sales | Non-Taxable Sales | Taxable Sales | Tax Rate | Tax Collected | Sales Tax Payable As of Jan 31, 17 |
|---|------------|-------------------|---------------|----------|---------------|-----------------------------------|
| ▼ Comptroller of Maryland | | | | | | |
| MD Sales at 6% | 1,050.00 ◀ | 50.00 | 1,000.00 | 6.0% | 60.00 | 60.00 |
| Comptroller of Maryland - Other | 0.00 | 0.00 | 0.00 | | 0.00 | -0.72 |
| Total Comptroller of Maryland | 1,050.00 | 50.00 | 1,000.00 | | 60.00 | 59.28 |
| ▼ Virginia Department of Taxation | | | | | | |
| VA Local Tax - Fairfax City | 800.00 | 0.00 | 800.00 | 1.0% | 8.00 | 8.00 |
| VA North Region - Fairfax City | 800.00 | 0.00 | 800.00 | 0.7% | 5.60 | 5.60 |
| VA State Sales Tax | 800.00 | 0.00 | 800.00 | 4.3% | 34.40 | 34.40 |
| Multiple taxes for Virginia Department of Taxa... | -1,600.00 | 0.00 | -1,600.00 | | 0.00 | 0.00 |
| Total Virginia Department of Taxation | 800.00 | 0.00 | 800.00 | | 48.00 | 48.00 |
| **TOTAL** | **1,850.00** | **50.00** | **1,800.00** | | **108.00** | **107.28** |

---

The sales tax payable amount shown above matches the liability on the balance sheet below:

**Sample Truck Dealership**
**Balance Sheet**
As of January 31, 2017

| | Jan 31, 17 |
|---|---|
| ▼ ASSETS | |
| ▼ Current Assets | |
| ▶ Checking/Savings | 10,000.00 |
| ▶ Accounts Receivable | 1,958.00 |
| ▼ Other Current Assets | |
|    Inventory Asset | 900.00 |
|   Total Other Current Assets | 900.00 |
| Total Current Assets | 12,858.00 |
| TOTAL ASSETS | 12,858.00 |
| ▼ LIABILITIES & EQUITY | |
| ▼ Liabilities | |
| ▼ Current Liabilities | |
| ▶ Accounts Payable | 900.00 |
| ▼ Other Current Liabilities | |
|    Sales Tax Payable | 107.28 |
|   Total Other Current Liabilities | 107.28 |
| Total Current Liabilities | 1,007.28 |
| Total Liabilities | 1,007.28 |
| ▼ Equity | |
|   Opening Balance Equity | 10,000.00 |
|   Net Income | 1,850.72 |
| Total Equity | 11,850.72 |
| TOTAL LIABILITIES & EQUITY | 12,858.00 |

# Resolving Issues With Sales Tax Liability Report

When the balances referred to above do not match, the most common reason is that transactions have been recorded to the Sales Tax Payable account that are not related to sales tax and need to be reclassified. This could be for a myriad of reasons; possibilities include:

- Vendor bills or checks not related to sales taxes coded to the sales tax payable account;
- Item codes that are not related to sales taxes incorrectly "mapped" to the sales tax payable account;
- Deposits were recorded using the sales tax payable account (possibly for sales tax refunds).

Another problem that can surface is when the totals on the Sales Tax Liability Report match the general ledger, but the individual lines on the report show balances that have been paid. The most common reason for this is when payments for sales taxes have been processed outside of the Vendor/Sales Tax section of QuickBooks. Even though warnings are given when recording these disbursements, ignoring the warnings will result in individual line items not zeroing out.

To illustrate issues that will appear on the Sales Tax Liability Report when payments are made outside of the Vendor/Sales Tax area, the sales taxes collected on the above invoices were paid with "regular" checks prepared in the Banking section of QuickBooks instead of being processed in the Vendor/Sales Tax area. The checks were charged to the Sales Tax Payable account. In this example, a payment to Comptroller of Maryland for $59.28 and another to Virginia Department of Taxation for $48.00 were recorded.

Below shows the Sales Tax Liability report after recording these two checks. (Compare with the liability report before the taxes were paid shown previously). Note that while the total shown as due each sales tax agency is zero, some lines show as due while others show negative amounts.

**Sample Truck Dealership**
**Sales Tax Liability**
January through February 2017

| | Total Sales | Non-Taxable Sales | Taxable Sales | Tax Rate | Tax Collected | Sales Tax Payable As of Feb 28, 17 |
|---|---|---|---|---|---|---|
| Comptroller of Maryland | | | | | | |
| MD Sales at 6% | 1,550.00 | 550.00 | 1,000.00 | 6.0% | 60.00 | 60.00 |
| Comptroller of Maryland - Other | 0.00 | 0.00 | 0.00 | | 0.00 | -60.00 |
| Total Comptroller of Maryland | 1,550.00 | 550.00 | 1,000.00 | | 60.00 | 0.00 |
| Virginia Department of Taxation | | | | | | |
| VA Local Tax - Fairfax City | 800.00 | 0.00 | 800.00 | 1.0% | 8.00 | 8.00 |
| VA North Region - Fairfax City | 800.00 | 0.00 | 800.00 | 0.7% | 5.60 | 5.60 |
| VA State Sales Tax | 800.00 | 0.00 | 800.00 | 4.3% | 34.40 | 34.40 |
| Virginia Department of Taxation - Other | 0.00 | 0.00 | 0.00 | | 0.00 | -48.00 |
| Multiple taxes for Virginia Department of Taxa... | -1,600.00 | 0.00 | -1,600.00 | | 0.00 | 0.00 |
| Total Virginia Department of Taxation | 800.00 | 0.00 | 800.00 | | 48.00 | 0.00 |
| TOTAL | 2,350.00 | 550.00 | 1,800.00 | | 108.00 | 0.00 |

The client data review section in the QuickBooks Accountant and Enterprise Solutions versions have a screen that can correct this problem. However, there are limitations for using this fix option. Users with the situations shown below will need to take steps other than using the Client Data Review to correct issues with the Sales Tax Liability Report related to payments:

- Not using the Accountant's or Enterprise version
- Have multiple Sales Tax Item codes set up under one tax agency
- Use Group Sales Tax item codes

# Correcting Payments for Single Sales Tax Item Codes Using Client Data Review

From the main menu, select Accountant, then Client Data Review, then Fix Incorrectly Recorded Sales Tax, which will bring up the screen below. In this example, the $59.28 check was chosen and the "Void and Replace" box clicked to correct the transaction.

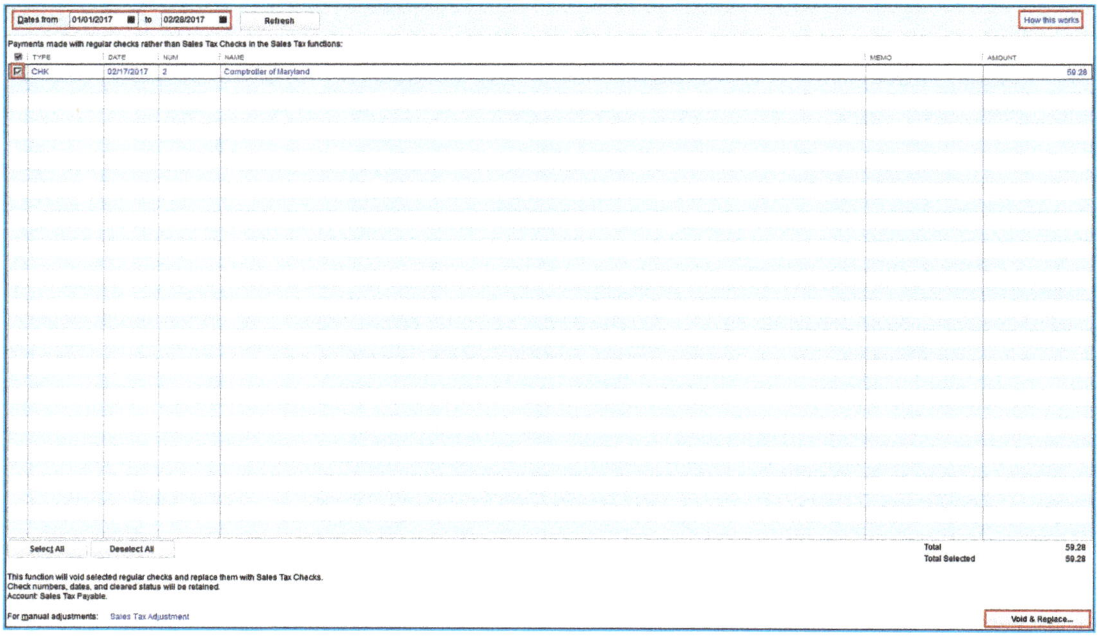

Clicking on "How this Works" in the upper right corner of the screen provides the details shown next about how the Fix Incorrectly Recorded Sales Tax screen works.

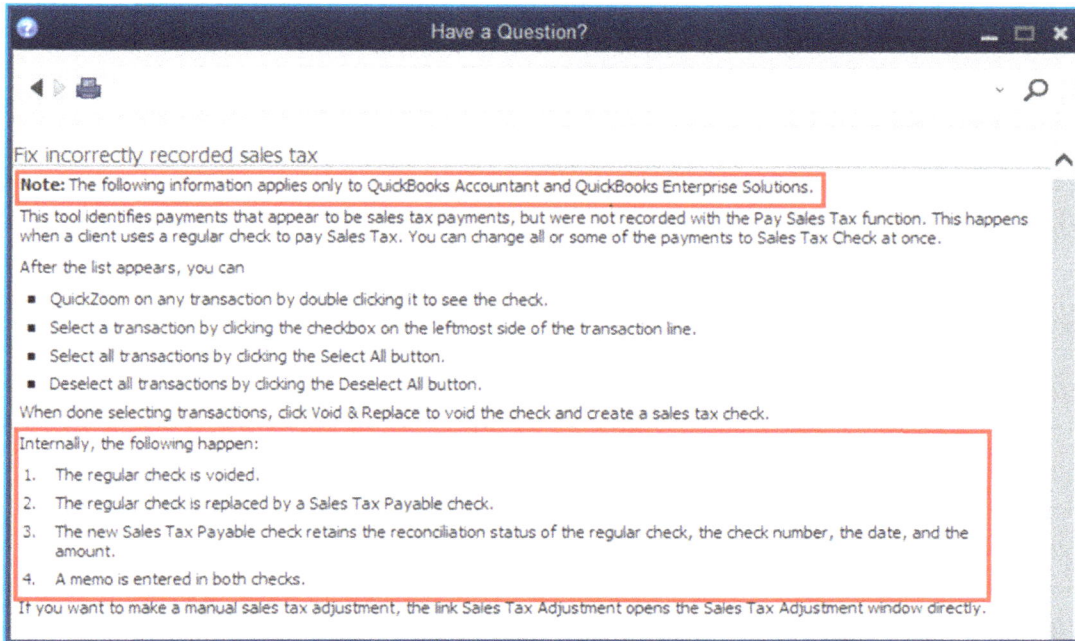

**Fix incorrectly recorded sales tax**

**Note:** The following information applies only to QuickBooks Accountant and QuickBooks Enterprise Solutions.

This tool identifies payments that appear to be sales tax payments, but were not recorded with the Pay Sales Tax function. This happens when a client uses a regular check to pay Sales Tax. You can change all or some of the payments to Sales Tax Check at once.

After the list appears, you can

- QuickZoom on any transaction by double clicking it to see the check.
- Select a transaction by clicking the checkbox on the leftmost side of the transaction line.
- Select all transactions by clicking the Select All button.
- Deselect all transactions by clicking the Deselect All button.

When done selecting transactions, click Void & Replace to void the check and create a sales tax check.

Internally, the following happen:

1. The regular check is voided.
2. The regular check is replaced by a Sales Tax Payable check.
3. The new Sales Tax Payable check retains the reconciliation status of the regular check, the check number, the date, and the amount.
4. A memo is entered in both checks.

If you want to make a manual sales tax adjustment, the link Sales Tax Adjustment opens the Sales Tax Adjustment window directly.

In summary, the fix voids the check prepared outside of the Sales Tax area and replaces it with a Sales Tax Payment check transferring the cleared status of the original check to the replacement check. Below are the details of the correction in the Cash and Sales Tax Payable accounts, showing the void of the original check and replacement with a Sales Tax Payment. This report was created by first running a balance sheet, then double clicking on the cash balance to bring up the Transactions by Account Report, then filtering the report to only include the Cash and Sales Tax Payable account.

**Sample Truck Dealership**
**Transactions by Account**
As of February 17, 2017

| Type | Date | Num | Name | Memo | Clr | Split | Debit | Credit | Balance |
|---|---|---|---|---|---|---|---|---|---|
| **First National** | | | | | | | | | **10,000.00** |
| Check | 02/17/2017 | 2 | Comptroller of Maryland | VOID: Replaced by Sales Tax Check | ✓ | Sales Tax Payable | 0.00 | | 10,000.00 |
| Sales Tax Paym.. | 02/17/2017 | 2 | Comptroller of Maryland | Replaces check #2 | | Sales Tax Payable | | 59.28 | 9,940.72 |
| Total First National | | | | | | | 0.00 | 59.28 | 9,940.72 |
| **Sales Tax Payable** | | | | | | | | | **-107.28** |
| Check | 02/17/2017 | 2 | Comptroller of Maryland | VOID: Replaced by Sales Tax Check | ✓ | First National | 0.00 | | -107.28 |
| Sales Tax Paym.. | 02/17/2017 | 2 | Comptroller of Maryland | Replaces check #2 | | First National | 59.28 | | -48.00 |
| Total Sales Tax Payable | | | | | | | 59.28 | 0.00 | -48.00 |
| **TOTAL** | | | | | | | 59.28 | 59.28 | 9,892.72 |

# Correcting Sales Tax Payments
# Without Client Data Review

In the scenarios that the Client Data Review functionality won't correctly fix the problem, the following approach is recommended:

> A "zero dollar" check should be issued in the Vendor/Sales Tax area to offset sales taxes that still show as open because the payment was made outside the Vendor/Sales Tax area. By clicking on both sales taxes that still show as open and the corresponding negative, all items are offset and a "zero dollar" check is generated. This clears all of the items and the sales taxes due will show correctly on the Sales Tax Liability report.

To illustrate this approach, the above example of the $48 check issued to the Virginia Department of Revenue in the banking module will be used. The two screens below show the Pay Sales Tax screen with the sales taxes checked off, indicating that those taxes are to be paid. Because the screen only shows three lines, the second screen image is needed to also show checking off the payment, made visible by scrolling down using the arrows on the right. Note that the amount of the check is shown as zero.

The individual line items for the Virginia taxes are now shown correctly on the Sales Tax Liability report:

| | | Sales Tax Liability | | | | — □ ✕ |
|---|---|---|---|---|---|---|

| Customize Report | Comment on Report | Share Template | Memorize | Print ▾ | E-mail ▾ | Excel ▾ | Hide Header | Collapse | Refresh |
|---|---|---|---|---|---|---|---|---|---|

Dates Custom ▾ From 01/01/2017 📅 To 02/28/2017 📅 Sort By Default ▾

8:04 PM
03/08/17
Accrual Basis

**Sample Truck Dealership**
**Sales Tax Liability**
January through February 2017

| | Total Sales | Non-Taxable Sales | Taxable Sales | Tax Rate | Tax Collected | Sales Tax Payable As of Feb 28, 17 |
|---|---|---|---|---|---|---|
| ▽ **Comptroller of Maryland** | | | | | | |
| MD Sales at 6% | 1,050.00 ◀ | 50.00 | 1,000.00 | 6.0% | 60.00 | 0.00 |
| Comptroller of Maryland - Other | 0.00 | 0.00 | 0.00 | | 0.00 | 0.00 |
| Total Comptroller of Maryland | 1,050.00 | 50.00 | 1,000.00 | | 60.00 | 0.00 |
| ▽ **Virginia Department of Taxation** | | | | | | |
| VA Local Tax - Fairfax City | 800.00 | 0.00 | 800.00 | 1.0% | 8.00 | 0.00 |
| VA North Region - Fairfax City | 800.00 | 0.00 | 800.00 | 0.7% | 5.60 | 0.00 |
| VA State Sales Tax | 800.00 | 0.00 | 800.00 | 4.3% | 34.40 | 0.00 |
| Virginia Department of Taxation - Other | 0.00 | 0.00 | 0.00 | | 0.00 | 0.00 |
| Multiple taxes for Virginia Department of Taxa... | -1,600.00 | 0.00 | -1,600.00 | | 0.00 | 0.00 |
| Total Virginia Department of Taxation | 800.00 | 0.00 | 800.00 | | 48.00 | 0.00 |
| TOTAL | 1,850.00 | 50.00 | 1,800.00 | | 108.00 | 0.00 |

Notes:

# Chapter Nineteen
# Tax Reports

QuickBooks will generate three tax reports that are useful in the preparation of US federal income tax returns. These QB reports can be run on either an accrual or cash basis. The reporting is driven by the type of entity chosen when setting up your company file. Accounts are "mapped" to a tax line on income tax returns to generate the reporting.

## Selection of Entity Type

To effectively use these reports, the proper entity must be selected as the reports and tax lines differ depending on the entity chosen. The following legal entity types and tax return forms are supported:

- Form 1120 (C Corporation)
- Form 1120S (S Corporation)
- Form 1065 (Partnership)
- Form 990 (Exempt Organization)
- Form 990-PF (Private Foundation)
- Form 990-T (Exempt Organization Business Income)
- Form 1040 (Sole Proprietorship)

To choose an entity type, from the main menu, select Company, then My Company, which will bring up the screen below:

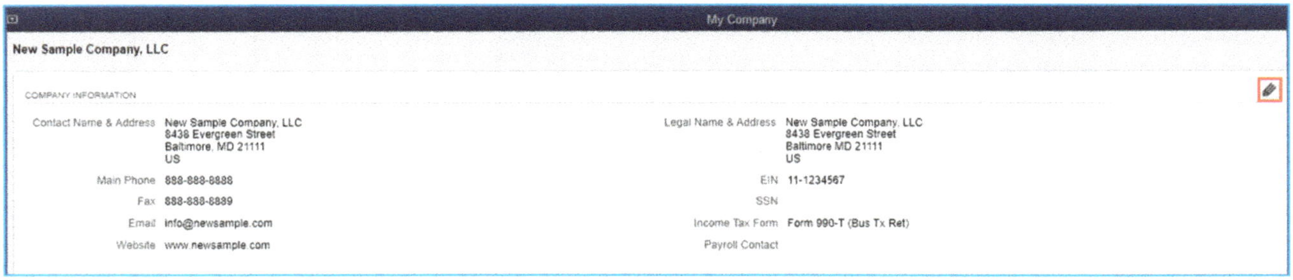

Clicking on the Edit (pencil) button in the upper right of the screen will bring up the Company Information Screen. The Report Information section (on the left side bar) is selected and, using the drop-down menu for the "Income Tax Form Used" area, the user can select the entity type as shown below:

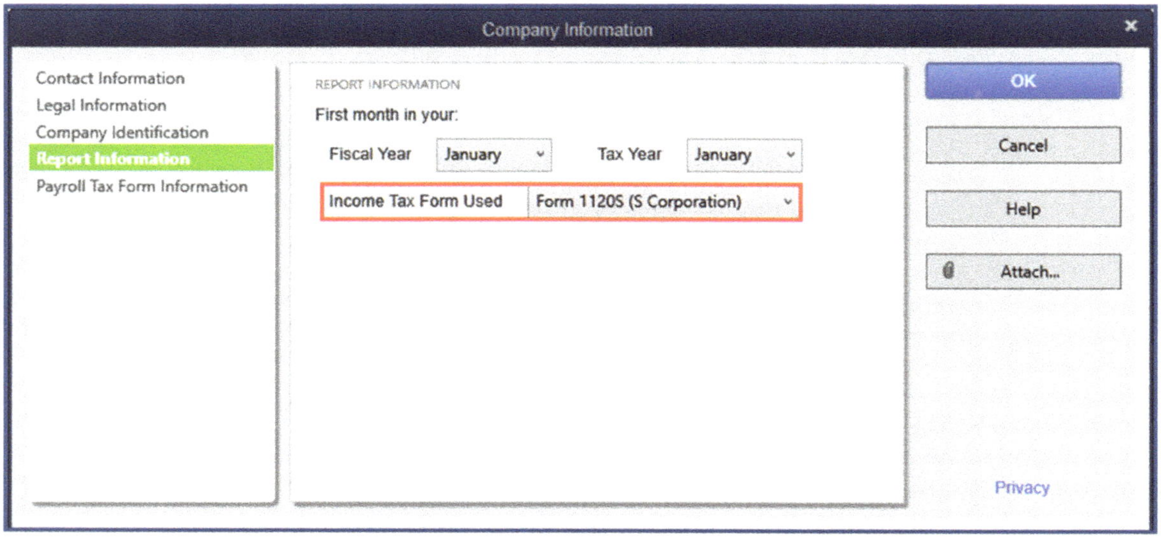

The drop-down list will display all the entity types listed in the beginning of this chapter. The entity type can be changed later, but will result in the deletion of mappings that may have already been set up. The following message will be displayed if the entity type is changed:

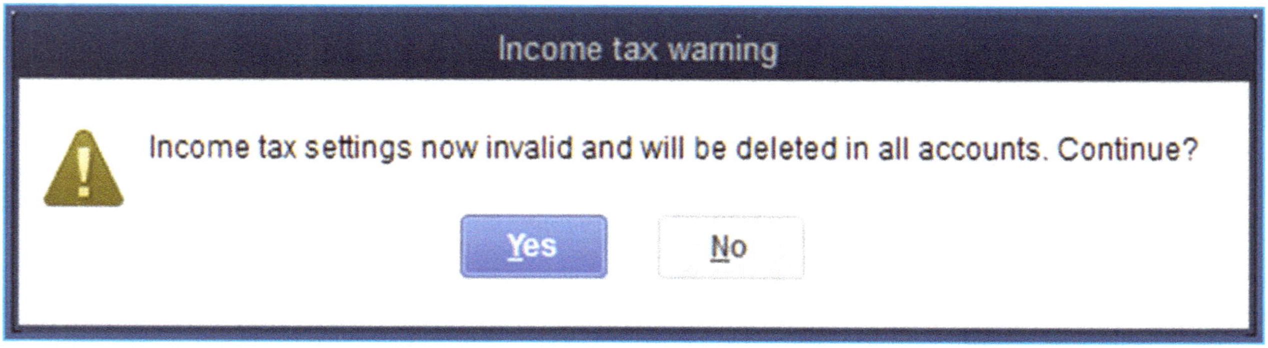

# Mapping Accounts to Tax Lines

Assigning or "Mapping" accounts to tax lines is done by editing the accounts. From the main menu, select Lists, then Chart of Accounts. Select the account you want to edit, then right click on the account and choose the "Edit Account" option, which will bring up the screen below:

Select the appropriate income tax "tax line" for the account from the drop-down list in the Tax Line Mapping area. The tax lines are preset based on the appropriate tax form for the type of entity chosen and it is not possible to add new tax lines to the list. Since forms 990T and 1040 do not require balance sheet reporting, mapping for entities selecting those forms is only available for income statement accounts. For all other entities, mapping is available for both income statement and balance sheet accounts.

It may be appropriate to have multiple accounts mapped to the same tax line if those accounts track the same category of transaction. For example, some companies may have multiple travel expense accounts for management reporting, and those accounts should all be mapped to one tax line.

# QuickBooks For Accounting Professionals

Below is the chart of accounts for a sample company showing the tax line mapping for each account:

| NAME | TYPE ▲ | TAX LINE |
|---|---|---|
| First Bank of Anytown | Bank | B/S-Assets: Cash |
| Accounts Receivable | Accounts Receivable | B/S-Assets: Accts. Rec. and trade notes |
| Undeposited Funds | Other Current Asset | B/S-Assets: Accts. Rec. and trade notes |
| Accumulated Depreciati... | Fixed Asset | B/S-Assets: Accumulated depreciation |
| Furniture and Equipment | Fixed Asset | B/S-Assets: Buildings/oth. depr. assets |
| Security Deposits Rece... | Other Asset | B/S-Assets: Other assets |
| Accounts Payable | Accounts Payable | B/S-Liabs/Eq.: Accounts payable |
| Visa Card 12345 | Credit Card | B/S-Liabs/Eq.: Other current liabilities |
| Payroll Liabilities | Other Current Liability | B/S-Liabs/Eq.: Other current liabilities |
| Sales Tax Payable | Other Current Liability | B/S-Liabs/Eq.: Other current liabilities |
| Members Draw | Equity | Schedule K-Other Items: Prop. distribs.(incl.cash) |
| Members Equity | Equity | B/S-Liabs/Eq.: Paid-in or capital surplus |
| Opening Balance Equity | Equity | B/S-Liabs/Eq.: Paid-in or capital surplus |
| Accounting Services Inc... | Income | Income: Gross receipts or sales not on line 1a |
| Consulting Income | Income | Income: Gross receipts or sales not on line 1a |
| Tax Preparation Service... | Income | Income: Gross receipts or sales not on line 1a |
| Contracted Services | Cost of Goods Sold | Other Deductions: Independent contractors |
| Advertising and Promoti... | Expense | Deductions: Advertising |
| Automobile Expense | Expense | Other Deductions: Auto and truck |
| Bank Service Charges | Expense | Other Deductions: Bank charges |
| Business Licenses an... | Expense | Deductions: Licenses |
| Computer and Internet ... | Expense | Other Deductions: Office expenses |
| Continuing Education | Expense | Other Deductions: Continuing/professional education |
| Depreciation Expense | Expense | Schedule M-1: Depreciation per books |
| Dues and Subscriptions | Expense | Other Deductions: Dues and subscriptions |
| Insurance Expense | Expense | Other Deductions: Insurance |
| General Liability Ins... | Expense | Other Deductions: Insurance |
| Life and Disability In... | Expense | Other Deductions: Insurance |
| Professional Liability | Expense | Other Deductions: Insurance |
| Worker's Compensa... | Expense | Other Deductions: Insurance |
| Interest Expense | Expense | Deductions: Interest expense |
| Meals and Entertainment | Expense | Deductions: Meals and entertainment (subj to 50% l |
| Office Supplies | Expense | Other Deductions: Office expenses |
| Payroll Expenses | Expense | Deductions: Salaries and wages |
| Postage and Delivery | Expense | Other Deductions: Postage & delivery |
| Professional Fees | Expense | Other Deductions: Legal & professional fees |
| Rent Expense | Expense | Deductions: Rents |
| Repairs and Maintenan... | Expense | Deductions: Repairs and maintenance |
| Telephone Expense | Expense | Other Deductions: Telephone |
| Travel Expense | Expense | Other Deductions: Travel |

Account ▼   Activities ▼   Reports ▼   Attach   Include inactive

Before running a tax related report, review the chart of accounts to make sure all accounts have been mapped or assigned to a tax line. Accounts that are not assigned a tax line code will show as unassigned.

# Reports

From the main menu, select Reports, then Accountant and Taxes, then one of the three reports discussed below.

**Income Tax Preparation Report**

This report is similar to a trial balance report. An accrual basis version of this report is shown below. Note that accounts with credit balances are shown as negatives.

**New Sample Company, LLC**
**Income Tax Preparation**
January through December 2016

| Account Type | Account | Amount | Tax Line |
|---|---|---|---|
| **Jan - Dec 16** | | | |
| Bank | First Bank of Anyt... | 116,043.00 | B/S-Assets: Cash |
| Accounts Receivable | Accounts Receiva... | 27,500.00 | B/S-Assets: Accts. Rec. and trade notes |
| Other Asset | Security Deposits ... | 2,000.00 | B/S-Assets: Other assets |
| Accounts Payable | Accounts Payable | -2,500.00 | B/S-Liabs/Eq.: Accounts payable |
| Credit Card | Visa Card 12345 | -800.00 | B/S-Liabs/Eq.: Other current liabilities |
| Other Current Liability | Sales Tax Payable | 0.00 | B/S-Liabs/Eq.: Other current liabilities |
| Equity | Members Equity | -30,000.00 | B/S-Liabs/Eq.: Paid-in or capital surplus |
| Equity | Members Draw | 25,000.00 | Schedule K-Other Items: Prop. distribs.(incl.cash) |
| Income | Consulting Income | -171,250.00 | Income: Gross receipts or sales not on line 1a |
| Expense | Postage and Delive... | 1,500.00 | Other Deductions: Postage & delivery |
| Expense | Utilities | 752.00 | Other Deductions: Utilities |
| Expense | Interest Expense | 5.00 | Deductions: Interest expense |
| Expense | Rent Expense | 2,000.00 | Deductions: Rents |
| Expense | Professional Fees | 29,750.00 | Other Deductions: Legal & professional fees |
| **Jan - Dec 16** | | 0.00 | |

Below is the same report run on a cash basis. Note that the accounts receivable and payable are both zero. Further, the income account amount is lower, reflecting only cash received and omitting uncollected receivables.

**New Sample Company, LLC**
**Income Tax Preparation**
January through December 2016

| Account Type | Account | Original Amount | Paid Amount | Tax Line |
|---|---|---|---|---|
| **Jan - Dec 16** | | | | |
| Bank | First Bank of Anyt... | 116,043.00 | 116,043.00 | B/S-Assets: Cash |
| Accounts Receivable | Accounts Receiva... | 0.00 | 0.00 | B/S-Assets: Accts. Rec. and trade notes |
| Other Asset | Security Deposits ... | 2,000.00 | 2,000.00 | B/S-Assets: Other assets |
| Accounts Payable | Accounts Payable | 0.00 | 0.00 | B/S-Liabs/Eq.: Accounts payable |
| Credit Card | Visa Card 12345 | -800.00 | -800.00 | B/S-Liabs/Eq.: Other current liabilities |
| Equity | Members Equity | -30,000.00 | -30,000.00 | B/S-Liabs/Eq.: Paid-in or capital surplus |
| Equity | Members Draw | 25,000.00 | 25,000.00 | Schedule K-Other Items: Prop. distribs. (incl.cash) |
| Income | Consulting Income | -143,750.00 | -143,750.00 | Income: Gross receipts or sales not on line 1a |
| Expense | Professional Fees | 27,250.00 | 27,250.00 | Other Deductions: Legal & professional fees |
| Expense | Postage and Delive... | 1,500.00 | 1,500.00 | Other Deductions: Postage & delivery |
| Expense | Utilities | 752.00 | 752.00 | Other Deductions: Utilities |
| Expense | Interest Expense | 5.00 | 5.00 | Deductions: Interest expense |
| Expense | Rent Expense | 2,000.00 | 2,000.00 | Deductions: Rents |
| **Jan - Dec 16** | | | 0.00 | |

## Income Tax Summary Report

An accrual basis version of this report is shown next. This report shows the accounts that make up the balance in income tax return groupings.

### New Sample Company, LLC
### Income Tax Summary
As of December 31, 2016

| | Dec 31, 16 |
|---|---|
| **Income** | |
| Gross receipts or sales not on line 1a | 171,250.00 |
| **Deductions** | |
| Rents | 2,000.00 |
| Interest expense | 5.00 |
| **Other Deductions** | |
| Legal & professional fees | 29,750.00 |
| Postage & delivery | 1,500.00 |
| Utilities | 752.00 |
| **Schedule K-Other Items** | |
| Prop. distribs.(incl.cash) | 25,000.00 |
| **B/S-Assets** | |
| Cash | 116,043.00 |
| Accts. Rec. and trade notes | 27,500.00 |
| Other assets | 2,000.00 |
| **B/S-Liabs/Eq.** | |
| Accounts payable | 2,500.00 |
| Other current liabilities | 800.00 |
| Paid-in or capital surplus | 30,000.00 |

## Income Tax Detail Report

This report shows all of the transactions in accounts shown on the Income Tax Summary report. By reviewing this report, miscoded transactions can be identified and corrected. The default setting for this report is to show only Income and Expense accounts; however, by changing the filters on the report, it can be run for all accounts. Below is a portion of the report:

**New Sample Company, LLC**
**Income Tax Detail**
January through December 2016

| Type | Date | Num | Adj | Name | Memo | Account | Debit | Credit | Balance |
|------|------|-----|-----|------|------|---------|-------|--------|---------|
| **Income** | | | | | | | | | |
| Gross receipts or sales not on line 1a | | | | | | | | | |
| Invoice | 04/01/2016 | 1 | | Acme Novelty Com... | Services for... | Consulting Income | | 60,000.00 | 60,000.00 |
| Invoice | 07/01/2016 | 2 | | Acme Novelty Com... | Services for... | Consulting Income | | 50,000.00 | 110,000.00 |
| Invoice | 09/01/2016 | 3 | | Acme Novelty Com... | Services for... | Consulting Income | | 33,750.00 | 143,750.00 |
| Invoice | 12/31/2016 | 4 | | Acme Novelty Com... | services for... | Consulting Income | | 27,500.00 | 171,250.00 |
| Total Gross receipts or sales not on line 1a | | | | | | | 0.00 | 171,250.00 | 171,250.00 |
| **Deductions** | | | | | | | | | |
| Rents | | | | | | | | | |
| Check | 12/31/2016 | 1002 | | Real Estate Holding... | | Rent Expense | 2,000.00 | | 2,000.00 |
| Total Rents | | | | | | | 2,000.00 | 0.00 | 2,000.00 |
| Interest expense | | | | | | | | | |
| Check | 12/28/2016 | | | Visa Bankcard | | Interest Expense | 5.00 | | 5.00 |
| Total Interest expense | | | | | | | 5.00 | 0.00 | 5.00 |
| **Other Deductions** | | | | | | | | | |
| Legal & professional fees | | | | | | | | | |
| Credit Card Char... | 12/01/2016 | | | Smith Services | | Professional Fees | 1,000.00 | | 1,000.00 |
| Bill | 12/06/2016 | | | Richard Jones | | Professional Fees | 2,500.00 | | 3,500.00 |
| Bill | 12/15/2016 | | | Richard Jones | | Professional Fees | 10,000.00 | | 13,500.00 |
| Bill | 12/15/2016 | | | XYZ Company | | Professional Fees | 10,000.00 | | 23,500.00 |
| Credit | 12/20/2016 | cr me... | | XYZ Company | | Professional Fees | | 1,750.00 | 21,750.00 |
| Check | 12/28/2016 | | | Charles Wilson | | Professional Fees | 1,000.00 | | 22,750.00 |
| General Journal | 12/31/2016 | 1 | ✓ | ABC Services | | Professional Fees | 2,000.00 | | 24,750.00 |
| General Journal | 12/31/2016 | 1 | ✓ | XYZ Company | | Professional Fees | 5,000.00 | | 29,750.00 |
| Total Legal & professional fees | | | | | | | 31,500.00 | 1,750.00 | 29,750.00 |
| Postage & delivery | | | | | | | | | |
| Bill | 12/01/2016 | | | William McNight | | Postage and Delive... | 1,500.00 | | 1,500.00 |
| Total Postage & delivery | | | | | | | 1,500.00 | 0.00 | 1,500.00 |
| Utilities | | | | | | | | | |
| Check | 12/28/2016 | | | Consolidated Elect... | | Utilities | 752.00 | | 752.00 |
| Total Utilities | | | | | | | 752.00 | 0.00 | 752.00 |
| **Schedule K-Other Items** | | | | | | | | | |
| Prop. distribs.(incl.cash) | | | | | | | | | |
| Check | 01/01/2016 | | | Charles Wilson | | Members Draw | 25,000.00 | | 25,000.00 |
| Total Prop. distribs.(incl.cash) | | | | | | | 25,000.00 | 0.00 | 25,000.00 |

Notes:

# Chapter Twenty
# QuickBooks Cash Basis Financial Statements

QuickBooks cash basis income statements and balance sheets can be very helpful to tax accountants in preparing tax returns on that basis. There are, however, some issues with cash basis financial statements that may call for adjustments so accurate returns can be filed.

In general, QuickBooks cash basis reports "ignore" certain transactions for which cash is not involved. As such, the debits and credits related to these transactions are not reflected on cash basis financial statements. The best examples of transactions *not* included as part of a cash basis financial statement are:

- Customer invoices for revenues that have not been paid by the customer.
- Vendor bills for expenses that have not been paid to the vendor.

These two examples cover what are typically the largest adjustments for cash basis financial statements. However, other types of transactions may or may not be reflected on cash basis financial statements depending on the transaction and accounts used.

Most of the issues that arise with cash basis financial statements relate to transactions that are not complete in terms of the accounting cycle they are related to. The two examples above are the most typical as in both cases, the accounting cycle is not complete. Invoices to customers that have been invoiced and paid as well as vendor bills that have been recorded and paid, in most cases, will be reflected on cash basis financial statements.

This chapter will:

- provide an overview of cash basis reporting and issues that can arise, and
- an in-depth review of a multitude of transaction types detailing what is and what is not included on a cash basis financial statement.

The information presented in this chapter was derived by setting up a company in QuickBooks and testing transactions one by one to see the impact on cash basis financial statements. Financial statements will be presented, showing the impact of transactions on both accrual and cash basis reports.

The Cash Basis Test Company was set up with the following assumptions:

- Initial $500,000 cash deposit for equity capitalization on 1/1/2017.
- Land and building acquired on 1/1/2017 for $300,000, financed with $60,000 from the corporation and a 10-year, $240,000 loan at 6% interest.
- The corporation paid $30,000 in financing costs related to the building loan, which will be amortized over the 10-year term of the loan.
- The building loan is payable in quarterly installments of principal and interest totaling $8.022.50 based on a ten-year amortization. Loan payments are due 10 days after the end of each quarter.
- The company sells, installs, and maintains commercial HVAC systems.
- Payments by the company's customers include both customers who pay individual invoices when due and customers who make payments "on account," i.e. not paying individual invoices but rather paying in lump sum amounts to be applied to existing and/or future invoices.
- Some invoices are generated for long-term maintenance contracts that require the underlying revenue be treated as deferred revenue.
- The company has payment terms from its vendors so that some are paid for specific bills when due while others are paid "on account."
- Company carries inventory of HVAC systems, which it purchases from manufacturers and sells to customers using various markups.
- The company uses a credit card to pay for certain expenses.
- Journal entries are used to record non-cash transactions such as depreciation, amortization, and expense accruals.
- Journal entries are also used to record adjustments to accounts receivable and accounts payable.

# Running Accrual and Cash Basis Reports

In the Reports and Graphs section of Preferences, reports can be set to run either on an accrual or cash basis as shown below:

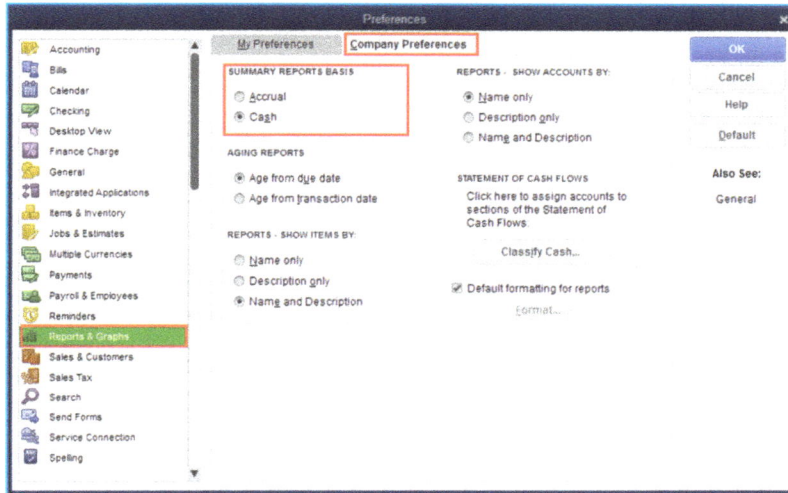

Users can also change reports between accrual and cash basis in the Display area of report customization here:

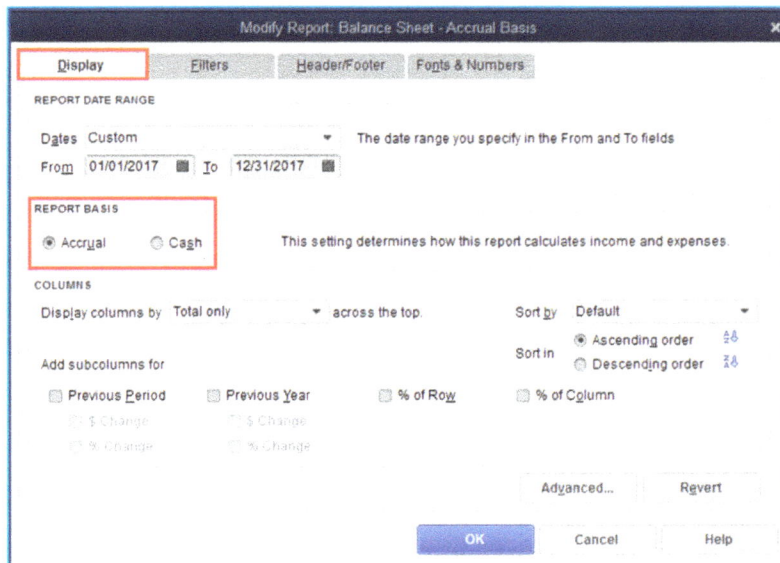

# Analysis of Transactions

The transactions for our test company will be discussed in the order listed, along with how QuickBooks handles cash basis reporting. The reports presented will assume year end reporting of 12/31/2017.

**Initial Capitalization, Building Acquisition, Depreciation, and Loan Fee Amortization**

The initial $500,000 capitalization was recorded with a bank deposit. The building acquisition and related loan, depreciation expense, and amortization of the loan fees were recorded with journal entries. For these transactions, there is no difference between cash and accrual basis statements—Net Income is the same on both balance sheets as shown below:

| Cash Basis Test Company<br>Balance Sheet - Cash Basis<br>As of December 31, 2017 | | | Cash Basis Test Company<br>Balance Sheet - Cash Basis<br>As of December 31, 2017 | | |
|---|---|---|---|---|---|
| | | Dec 31, 17 | | | Dec 31, 17 |
| **ASSETS** | | | **ASSETS** | | |
| Current Assets | | | Current Assets | | |
| ▾ Checking/Savings | | | ▾ Checking/Savings | | |
| First National Bank | ▶ | 410,000.00 | First National Bank | ▶ | 410,000.00 |
| Total Checking/Savings | | 410,000.00 | Total Checking/Savings | | 410,000.00 |
| Total Current Assets | | 410,000.00 | Total Current Assets | | 410,000.00 |
| Fixed Assets | | | Fixed Assets | | |
| Buildings | | 220,000.00 | Buildings | | 220,000.00 |
| Land | | 80,000.00 | Land | | 80,000.00 |
| Accumulated Depreciation | | -5,640.00 | Accumulated Depreciation | | -5,640.00 |
| Total Fixed Assets | | 294,360.00 | Total Fixed Assets | | 294,360.00 |
| Other Assets | | | Other Assets | | |
| ▾ Deferred Financing Costs | | | ▾ Deferred Financing Costs | | |
| Deferred Financing - Orig Cost | | 30,000.00 | Deferred Financing - Orig Cost | | 30,000.00 |
| Accum Amort - Def Financing | | -3,000.00 | Accum Amort - Def Financing | | -3,000.00 |
| Total Deferred Financing Costs | | 27,000.00 | Total Deferred Financing Costs | | 27,000.00 |
| Total Other Assets | | 27,000.00 | Total Other Assets | | 27,000.00 |
| **TOTAL ASSETS** | | **731,360.00** | **TOTAL ASSETS** | | **731,360.00** |
| **LIABILITIES & EQUITY** | | | **LIABILITIES & EQUITY** | | |
| Liabilities | | | Liabilities | | |
| ▾ Long Term Liabilities | | | ▾ Long Term Liabilities | | |
| Building Mortgage | | 240,000.00 | Building Mortgage | | 240,000.00 |
| Total Long Term Liabilities | | 240,000.00 | Total Long Term Liabilities | | 240,000.00 |
| Total Liabilities | | 240,000.00 | Total Liabilities | | 240,000.00 |
| Equity | | | Equity | | |
| Additional Paid in Capital | | 499,000.00 | Additional Paid in Capital | | 499,000.00 |
| Capital Stock | | 1,000.00 | Capital Stock | | 1,000.00 |
| Net Income | | -8,640.00 | Net Income | | -8,640.00 |
| Total Equity | | 491,360.00 | Total Equity | | 491,360.00 |
| **TOTAL LIABILITIES & EQUITY** | | **731,360.00** | **TOTAL LIABILITIES & EQUITY** | | **731,360.00** |

## Loan Accounting – Loan Payments, Accrual of Interest, Classification of Current Portion

For the first example, loan payments with the split of principal and interest were recorded as checks for the payments due for the first, second, and third quarters. Since the interest expense for the fourth quarter won't be paid to the bank until the next year, an accrual for interest expense was made with a journal entry. The current portion of long-term debt was set up using a journal entry. For these transactions, there is no difference between cash and accrual basis statements—Net Income is the same on both balance sheets as shown below.

**Cash Basis Test Company**
**Balance Sheet - Accrual Basis**
As of December 31, 2017

| | Dec 31, 17 |
|---|---|
| Checking/Savings | |
| First National Bank | 385,932.50 |
| Total Checking/Savings | 385,932.50 |
| Total Current Assets | 385,932.50 |
| Fixed Assets | |
| Buildings | 220,000.00 |
| Land | 80,000.00 |
| Accumulated Depreciation | -5,640.00 |
| Total Fixed Assets | 294,360.00 |
| Other Assets | |
| Deferred Financing Costs | |
| Deferred Financing - Orig Cost | 30,000.00 |
| Accum Amort - Def Financing | -3,000.00 |
| Total Deferred Financing Costs | 27,000.00 |
| Total Other Assets | 27,000.00 |
| TOTAL ASSETS | 707,292.50 |
| LIABILITIES & EQUITY | |
| Liabilities | |
| Current Liabilities | |
| Other Current Liabilities | |
| Current Portion Long Term Debt | 61,214.00 |
| Accrued Interest | 3,397.99 |
| Total Other Current Liabilities | 64,611.99 |
| Total Current Liabilities | 64,611.99 |
| Long Term Liabilities | |
| Building Mortgage | 165,318.49 |
| Total Long Term Liabilities | 165,318.49 |
| Total Liabilities | 229,930.48 |
| Equity | |
| Additional Paid in Capital | 499,000.00 |
| Capital Stock | 1,000.00 |
| Net Income | -22,637.98 |
| Total Equity | 477,362.02 |
| TOTAL LIABILITIES & EQUITY | 707,292.50 |

**Cash Basis Test Company**
**Balance Sheet - Cash Basis**
As of December 31, 2017

| | Dec 31, 17 |
|---|---|
| ASSETS | |
| Current Assets | |
| Checking/Savings | |
| First National Bank | 385,932.50 |
| Total Checking/Savings | 385,932.50 |
| Total Current Assets | 385,932.50 |
| Fixed Assets | |
| Buildings | 220,000.00 |
| Land | 80,000.00 |
| Accumulated Depreciation | -5,640.00 |
| Total Fixed Assets | 294,360.00 |
| Other Assets | |
| Deferred Financing Costs | |
| Deferred Financing - Orig Cost | 30,000.00 |
| Accum Amort - Def Financing | -3,000.00 |
| Total Deferred Financing Costs | 27,000.00 |
| Total Other Assets | 27,000.00 |
| TOTAL ASSETS | 707,292.50 |
| LIABILITIES & EQUITY | |
| Liabilities | |
| Current Liabilities | |
| Other Current Liabilities | |
| Current Portion Long Term Debt | 61,214.00 |
| Accrued Interest | 3,397.99 |
| Total Other Current Liabilities | 64,611.99 |
| Total Current Liabilities | 64,611.99 |
| Long Term Liabilities | |
| Building Mortgage | 165,318.49 |
| Total Long Term Liabilities | 165,318.49 |
| Total Liabilities | 229,930.48 |
| Equity | |
| Additional Paid in Capital | 499,000.00 |
| Capital Stock | 1,000.00 |
| Net Income | -22,637.98 |
| Total Equity | 477,362.02 |
| TOTAL LIABILITIES & EQUITY | 707,292.50 |

For the second example, the accrual for interest expense was deleted and replaced with a vendor bill payable to the bank for the payment due in the next year. The bill is unpaid as of 12/31/2017. Since some companies process their loan payments as bills when statements are received from the bank and later paid when due, accountants may run into this scenario. There will be differences between the accrual basis balance sheet and the cash basis. Those differences are shown on the balance sheets below, and are as follows:

- Accounts payable on the accrual basis balance sheet shows the total of the loan payment ($8,022.50), but the cash basis balance sheet only shows the principal portion of the bill ($4,624.51). The interest portion of the bill is not reflected on the cash basis balance sheet.
- Net income on an accrual basis reflects the recording of the interest expense portion of the quarterly loan payment, but the cash basis statement does not.
- Recording the loan payment in the current year that is due next year incorrectly transfers the loan due to accounts payable, and an adjustment would be needed to correct this.

| Cash Basis Test Company<br>Balance Sheet - Accrual Basis<br>As of December 31, 2017 | | Cash Basis Test Company<br>Balance Sheet - Cash Basis<br>As of December 31, 2017 | |
|---|---|---|---|
| | Dec 31, 17 | | Dec 31, 17 |
| **ASSETS** | | **ASSETS** | |
| Current Assets | | Current Assets | |
| ⯆ Checking/Savings | | ⯆ Checking/Savings | |
| First National Bank | 385,932.50 | First National Bank | 385,932.50 |
| Total Checking/Savings | 385,932.50 | Total Checking/Savings | 385,932.50 |
| Total Current Assets | 385,932.50 | Total Current Assets | 385,932.50 |
| Fixed Assets | | Fixed Assets | |
| Buildings | 220,000.00 | Buildings | 220,000.00 |
| Land | 80,000.00 | Land | 80,000.00 |
| Accumulated Depreciation | -5,640.00 | Accumulated Depreciation | -5,640.00 |
| Total Fixed Assets | 294,360.00 | Total Fixed Assets | 294,360.00 |
| Other Assets | | Other Assets | |
| ▷ Deferred Financing Costs | 27,000.00 | ▷ Deferred Financing Costs | 27,000.00 |
| Total Other Assets | 27,000.00 | Total Other Assets | 27,000.00 |
| **TOTAL ASSETS** | 707,292.50 | **TOTAL ASSETS** | 707,292.50 |
| **LIABILITIES & EQUITY** | | **LIABILITIES & EQUITY** | |
| Liabilities | | Liabilities | |
| ⯆ Current Liabilities | | ⯆ Current Liabilities | |
| ▷ Accounts Payable | 8,022.50 | ▷ Accounts Payable | 4,624.51 |
| ⯆ Other Current Liabilities | | ⯆ Other Current Liabilities | |
| Current Portion Long Term Debt | 61,214.00 | Current Portion Long Term Debt | 61,214.00 |
| Total Other Current Liabilities | 61,214.00 | Total Other Current Liabilities | 61,214.00 |
| Total Current Liabilities | 69,236.50 | Total Current Liabilities | 65,838.51 |
| ⯆ Long Term Liabilities | | ⯆ Long Term Liabilities | |
| Building Mortgage | 160,693.98 | Building Mortgage | 160,693.98 |
| Total Long Term Liabilities | 160,693.98 | Total Long Term Liabilities | 160,693.98 |
| Total Liabilities | 229,930.48 | Total Liabilities | 226,532.49 |
| Equity | | Equity | |
| Additional Paid in Capital | 499,000.00 | Additional Paid in Capital | 499,000.00 |
| Capital Stock | 1,000.00 | Capital Stock | 1,000.00 |
| Net Income | -22,637.98 | Net Income | -19,239.99 |
| Total Equity | 477,362.02 | Total Equity | 480,760.01 |
| **TOTAL LIABILITIES & EQUITY** | 707,292.50 | **TOTAL LIABILITIES & EQUITY** | 707,292.50 |

Before going into the next section, the test company's vendor bill payable to the bank was replaced with the journal entry discussed in the first example to record accrued interest, returning the company to a position where the two balance sheets match.

**Revenue and Accounts Receivable Accounting**

A series of transactions affecting cash, accounts receivable, revenues, and a deferred revenue liability account will be analyzed. Inventory related revenue transactions will be covered in a later section. The transactions analyzed will only include transactions for which the accounting cycle has not been completed. Transactions analyzed will include the following:

- Customer Invoice recorded to a revenue account, not paid by statement date;
- Customer invoice recorded to a balance sheet account, not paid by statement date;
- Payments by a customer on account not offset to specific invoices;
- Revenue recorded with journal entry with offset to accounts receivable, not paid by statement date.

Keep in mind that in the test company, the accrual and cash basis balance sheets are the same at this point.

In the first example, an invoice for $10,000 is issued to a customer using an item code that maps the transaction to a revenue account and is unpaid as of 12/31/2017. In this case, the income and accounts receivable do not appear on the cash basis balance sheet as shown below:

| **Cash Basis Test Company**<br>**Balance Sheet - Accrual Basis**<br>As of December 31, 2017 | Dec 31, 17 |
|---|---|
| **ASSETS** | |
| Current Assets | |
| Checking/Savings | |
| First National Bank | 385,932.50 |
| Total Checking/Savings | 385,932.50 |
| Accounts Receivable | |
| Accounts Receivable | 10,000.00 |
| Total Accounts Receivable | 10,000.00 |
| Total Current Assets | 395,932.50 |
| Fixed Assets | 294,360.00 |
| Other Assets | |
| Deferred Financing Costs | 27,000.00 |
| Total Other Assets | 27,000.00 |
| TOTAL ASSETS | 717,292.50 |
| **LIABILITIES & EQUITY** | |
| Liabilities | |
| Current Liabilities | |
| Other Current Liabilities | |
| Current Portion Long Term Debt | 61,214.00 |
| Accrued Interest | 3,397.99 |
| Total Other Current Liabilities | 64,611.99 |
| Total Current Liabilities | 64,611.99 |
| Long Term Liabilities | 165,318.49 |
| Total Liabilities | 229,930.48 |
| Equity | |
| Additional Paid in Capital | 499,000.00 |
| Capital Stock | 1,000.00 |
| Net Income | -12,637.98 |
| Total Equity | 487,362.02 |
| TOTAL LIABILITIES & EQUITY | 717,292.50 |

| **Cash Basis Test Company**<br>**Balance Sheet - Cash Basis**<br>As of December 31, 2017 | Dec 31, 17 |
|---|---|
| **ASSETS** | |
| Current Assets | |
| Checking/Savings | |
| First National Bank | 385,932.50 |
| Total Checking/Savings | 385,932.50 |
| Total Current Assets | 385,932.50 |
| Fixed Assets | 294,360.00 |
| Other Assets | |
| Deferred Financing Costs | 27,000.00 |
| Total Other Assets | 27,000.00 |
| TOTAL ASSETS | 707,292.50 |
| **LIABILITIES & EQUITY** | |
| Liabilities | |
| Current Liabilities | |
| Other Current Liabilities | |
| Current Portion Long Term Debt | 61,214.00 |
| Accrued Interest | 3,397.99 |
| Total Other Current Liabilities | 64,611.99 |
| Total Current Liabilities | 64,611.99 |
| Long Term Liabilities | 165,318.49 |
| Total Liabilities | 229,930.48 |
| Equity | |
| Additional Paid in Capital | 499,000.00 |
| Capital Stock | 1,000.00 |
| Net Income | -22,637.98 |
| Total Equity | 477,362.02 |
| TOTAL LIABILITIES & EQUITY | 707,292.50 |

In the second example, the invoice to the customer was changed to $12,000 and an item code was used that recorded the billing to deferred revenue billing, a liability account. Additionally, a journal entry was recorded to recognize 1/12th of the billing as revenue. For these transactions, there is no difference between cash and accrual basis statements as demonstrated below. For accountants who have cash balance sheets that are showing a receivable, this type of transaction is one likely reason.

| Cash Basis Test Company<br>Balance Sheet - Accrual Basis<br>As of December 31, 2017 | | Cash Basis Test Company<br>Balance Sheet - Cash Basis<br>As of December 31, 2017 | |
|---|---|---|---|
| | Dec 31, 17 | | Dec 31, 17 |
| ASSETS | | ASSETS | |
| Current Assets | | Current Assets | |
| ▾ Checking/Savings | | ▾ Checking/Savings | |
| First National Bank | 385,932.50 | First National Bank | 385,932.50 |
| Total Checking/Savings | 385,932.50 | Total Checking/Savings | 385,932.50 |
| ▾ Accounts Receivable | | ▾ Accounts Receivable | |
| Accounts Receivable | 12,000.00 | Accounts Receivable | 12,000.00 |
| Total Accounts Receivable | 12,000.00 | Total Accounts Receivable | 12,000.00 |
| Total Current Assets | 397,932.50 | Total Current Assets | 397,932.50 |
| Fixed Assets | 294,360.00 | Fixed Assets | 294,360.00 |
| Other Assets | | Other Assets | |
| ▸ Deferred Financing Costs | 27,000.00 | ▸ Deferred Financing Costs | 27,000.00 |
| Total Other Assets | 27,000.00 | Total Other Assets | 27,000.00 |
| TOTAL ASSETS | 719,292.50 | TOTAL ASSETS | 719,292.50 |
| LIABILITIES & EQUITY | | LIABILITIES & EQUITY | |
| Liabilities | | Liabilities | |
| ▾ Current Liabilities | | ▾ Current Liabilities | |
| ▾ Other Current Liabilities | | ▾ Other Current Liabilities | |
| Current Portion Long Term Debt | 61,214.00 | Current Portion Long Term Debt | 61,214.00 |
| Accrued Interest | 3,397.99 | Accrued Interest | 3,397.99 |
| Deferred Mtce Plan Billing | 11,000.00 | Deferred Mtce Plan Billing | 11,000.00 |
| Total Other Current Liabilities | 75,611.99 | Total Other Current Liabilities | 75,611.99 |
| Total Current Liabilities | 75,611.99 | Total Current Liabilities | 75,611.99 |
| ▾ Long Term Liabilities | | ▾ Long Term Liabilities | |
| Building Mortgage | 165,318.49 | Building Mortgage | 165,318.49 |
| Total Long Term Liabilities | 165,318.49 | Total Long Term Liabilities | 165,318.49 |
| Total Liabilities | 240,930.48 | Total Liabilities | 240,930.48 |
| Equity | | Equity | |
| Additional Paid in Capital | 499,000.00 | Additional Paid in Capital | 499,000.00 |
| Capital Stock | 1,000.00 | Capital Stock | 1,000.00 |
| Net Income | -21,637.98 | Net Income | -21,637.98 |
| Total Equity | 478,362.02 | Total Equity | 478,362.02 |
| TOTAL LIABILITIES & EQUITY | 719,292.50 | TOTAL LIABILITIES & EQUITY | 719,292.50 |

For the third example, the invoice to the customer is changed back to the invoice in the first example: a $10,000 invoice coded with an item code that maps the transaction to a revenue account. Then a payment from the customer of $10,000 "on account" is recorded on 12/31/2017. As shown below, when a customer payment is recorded without checking off an invoice in the Customer Payment screen, QuickBooks considers the invoice still open. Checking off specific invoices to apply the payment is done in the red boxed area on the left of the screen below:

Recording customer payments "on account" rather than applying payments to specific invoices causes issues with cash basis statements.

- Because QuickBooks treats these invoices as unpaid, they are not included as revenue, causing an understatement of revenue and profits.
- Payments "on account" cause a negative balance in accounts receivable.

In essence, the entry QuickBooks makes in the background to record an invoice (a debit to Accounts Receivable and a credit to Revenue) is ignored while the entry to record a payment (a debit to cash and a credit to Accounts Receivable) is reflected.

To avoid this situation, it is advisable to apply all payments to customers to specific invoices. Below are the accrual and cash basis balance sheets for this example, showing the negative $10,000 receivable:

| Cash Basis Test Company<br>Balance Sheet - Accrual Basis<br>As of December 31, 2017 | |
| --- | --- |
| | Dec 31, 17 |
| **ASSETS** | |
| Current Assets | |
| ▼ Checking/Savings | |
| First National Bank | 395,932.50 |
| Total Checking/Savings | 395,932.50 |
| **Total Current Assets** | 395,932.50 |
| Fixed Assets | 294,360.00 |
| Other Assets | |
| ▶ Deferred Financing Costs | 27,000.00 |
| Total Other Assets | 27,000.00 |
| **TOTAL ASSETS** | **717,292.50** |
| **LIABILITIES & EQUITY** | |
| Liabilities | |
| ▼ Current Liabilities | |
| ▼ Other Current Liabilities | |
| Current Portion Long Term Debt | 61,214.00 |
| Accrued Interest | 3,397.99 |
| Total Other Current Liabilities | 64,611.99 |
| Total Current Liabilities | 64,611.99 |
| ▼ Long Term Liabilities | |
| Building Mortgage | 165,318.49 |
| Total Long Term Liabilities | 165,318.49 |
| Total Liabilities | 229,930.48 |
| Equity | |
| Additional Paid in Capital | 499,000.00 |
| Capital Stock | 1,000.00 |
| Net Income | -12,637.98 |
| Total Equity | 487,362.02 |
| **TOTAL LIABILITIES & EQUITY** | **717,292.50** |

| Cash Basis Test Company<br>Balance Sheet - Cash Basis<br>As of December 31, 2017 | |
| --- | --- |
| | Dec 31, 17 |
| **ASSETS** | |
| Current Assets | |
| ▼ Checking/Savings | |
| First National Bank | 395,932.50 |
| Total Checking/Savings | 395,932.50 |
| ▼ Accounts Receivable | |
| Accounts Receivable | -10,000.00 |
| Total Accounts Receivable | -10,000.00 |
| Total Current Assets | 385,932.50 |
| Fixed Assets | 294,360.00 |
| Other Assets | |
| ▶ Deferred Financing Costs | 27,000.00 |
| Total Other Assets | 27,000.00 |
| **TOTAL ASSETS** | **707,292.50** |
| **LIABILITIES & EQUITY** | |
| Liabilities | |
| ▼ Current Liabilities | |
| ▼ Other Current Liabilities | |
| Current Portion Long Term Debt | 61,214.00 |
| Accrued Interest | 3,397.99 |
| Total Other Current Liabilities | 64,611.99 |
| Total Current Liabilities | 64,611.99 |
| ▼ Long Term Liabilities | |
| Building Mortgage | 165,318.49 |
| Total Long Term Liabilities | 165,318.49 |
| Total Liabilities | 229,930.48 |
| Equity | |
| Additional Paid in Capital | 499,000.00 |
| Capital Stock | 1,000.00 |
| Net Income | -22,637.98 |
| Total Equity | 477,362.02 |
| **TOTAL LIABILITIES & EQUITY** | **707,292.50** |

**Researching Transactions – Accounts Receivable Balance Showing on a Cash Basis Balance Sheet**

When "drilling down" on the accounts receivable balance of a cash basis financial statement by double clicking on the amount, QuickBooks displays all of the transactions that were processed through accounts receivable, including invoice and payment transactions that offset. A list comprising only the transactions is not presented.

To get just the transactions that comprise the balance, the transaction detail report must be filtered for a paid status of "open." To illustrate, several invoices were entered and payments applied against those payments to offset or close them out. Further, the payment "on account" and the invoice with deferred revenue examples were entered. These transactions show a balance of $2,000 in accounts receivable on the cash basis financial statement:

|  | Dec 31, 17 |
|---|---|
| **Cash Basis Test Company** | |
| **Balance Sheet - Cash Basis** | |
| As of December 31, 2017 | |
| **ASSETS** | |
| Current Assets | |
| ▼ Checking/Savings | |
| First National Bank | 406,432.50 |
| Total Checking/Savings | 406,432.50 |
| ▼ Accounts Receivable | |
| Accounts Receivable | 2,000.00 |
| Total Accounts Receivable | 2,000.00 |
| Total Current Assets | 408,432.50 |
| Fixed Assets | 294,360.00 |
| Other Assets | |
| ▶ Deferred Financing Costs ▶ | 27,000.00 |
| Total Other Assets | 27,000.00 |
| TOTAL ASSETS | 729,792.50 |
| **LIABILITIES & EQUITY** | |
| Liabilities | |
| ▼ Current Liabilities | |
| ▼ Other Current Liabilities | |
| Current Portion Long Term Debt | 61,214.00 |
| Accrued Interest | 3,397.99 |
| Deferred Mtce Plan Billing | 12,000.00 |
| Total Other Current Liabilities | 76,611.99 |
| Total Current Liabilities | 76,611.99 |
| ▼ Long Term Liabilities | |
| Building Mortgage | 165,318.49 |
| Total Long Term Liabilities | 165,318.49 |
| Total Liabilities | 241,930.48 |
| Equity | |
| Additional Paid in Capital | 499,000.00 |
| Capital Stock | 1,000.00 |
| Net Income | -12,137.98 |
| Total Equity | 487,862.02 |
| TOTAL LIABILITIES & EQUITY | 729,792.50 |

Double clicking on the $2,000 receivable amount brings up the transaction detail report below, which shows all the transactions in 2017, not just the transactions that make up the $2,000 balance. As shown below, several of the transactions offset and are not part of the ending balance:

### Cash Basis Test Company
### Transactions by Account
As of December 31, 2017

| Type | Date | Num | Adj | Name | Memo | Split | Debit | Credit | Balance |
|------|------|-----|-----|------|------|-------|-------|--------|---------|
| **Accounts Receivable** | | | | | | | | | 0.00 |
| Payment | 03/24/2017 | | | ABC Contracting C... | | First National... | 2,500.00 | | 2,500.00 |
| Payment | 03/24/2017 | | | ABC Contracting C... | | First National... | | 2,500.00 | 0.00 |
| Payment | 07/31/2017 | | | The Property Mana... | | First National... | | 7,000.00 | -7,000.00 |
| Payment | 07/31/2017 | | | The Property Mana... | | First National... | 7,000.00 | | 0.00 |
| Payment | 10/05/2017 | | | ABC Contracting C... | | First National... | | 1,000.00 | -1,000.00 |
| Payment | 10/05/2017 | | | ABC Contracting C... | | First National... | 1,000.00 | | 0.00 |
| Invoice | 12/15/2017 | 7 | | The Property Mana... | Annual Maintenance Plan | Deferred Mtc... | 12,000.00 | | 12,000.00 |
| Payment | 12/31/2017 | chec... | | The Property Mana... | | First National... | | 10,000.00 | 2,000.00 |
| Total Accounts Receivable | | | | | | | 22,500.00 | 20,500.00 | 2,000.00 |
| **TOTAL** | | | | | | | 22,500.00 | 20,500.00 | 2,000.00 |

Filtering the report by paid status of "Open" will create the desired report:

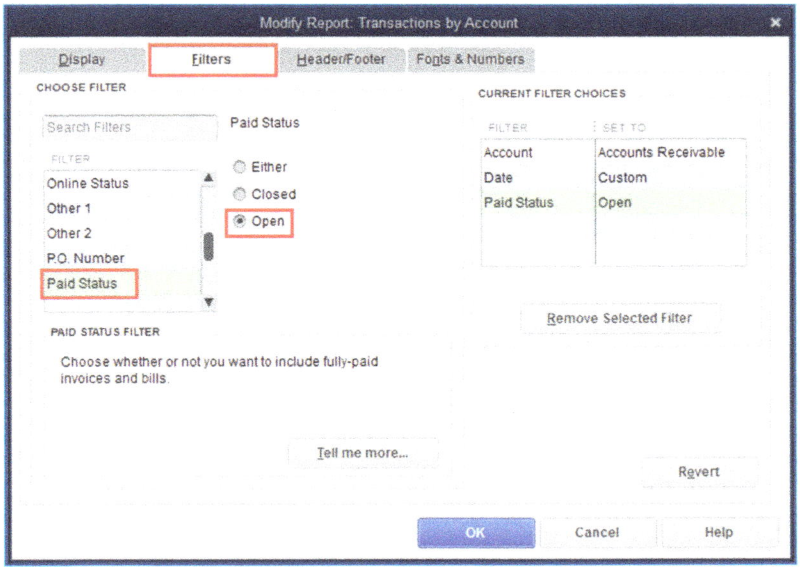

© The CFO Source, LLC 2017

The filtered report shows only the transactions comprising the balance in the account. Note that the beginning balance is zero, but when that is not the case, the range of dates for the report will need to be set back to an earlier date.

**Cash Basis Test Company**
**Transactions by Account**
As of December 31, 2017

| Type | Date | Num | Name | Memo | Split | Debit | Credit | Balance |
|------|------|-----|------|------|-------|-------|--------|---------|
| **Accounts Receivable** | | | | | | | | 0.00 |
| Invoice | 12/15/2017 | 7 | The Property Mana... | Annual Maintenance Plan | Deferred Mtce Plan Billing | 12,000.00 | | 12,000.00 |
| Payment | 12/31/2017 | chec... | The Property Mana... | | First National Bank | | 10,000.00 | 2,000.00 |
| Total Accounts Receivable | | | | | | 12,000.00 | 10,000.00 | 2,000.00 |
| **TOTAL** | | | | | | 12,000.00 | 10,000.00 | 2,000.00 |

## Expenses and Accounts Payable Accounting

A series of transactions affecting cash, accounts payable, expenses, and a fixed asset account will be analyzed. The transactions will only include those for which the "accounting cycle" has not been completed:

- Vendor bill recorded to an expense account not paid by statement date;
- Vendor bill recorded to a balance sheet account not paid by statement date;
- Payments to a Vendor on account rather than payment of specific bills.

The test company has been adjusted such that the accrual and cash basis balance sheets are the same at this point.

In the first example, a bill for $8,000 is recorded as payable to a vendor using a supplies expense account and is unpaid as of 12/31/2017. In this case, the related changes in net income and accounts payable are not displayed on the cash basis balance sheet as shown below:

**Cash Basis Test Company**
**Balance Sheet - Accrual Basis**
As of December 31, 2017

| | Dec 31, 17 |
|---|---|
| **ASSETS** | |
| **Current Assets** | |
| ▼ Checking/Savings | |
| First National Bank | 396,432.50 |
| Total Checking/Savings | 396,432.50 |
| Total Current Assets | 396,432.50 |
| **Fixed Assets** | |
| Buildings | 220,000.00 |
| Land | 80,000.00 |
| Accumulated Depreciation | -5,640.00 |
| Total Fixed Assets | 294,360.00 |
| **Other Assets** | |
| ▶ Deferred Financing Costs ▶ | 27,000.00 |
| Total Other Assets | 27,000.00 |
| **TOTAL ASSETS** | 717,792.50 |
| **LIABILITIES & EQUITY** | |
| Liabilities | |
| ▼ Current Liabilities | |
| ▼ Accounts Payable | |
| Accounts Payable | 8,000.00 |
| Total Accounts Payable | 8,000.00 |
| ▼ Other Current Liabilities | |
| Current Portion Long Term Debt | 61,214.00 |
| Accrued Interest | 3,397.99 |
| Total Other Current Liabilities | 64,611.99 |
| Total Current Liabilities | 72,611.99 |
| ▼ Long Term Liabilities | |
| Building Mortgage | 165,318.49 |
| Total Long Term Liabilities | 165,318.49 |
| Total Liabilities | 237,930.48 |
| Equity | |
| Additional Paid in Capital | 499,000.00 |
| Capital Stock | 1,000.00 |
| Net Income | -20,137.98 |
| Total Equity | 479,862.02 |
| **TOTAL LIABILITIES & EQUITY** | 717,792.50 |

**Cash Basis Test Company**
**Balance Sheet - Cash Basis**
As of December 31, 2017

| | Dec 31, 17 |
|---|---|
| **ASSETS** | |
| **Current Assets** | |
| ▼ Checking/Savings | |
| First National Bank | 396,432.50 |
| Total Checking/Savings | 396,432.50 |
| Accounts Receivable | 0.00 |
| Total Current Assets | 396,432.50 |
| **Fixed Assets** | |
| Buildings | 220,000.00 |
| Land | 80,000.00 |
| Accumulated Depreciation | -5,640.00 |
| Total Fixed Assets | 294,360.00 |
| **Other Assets** | |
| ▶ Deferred Financing Costs ▶ | 27,000.00 |
| Total Other Assets | 27,000.00 |
| **TOTAL ASSETS** | 717,792.50 |
| **LIABILITIES & EQUITY** | |
| Liabilities | |
| ▼ Current Liabilities | |
| ▼ Other Current Liabilities | |
| Current Portion Long Term Debt | 61,214.00 |
| Accrued Interest | 3,397.99 |
| Total Other Current Liabilities | 64,611.99 |
| Total Current Liabilities | 64,611.99 |
| ▼ Long Term Liabilities | |
| Building Mortgage | 165,318.49 |
| Total Long Term Liabilities | 165,318.49 |
| Total Liabilities | 229,930.48 |
| Equity | |
| Additional Paid in Capital | 499,000.00 |
| Capital Stock | 1,000.00 |
| Net Income | -12,137.98 |
| Total Equity | 487,862.02 |
| **TOTAL LIABILITIES & EQUITY** | 717,792.50 |

# QuickBooks For Accounting Professionals

In the second example, the vendor bill was changed to $20,000 and charged to a fixed asset account. For this transaction, there is no difference between cash and accrual basis statements as shown below. Net Income is the same on both balance sheets as a transaction charged to a fixed asset account does not affect income. For accountants who have cash balance sheets that are showing a balance in accounts payable, this type of transaction is one likely reason.

| Cash Basis Test Company Balance Sheet - Accrual Basis As of December 31, 2017 | Dec 31, 17 |
|---|---|
| ASSETS | |
| Current Assets | |
| ▸ Checking/Savings | 396,432.50 |
| Total Current Assets | 396,432.50 |
| Fixed Assets | |
| Buildings | 220,000.00 |
| Furniture and Equipment | 20,000.00 |
| Land | 80,000.00 |
| Accumulated Depreciation | -5,640.00 |
| Total Fixed Assets | 314,360.00 |
| Other Assets | |
| ▸ Deferred Financing Costs | 27,000.00 |
| Total Other Assets | 27,000.00 |
| TOTAL ASSETS | 737,792.50 |
| LIABILITIES & EQUITY | |
| Liabilities | |
| ▾ Current Liabilities | |
| ▾ Accounts Payable | |
| Accounts Payable | 20,000.00 |
| Total Accounts Payable | 20,000.00 |
| ▾ Other Current Liabilities | |
| Current Portion Long Term Debt | 61,214.00 |
| Accrued Interest | 3,397.99 |
| Total Other Current Liabilities | 64,611.99 |
| Total Current Liabilities | 84,611.99 |
| ▾ Long Term Liabilities | |
| Building Mortgage | 165,318.49 |
| Total Long Term Liabilities | 165,318.49 |
| Total Liabilities | 249,930.48 |
| Equity | |
| Additional Paid in Capital | 499,000.00 |
| Capital Stock | 1,000.00 |
| Net Income | -12,137.98 |
| Total Equity | 487,862.02 |
| TOTAL LIABILITIES & EQUITY | 737,792.50 |

| Cash Basis Test Company Balance Sheet - Cash Basis As of December 31, 2017 | Dec 31, 17 |
|---|---|
| ASSETS | |
| Current Assets | |
| ▸ Checking/Savings | 396,432.50 |
| Total Current Assets | 396,432.50 |
| Fixed Assets | |
| Buildings | 220,000.00 |
| Furniture and Equipment | 20,000.00 |
| Land | 80,000.00 |
| Accumulated Depreciation | -5,640.00 |
| Total Fixed Assets | 314,360.00 |
| Other Assets | |
| ▸ Deferred Financing Costs | 27,000.00 |
| Total Other Assets | 27,000.00 |
| TOTAL ASSETS | 737,792.50 |
| LIABILITIES & EQUITY | |
| Liabilities | |
| ▾ Current Liabilities | |
| ▾ Accounts Payable | |
| Accounts Payable | 20,000.00 |
| Total Accounts Payable | 20,000.00 |
| ▾ Other Current Liabilities | |
| Current Portion Long Term Debt | 61,214.00 |
| Accrued Interest | 3,397.99 |
| Total Other Current Liabilities | 64,611.99 |
| Total Current Liabilities | 84,611.99 |
| ▾ Long Term Liabilities | |
| Building Mortgage | 165,318.49 |
| Total Long Term Liabilities | 165,318.49 |
| Total Liabilities | 249,930.48 |
| Equity | |
| Additional Paid in Capital | 499,000.00 |
| Capital Stock | 1,000.00 |
| Net Income | -12,137.98 |
| Total Equity | 487,862.02 |
| TOTAL LIABILITIES & EQUITY | 737,792.50 |

For the third example, the vendor bill is changed back to the bill in the first example: an $8,000 bill charged to a supplies expense account. Then a payment to the vendor of $8,000 "on account" is recorded on 12/31/2017 using a journal entry. A journal entry is not the desired method for recording payments to vendors as these should be recorded in the Vendor section in the Pay Bills screen so that the bills can be shown as paid. It is not uncommon, however, to see ACH payments to vendors recorded with journal entries. When payments are recorded in this fashion, QuickBooks considers the vendor bill as still open. As such, a negative balance in accounts payable will be shown on a cash basis balance sheet (as shown below) because QuickBooks ignores the bill but recognizes the payment. The same happens if the payment is recorded with a check in the banking section when the check disbursement is recorded to accounts payable.

**Cash Basis Test Company**
**Balance Sheet - Accrual Basis**
As of December 31, 2017

| | Dec 31, 17 |
|---|---|
| **ASSETS** | |
| Current Assets | |
| ▼ Checking/Savings | |
| First National Bank | 388,432.50 |
| Total Checking/Savings | 388,432.50 |
| Total Current Assets | 388,432.50 |
| Fixed Assets | |
| Buildings | 220,000.00 |
| Land | 80,000.00 |
| Accumulated Depreciation | -5,640.00 |
| Total Fixed Assets | 294,360.00 |
| Other Assets | |
| ▶ Deferred Financing Costs | 27,000.00 |
| Total Other Assets | 27,000.00 |
| **TOTAL ASSETS** | **709,792.50** |
| **LIABILITIES & EQUITY** | |
| Liabilities | |
| ▼ Current Liabilities | |
| ▼ Other Current Liabilities | |
| Current Portion Long Term Debt | 61,214.00 |
| Accrued Interest | 3,397.99 |
| Total Other Current Liabilities | 64,611.99 |
| Total Current Liabilities | 64,611.99 |
| ▼ Long Term Liabilities | |
| Building Mortgage | 165,318.49 |
| Total Long Term Liabilities | 165,318.49 |
| Total Liabilities | 229,930.48 |
| Equity | |
| Additional Paid in Capital | 499,000.00 |
| Capital Stock | 1,000.00 |
| Net Income | -20,137.98 |
| Total Equity | 479,862.02 |
| **TOTAL LIABILITIES & EQUITY** | **709,792.50** |

**Cash Basis Test Company**
**Balance Sheet - Cash Basis**
As of December 31, 2017

| | Dec 31, 17 |
|---|---|
| **ASSETS** | |
| Current Assets | |
| ▼ Checking/Savings | |
| First National Bank | 388,432.50 |
| Total Checking/Savings | 388,432.50 |
| Total Current Assets | 388,432.50 |
| Fixed Assets | |
| Buildings | 220,000.00 |
| Land | 80,000.00 |
| Accumulated Depreciation | -5,640.00 |
| Total Fixed Assets | 294,360.00 |
| Other Assets | |
| ▶ Deferred Financing Costs | 27,000.00 |
| Total Other Assets | 27,000.00 |
| **TOTAL ASSETS** | **709,792.50** |
| **LIABILITIES & EQUITY** | |
| Liabilities | |
| ▼ Current Liabilities | |
| ▼ Accounts Payable | |
| Accounts Payable | -8,000.00 |
| Total Accounts Payable | -8,000.00 |
| ▼ Other Current Liabilities | |
| Current Portion Long Term Debt | 61,214.00 |
| Accrued Interest | 3,397.99 |
| Total Other Current Liabilities | 64,611.99 |
| Total Current Liabilities | 56,611.99 |
| ▼ Long Term Liabilities | |
| Building Mortgage | 165,318.49 |
| Total Long Term Liabilities | 165,318.49 |
| Total Liabilities | 221,930.48 |
| Equity | |
| Additional Paid in Capital | 499,000.00 |
| Capital Stock | 1,000.00 |
| Net Income | -12,137.98 |
| Total Equity | 487,862.02 |
| **TOTAL LIABILITIES & EQUITY** | **709,792.50** |

One way to clear up the negative amounts showing in accounts payable is to go to the Vendor Pay Bills screen and "Set Credits" as shown below:

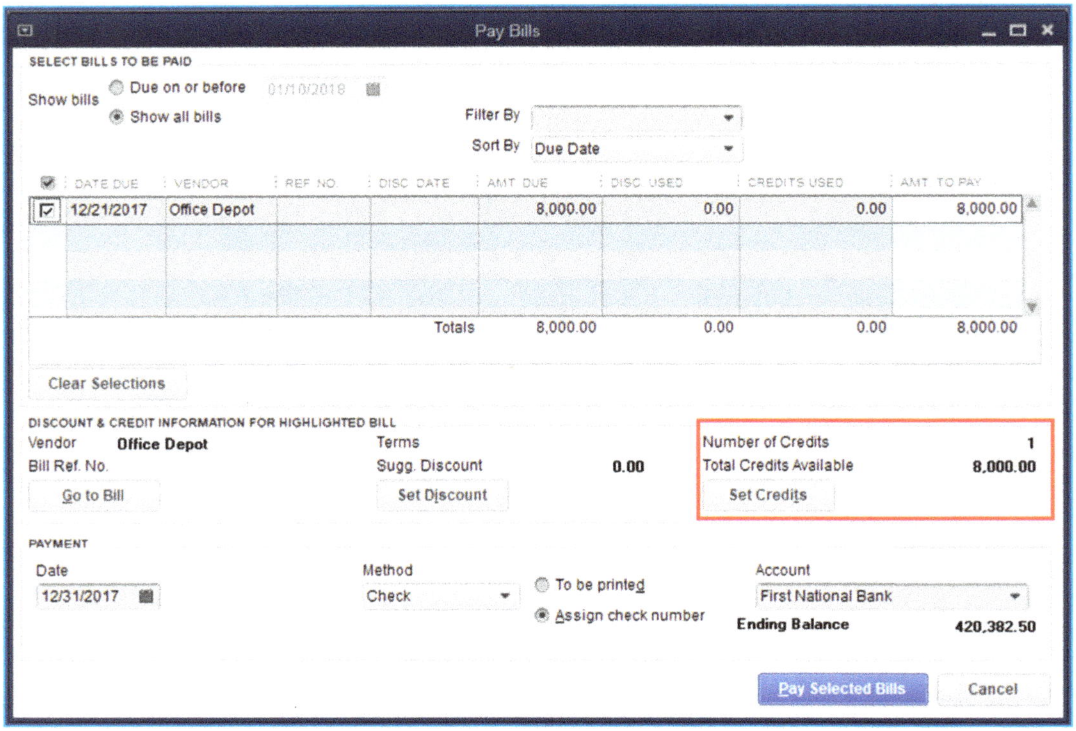

**Researching Transactions – Accounts Payable Balance Showing on a Cash Basis Balance Sheet**

When "drilling down" on the accounts payable balance on a cash basis financial statement by double clicking on the amount, QuickBooks displays *all* of the transactions that were processed through accounts payable, including bill and bill payment check transactions that offset. A list comprising only the transactions is not presented.

To get just the transactions that comprise the balance, the transaction detail report must be filtered for a paid status of "open." To illustrate, several bills were entered and checks issued to close those out. Further, the bill charged to a fixed asset account for $20,000 and the check paid "on account" for $8,000 were entered to create a balance of $12,000 in accounts payable on the cash basis financial statement:

### Cash Basis Test Company
### Balance Sheet - Cash Basis
As of December 31, 2017

| | Dec 31, 17 |
|---|---|
| **ASSETS** | |
| **Current Assets** | |
| ▶ Checking/Savings | 383,382.50 |
| Total Current Assets | 383,382.50 |
| **Fixed Assets** | |
| Buildings | 220,000.00 |
| Furniture and Equipment | 20,000.00 |
| Land | 80,000.00 |
| Accumulated Depreciation | -5,640.00 |
| Total Fixed Assets | 314,360.00 |
| **Other Assets** | |
| ▶ Deferred Financing Costs | 27,000.00 |
| Total Other Assets | 27,000.00 |
| **TOTAL ASSETS** | **724,742.50** |
| **LIABILITIES & EQUITY** | |
| **Liabilities** | |
| ▼ Current Liabilities | |
| ▼ Accounts Payable | |
| Accounts Payable | 12,000.00 |
| Total Accounts Payable | 12,000.00 |
| ▼ Other Current Liabilities | |
| Current Portion Long Term Debt | 61,214.00 |
| Accrued Interest | 3,397.99 |
| Total Other Current Liabilities | 64,611.99 |
| Total Current Liabilities | 76,611.99 |
| ▼ Long Term Liabilities | |
| Building Mortgage | 165,318.49 |
| Total Long Term Liabilities | 165,318.49 |
| Total Liabilities | 241,930.48 |
| **Equity** | |
| Additional Paid in Capital | 499,000.00 |
| Capital Stock | 1,000.00 |
| Net Income | -17,187.98 |
| Total Equity | 482,812.02 |
| **TOTAL LIABILITIES & EQUITY** | **724,742.50** |

Double clicking on the $12,000 accounts payable amount brings up the transaction detail report below, which shows all the transactions in 2017 for that account, not just the transactions that make up the $12,000 balance. Several of the transactions offset and are not part of the ending balance.

**Cash Basis Test Company**
**Transactions by Account**
As of December 31, 2017

| Type | Date | Num | Adj | Name | Memo | Clr | Split | Debit | Credit | Original Amount | Balance |
|---|---|---|---|---|---|---|---|---|---|---|---|
| **Accounts Payable** | | | | | | | | | | | 0.00 |
| Bill Pmt -Check | 01/10/2017 | 1005 | | Office Depot | | | First National... | | 250.00 | -250.00 | 250.00 |
| Bill Pmt -Check | 01/10/2017 | 1005 | | Office Depot | | | First National... | 250.00 | | -250.00 | 0.00 |
| Bill Pmt -Check | 05/09/2017 | 1006 | | Acme Product Sup... | | | First National... | 1,550.00 | | -1,550.00 | -1,550.00 |
| Bill Pmt -Check | 05/09/2017 | 1006 | | Acme Product Sup... | | | First National... | | 1,550.00 | -1,550.00 | 0.00 |
| Bill Pmt -Check | 08/24/2017 | 1007 | | Acme Product Sup... | | | First National... | 3,250.00 | | -3,250.00 | -3,250.00 |
| Bill Pmt -Check | 08/24/2017 | 1007 | | Acme Product Sup... | | | First National... | | 3,250.00 | -3,250.00 | 0.00 |
| General Journal | 10/31/2017 | | | Office Depot | | | First National... | 8,000.00 | | 8,000.00 | -8,000.00 |
| Bill | 10/31/2017 | | | Acme Product Sup... | | | Furniture and... | | 20,000.00 | -20,000.00 | 12,000.00 |
| Total Accounts Payable | | | | | | | | 13,050.00 | 25,050.00 | | 12,000.00 |
| **TOTAL** | | | | | | | | **13,050.00** | **25,050.00** | | **12,000.00** |

Filtering the report for a paid status of "Open" will create the desired report:

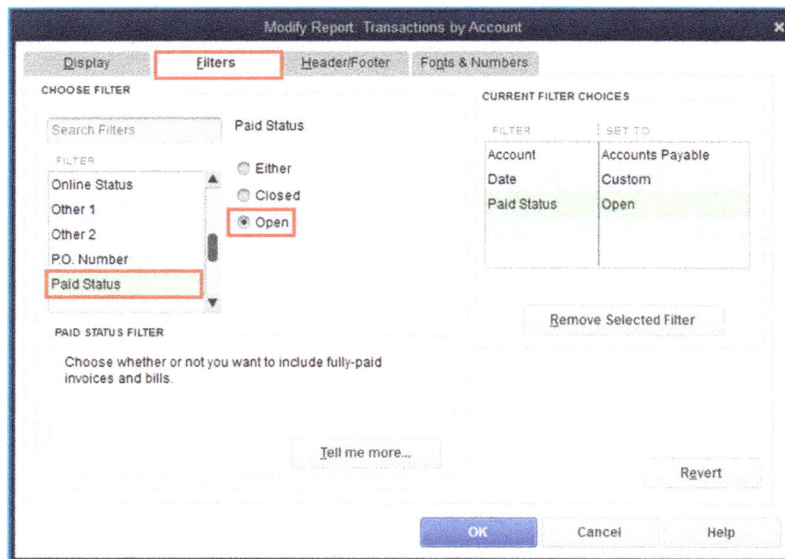

The filtered report is shown below with only the transactions comprising the balance in the account. Note that the beginning balance is zero. If this is not the case, the range of dates for the report will need to be set back to an earlier date.

| | Cash Basis Test Company | | | | | | | | | | |
|---|---|---|---|---|---|---|---|---|---|---|---|
| | **Transactions by Account** | | | | | | | | | | |
| | As of December 31, 2017 | | | | | | | | | | |
| Type | Date | Num | Adj | Name | Memo | Clr | Split | Debit | Credit | Original Amount | Balance |
| **Accounts Payable** | | | | | | | | | | | 0.00 |
| General Journal | 10/31/2017 | | | Office Depot | | | First National... | 8,000.00 | | 8,000.00 | -8,000.00 |
| Bill | 10/31/2017 | | | Acme Product Sup... | | | Furniture and... | | 20,000.00 | -20,000.00 | 12,000.00 |
| Total Accounts Payable | | | | | | | | 8,000.00 | 20,000.00 | | 12,000.00 |
| **TOTAL** | | | | | | | | **8,000.00** | **20,000.00** | | **12,000.00** |

## Inventory Accounting

A series of transactions affecting inventory, accounts receivable, accounts payable, revenues, and expenses will be analyzed. As before, the transactions analyzed will only include transactions for which the "accounting cycle" has not been completed. Transactions analyzed will include the following:

- Vendor bill recorded to an inventory account not paid by statement date;
- Customer invoice not paid by the statement date, with an item code that maps to a revenue code for the income side of the transaction and a cost of goods sold account for the expense side.

The test company has been adjusted such that the accrual and cash basis balance sheets are the same at this point.

In the first example, a bill for $100,000 is recorded payable to a vendor using an item code that maps to the inventory account and is unpaid at 12/31/2017. The accrual and cash basis balance sheets are the same as shown below. Since this transaction does not affect any profit or loss accounts, there is no change in Net Income. Note that both balance sheets below show inventory and accounts payable of $100,000:

| Cash Basis Test Company<br>Balance Sheet - Accrual Basis<br>As of December 31, 2017 | Dec 31, 17 |
| --- | --- |
| **ASSETS** | |
| Current Assets | |
| ▶ Checking/Savings | 391,382.50 |
| ▼ Other Current Assets | |
|    Inventory Asset | 100,000.00 |
|    Total Other Current Assets | 100,000.00 |
| Total Current Assets | 491,382.50 |
| Fixed Assets ▶ | 294,360.00 |
| Other Assets | |
| ▶ Deferred Financing Costs | 27,000.00 |
| Total Other Assets | 27,000.00 |
| **TOTAL ASSETS** | **812,742.50** |
| **LIABILITIES & EQUITY** | |
| Liabilities | |
| ▼ Current Liabilities | |
|   ▼ Accounts Payable | |
|     Accounts Payable | 100,000.00 |
|     Total Accounts Payable | 100,000.00 |
|   ▼ Other Current Liabilities | |
|     Current Portion Long Term Debt | 61,214.00 |
|     Accrued Interest | 3,397.99 |
|     Total Other Current Liabilities | 64,611.99 |
|   Total Current Liabilities | 164,611.99 |
| ▼ Long Term Liabilities | |
|   Building Mortgage | 165,318.49 |
|   Total Long Term Liabilities | 165,318.49 |
| Total Liabilities | 329,930.48 |
| Equity | |
|   Additional Paid in Capital | 499,000.00 |
|   Capital Stock | 1,000.00 |
|   Net Income | -17,187.98 |
| Total Equity | 482,812.02 |
| **TOTAL LIABILITIES & EQUITY** | **812,742.50** |

| Cash Basis Test Company<br>Balance Sheet - Cash Basis<br>As of December 31, 2017 | Dec 31, 17 |
| --- | --- |
| **ASSETS** | |
| Current Assets | |
| ▶ Checking/Savings ▶ | 391,382.50 |
| ▼ Other Current Assets | |
|    Inventory Asset | 100,000.00 |
|    Total Other Current Assets | 100,000.00 |
| Total Current Assets | 491,382.50 |
| Fixed Assets | 294,360.00 |
| Other Assets | |
| ▶ Deferred Financing Costs | 27,000.00 |
| Total Other Assets | 27,000.00 |
| **TOTAL ASSETS** | **812,742.50** |
| **LIABILITIES & EQUITY** | |
| Liabilities | |
| ▼ Current Liabilities | |
|   ▼ Accounts Payable | |
|     Accounts Payable | 100,000.00 |
|     Total Accounts Payable | 100,000.00 |
|   ▼ Other Current Liabilities | |
|     Current Portion Long Term Debt | 61,214.00 |
|     Accrued Interest | 3,397.99 |
|     Total Other Current Liabilities | 64,611.99 |
|   Total Current Liabilities | 164,611.99 |
| ▼ Long Term Liabilities | |
|   Building Mortgage | 165,318.49 |
|   Total Long Term Liabilities | 165,318.49 |
| Total Liabilities | 329,930.48 |
| Equity | |
|   Additional Paid in Capital | 499,000.00 |
|   Capital Stock | 1,000.00 |
|   Net Income | -17,187.98 |
| Total Equity | 482,812.02 |
| **TOTAL LIABILITIES & EQUITY** | **812,742.50** |

In the second example, a $30,000 invoice is issued to a customer with the same item code used to record the purchase of inventory. The item code is set up to record revenue and a corresponding receivable as well as cost of goods sold and a corresponding reduction in inventory. The transaction generates a $10,000 profit calculated as $30,000 in revenue less $20,000 of inventory/product cost. Note the following differences and similarities between the accrual versus cash basis balance sheets shown below:

- The accrual basis balance sheet shows the total receivable of $30,000 while the cash basis balance sheet only shows $20,000 (the cost of the product sold).
- Both balance sheets show an inventory balance of $80,000, which is the original cost of $100,000 less the $20,000 cost of the sale.
- Net Income is lower in the cash basis balance sheet by $10,000, the profit on the sale.

| Cash Basis Test Company Balance Sheet - Accrual Basis As of December 31, 2017 | | Cash Basis Test Company Balance Sheet - Cash Basis As of December 31, 2017 | |
|---|---|---|---|
| | Dec 31, 17 | | Dec 31, 17 |
| ASSETS | | ASSETS | |
| Current Assets | | Current Assets | |
| ▶ Checking/Savings | 391,382.50 | ▶ Checking/Savings | 391,382.50 |
| ▶ Accounts Receivable | 30,000.00 | ▶ Accounts Receivable | 20,000.00 |
| ▼ Other Current Assets | | ▼ Other Current Assets | |
|   Inventory Asset | 80,000.00 |   Inventory Asset | 80,000.00 |
|   Total Other Current Assets | 80,000.00 |   Total Other Current Assets | 80,000.00 |
| Total Current Assets | 501,382.50 | Total Current Assets | 491,382.50 |
| Fixed Assets | 294,360.00 | Fixed Assets | 294,360.00 |
| Other Assets | | Other Assets | |
| ▶ Deferred Financing Costs | 27,000.00 | ▶ Deferred Financing Costs | 27,000.00 |
| Total Other Assets | 27,000.00 | Total Other Assets | 27,000.00 |
| TOTAL ASSETS | 822,742.50 | TOTAL ASSETS | 812,742.50 |
| LIABILITIES & EQUITY | | LIABILITIES & EQUITY | |
| Liabilities | | Liabilities | |
| ▼ Current Liabilities | | ▼ Current Liabilities | |
|   ▼ Accounts Payable | |   ▼ Accounts Payable | |
|     Accounts Payable | 100,000.00 |     Accounts Payable | 100,000.00 |
|   Total Accounts Payable | 100,000.00 |   Total Accounts Payable | 100,000.00 |
|   ▼ Other Current Liabilities | |   ▼ Other Current Liabilities | |
|     Current Portion Long Term Debt | 61,214.00 |     Current Portion Long Term Debt | 61,214.00 |
|     Accrued Interest | 3,397.99 |     Accrued Interest | 3,397.99 |
|   Total Other Current Liabilities | 64,611.99 |   Total Other Current Liabilities | 64,611.99 |
| Total Current Liabilities | 164,611.99 | Total Current Liabilities | 164,611.99 |
| ▼ Long Term Liabilities | | ▼ Long Term Liabilities | |
|   Building Mortgage | 165,318.49 |   Building Mortgage | 165,318.49 |
| Total Long Term Liabilities | 165,318.49 | Total Long Term Liabilities | 165,318.49 |
| Total Liabilities | 329,930.48 | Total Liabilities | 329,930.48 |
| Equity | | Equity | |
| Additional Paid in Capital | 499,000.00 | Additional Paid in Capital | 499,000.00 |
| Capital Stock | 1,000.00 | Capital Stock | 1,000.00 |
| Net Income | -7,187.98 | Net Income | -17,187.98 |
| Total Equity | 492,812.02 | Total Equity | 482,812.02 |
| TOTAL LIABILITIES & EQUITY | 822,742.50 | TOTAL LIABILITIES & EQUITY | 812,742.50 |

## Credit Card Accounting

The recording of credit charges in QuickBooks does not create a difference between accrual and cash basis reports.

**Final Note**

Before using cash basis reports for preparation of tax returns, it is suggested to use an alternative method outside QuickBooks to verify the reports. This can be done by adjusting an accrual basis income statement to derive cash basis income. This approach starts with accrual basis income and then either increases or decreases income based on the net change in selected current asset and current liability accounts. For example, if accounts receivable has decreased from the start of the year to end of the year, accrual basis income would be increased by the change, and the reverse would hold true if accounts receivable increased. In a similar fashion, changes in accounts payable would drive a similar adjustment—if accounts payable increased year over year, this would create a reduction in expense (and corresponding increase in pre-tax income) and the reverse would hold true if accounts payable decreased.

Notes:

_____

_____

_____

_____

_____

_____

_____

_____

_____

_____

_____

_____

_____

_____

_____

_____

_____

_____

_____

_____

_____

_____

_____

_____

_____

_____

_____

_____

_____

_____

_____

_____

_____

_____

Notes:

Suggestions

# For Accountants and Bookkeepers

The field of accounting presents significant opportunities—all organizations need qualified accounting personnel no matter the state of the economy. Individuals with strong bookkeeping and accounting skills typically have steady employment and chances for advancement. As one of my first bosses said, "A good accountant is never out of work for long." This applies whether you are an employee or have struck out on your own.

Continued improvement in your technical skills, ability to communicate financial information, and your general business knowledge are key components to being successful in your career. I offer the following suggestions to enhance your success:

- As QuickBooks is the most widely used accounting software for small and medium size businesses, mastery of the program will give you numerous advantages: a leg up when applying for a better position, the ability to produce meaningful reports and make yourself a key part of an organizations' success, or being put in charge of training new users, to name a few.
- Become a QuickBooks Pro Advisor as this will provide you with the latest software, unlimited US based phone support, continuing education courses, and the ability to be listed on the QuickBooks Pro Advisor website so potential customers can find you. Pro Advisors are viewed by companies looking for accountants as the "best of the best."
- Go beyond just processing transactions and learn to use the information contained in QuickBooks to become a trusted financial advisor. Accountants are on the front line when it comes to "seeing the numbers" and those that can communicate critical financial information are invaluable to business owners.
- Understand that you can't do accounting just sitting at your desk. The best accountants learn about the organization(s) they work for by talking to people and seeing operations first hand. If you don't know what is going on in an organization, how can you do the accounting?
- Make a concerted effort to improve your skills and learn new things. There is always something new to learn about!

At The CFO Source, we are passionate about QuickBooks and hope that you have been able to use this book to improve your expertise. Please feel free to contact us if you have any questions. Our contact information is below:

Website – www.cfosource.net

Phone – (443) 487-7733

Email – info@cfosource.net

# Appendix A

# QuickBooks Transaction Code Types

| Module/<br>Main Menu | Transaction<br>Type Code | Typical Usage |
|---|---|---|
| Customers | Invoice | Invoice to customer |
| | Credit Memo | Credit Memo to Customer |
| | Sales Receipt | Record daily sales with no specific customer |
| | Payment | Record payments from customers to specific invoices |
| | Estimate | Estimate prepared for customer |
| | Sales Order | Sales order generated for customer |
| Employees | Paycheck | All facets of payroll – gross pay, deductions, payroll taxes, etc |
| | Liability Check | Payment of liabilities paid within QB payroll |
| Vendors | Bill | Bills from Vendors |
| | Credit | Credits from Vendors |
| | Bill Pmt – Check | Checks issued to Vendors within Vendor module |
| | Sales Tax Payment | Payment of sales tax liabilities within Vendor module |
| | Inventory Adjustment | Adjustments to Inventory |
| | Purchase Order | Purchase order issued to Vendor |
| Banking | Check | Checks issued within Banking module |
| | Deposits | Bank deposits, both from customers and non customers |
| | Transfer | Movement of cash between bank accounts |
| | Credit Card Charge | Charges made on credit cards |
| | Credit Card Credit | Credits to credit cards |
| Company or Accountant | General Journal | Journal Entries |

www.ingramcontent.com/pod-product-compliance
Lightning Source LLC
Chambersburg PA
CBHW050106220326
41598CB00043B/7394